EXCEL BASICS TO BLACKBELT

Excel Basics to Blackbelt is intended to serve as an accelerated guide to decision support designs. Its structure is designed to enhance the skills in Excel of those who have never used it for anything but possibly storing phone numbers, enabling them to reach a level of mastery that will allow them to develop user interfaces and automated applications. To accomplish this, the major theme of the text is the integration of the basics; as a result, readers will be able to develop decision support tools that are at once highly intuitive from a working components perspective but also highly significant from the perspective of practical use and distribution. Applications integration discussed includes the use of MicroSoft MapPoint, XLStat, and RISKOptimizer, as well as how to leverage Excel's iteration mode, Web queries, Visual Basic code, and interface development. There are ample examples throughout the text.

For the accompanying Web site material, please go to
http://www.cambridge.org/bendoly.

Elliot Bendoly is an associate professor at Emory University's Goizueta Business School. He holds a Ph.D. from Indiana University in operations management and decision sciences with an information systems specialization in enterprise resource planning (ERP) and knowledge management. Professor Bendoly serves on the editorial boards of the *Journal of Operations Management* and *Decision Sciences*. His research has been published in leading academic journals, including the *Journal of Operations Management, Production and Operations Management, MIS Quarterly, Information Systems Research, Journal of Applied Psychology, Decision Sciences*, and the *Journal of Service Research*. He is also the coeditor of *Strategic ERP Extension and Use*. He has served as the academic liaison for APICS: The Association for Operations Management and is a cofounder of the Behavioral Dynamics in Operations Management Network. He has lectured on decision support at research institutions such as Harvard University, as well as to practitioners at firms such as AT Kearney and Price Waterhouse Coopers Inc.

EXCEL BASICS TO BLACKBELT

An Accelerated Guide to Decision Support Designs

ELLIOT BENDOLY

Emory University

CAMBRIDGE
UNIVERSITY PRESS

CAMBRIDGE UNIVERSITY PRESS
Cambridge, New York, Melbourne, Madrid, Cape Town, Singapore, São Paulo, Delhi

Cambridge University Press
32 Avenue of the Americas, New York, NY 10013-2473, USA

www.cambridge.org
Information on this title: www.cambridge.org/9780521889056

© Elliot Bendoly 2008

This publication is in copyright. Subject to statutory exception
and to the provisions of relevant collective licensing agreements,
no reproduction of any part may take place without
the written permission of Cambridge University Press.

First published 2008

Printed in the United States of America

A catalog record for this publication is available from the British Library.

Library of Congress Cataloging in Publication Data
Bendoly, Elliot.
Excel basics to blackbelt : an accelerated guide to decision support
designs / Elliot Bendoly.
p.   cm.
Includes bibliographical references and index.
ISBN 978-0-521-88905-6 (hbk.)
1. Decision support systems.   2. Microsoft Excel (Computer file)   I. Title.
HD30.213.B46   2008
005.54 – dc22   2007050174

ISBN   978-0-521-88905-6 hardback

Cambridge University Press has no responsibility for
the persistence or accuracy of URLs for external or
third-party Internet Web sites referred to in this publication
and does not guarantee that any content on such
Web sites is, or will remain, accurate or appropriate.

Contents

Section 1

Getting Oriented

1

Necessary Foundations for Decision Support

Professionals are expected to make decisions on a daily basis. Some of these decisions may appear trivial, such as what shirt to wear, or what to have for lunch. Some may appear routine and almost free of in-depth consideration. Should I provide my PIN number when prompted by the ATM? Should I respond (in some fashion) to a question addressed to me by a colleague? Other decisions are more complex and potentially more significant. Should I recommend that my client invest in a particular firm? Should I offer to take on additional work now that one of my current projects appears to be nearing completion? Should I purchase a new technology, given my current knowledge of its potential benefits? Should I recommend a settlement in a lawsuit, given my expectations of how the other party is likely to act in the near term?

These aren't simple questions, and we can't expect individuals to always have immediate and appropriate answers. What we can expect, however, is some level of thought, and some level of a desire for assistance when good solutions are needed. The origin of this assistance can vary, but being the eternal tool builders that we are, we tend to find such assistance in the form of data analysis and interpretation mechanisms. Increasingly these are high-tech, information-intensive mechanisms, and are ever more within our own grasp to develop and master.

We can describe such mechanisms through a range of potential – if not typical – attributes and benefits of decision support systems (DSS). Some of these attributes and benefits are shown in Figure 1.1. For many developers and analysts, only a few of the above issues and attributes are viewed as worthy of rigorous pursuit. A truly practical and forward-thinking perspective of decision support, however, will ultimately suggest a development process and finished product that at least has taken each of these issues and attributes into consideration in some shape or form. Toward this goal, the power of visualization cannot be underemphasized. As such, an understanding of how to leverage the visualization of data analysis, its results, and its implications/suggestions are naturally critical to the development of DSS.

Typical Attributes

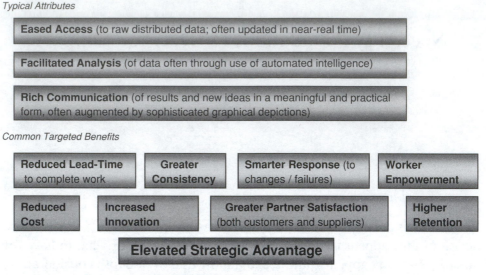

Figure 1.1. Elements of DSS.

Consider the following key principles put forward by Edward Tufte,* world-renowned scholar on data and relational visualization:

1) *Enforce Wise Visual Comparisons:* Comparison is a critical element in the development of understanding and, ultimately, practice. It allows for the illustration of practical relevance of effects and decisions that may give rise to them. It's the mechanism by which analytical and theoretical findings are vetted by intuition past real-world experience. It encourages faith in the diligence of the analyst, and hence any system, on the framework he or she is promoting the use of.

2) *Show Causality (IF possible to even "suggest"):* Most practical researchers cringe when people throw around claims of "causality" without really having appropriate evidence. However, in some cases, certain logically thought-out and reasoned explanations can definitely prove convincing towards such claims. The task of the developer is to provide enough temporal and situational information, as well as information regarding the binding relationships relevant, to allow individuals to understand any causal suggestions made or implied, as well as potentially critique them as appropriate. Developers should be willing to sufficiently provide representation to allow others to draw their own conclusions regarding causality rather than focusing on driving home their own hypotheses as immutable fact.

3) *The World We Seek to Understand Is Multivariate, as Our Displays Should Be (AND as our analysis that supports our displays should be):* Only meaningful dimensions should be incomplete (not multivariate for multivariation's sake – knowing the price of tea in Boston is seldom helpful in predicting stock values over time). Push for multidimensional considerations in analysis and visualization,

* Tufte, E. R., *Beautiful Evidence*. Cheshire, CT: Edward R. Tufte Graphic Press, 2006.

but do so as needed intelligently. Consider which multivariate depictions have the most critical meaning, juxtapose those, and don't clutter with others.

4) *Completely Integrate Words, Numbers, and Images:* Any disconnects between data and graphics only tend to weaken their potential. In some cases, the unintegrated presentation of both actually can mislead. Analysts need to view numerical and textual content as reinforcing graphics (and vice-versa) rather than idiosyncratic to specific elements of analysts. People need to be able to quickly understand what data and text graphics are driven by. This is another key to generating faith in the analyst and his/her tool.

5) *Most of What Happens in Design Depends upon the Quality, Relevance, and Integrity of Content:* Garbage fed into a graph results at best in beautiful garbage (i.e., it still has little practical value; it still stinks). Know the audience. Understand the context of practice. Be fully aware of what needs to be analyzed and presented – and do it the right way. Mistakes, insufficiency, and irrelevant detail can destroy many hours, days, and even months of work.

Regardless of the technical nature of the systems developed for support, a continued and serious consideration of these principles helps to guarantee that developed tools are used, valued, and worthy of future generations' development and use.

Aside from these recommendations, it is essential to reinforce a point here, particularly for those new to DSS development: Decision support systems quite literally refer to applications that are designed to *support*, not *replace*, decision making. Unfortunately, this is too often forgotten by decision support system users, or these users simply equate the notion of intelligent support of human decision making with automated decision making. Not only does that miss the point of the application development, it also sets up a sequence of potentially disruptive behaviors and events that include excessive anthropomorphism of technology, poor or impractical decisions based on incomplete knowledge and interpretation, disastrous results, and ultimately the scapegoating by technology decision makers, developers, and technicians that maintain these applications. *It's easy for decision makers to view decision support systems as remedies for difficult work, particularly if they can blame others for their own lack of effort.*

Although often difficult to codify, there is an implied contract between those who attest to deliver intelligent tools and those who accept their use: namely, that the analyst is not attempting to intentionally mislead. But what does that really mean? Simply not attempting to lead decision makers towards policies that benefit the confederates of a developer? Or does that also include omitting data and analysis considered for the sake of ease in development, with the knowledge that doing so may severely bias results?

Ultimately these issues relate to accountability and ethics in organizations, but they also relate to personal accountability and ethics on the part of those developing these applications. If you want to develop a strong decision support tool for yourself, you guarantee that any problems rest in your lap. But if you want to be able to pass the tool onto others (the most powerful implication of DSS development given the nature of modern, highly pervasive technologies), you have a responsibility to pay a great deal of attention to exactly how your applications might be used by others. Critical here is guiding usage through built-in assistance in analysis, clear visualization of how characteristics of problems and solutions relate, and formally structured interfaces that deter, if not prohibit, misuse. In my mind, it is difficult to distinguish those who intend to use their positions as knowledge brokers to the detriment of others; even those seemingly willing to discard diligence or accept obscured presentation in the pursuit of personal gains.

With this in mind, this text is written not only for the potential developer, but also for the potential user. Know what to expect as possibilities of DSS and you can know what to expect from the efforts of those pushing their tools on you. Developers be forewarned – DSS is becoming increasingly available for non-programmers. This text illustrates the beginning scope of that availability.

The basic structure builds upon past examples to illustrate how simple ideas can evolve, as does the skillful understanding of the potential for enriching decision support. The first few chapters of the text, grouped together in a section entitled "Getting Oriented," are designed to ease people into simple but effective use of the Excel 2007 environment as a platform for tool development and visualization. Navigation and data acquisition are central themes; however, basic logic concepts essential to the nature of discussions throughout the remainder of the text are also covered. Discussion of capabilities from external applications like MapPoint and the Internet are also provided.

In Section II, "Harvesting Intelligence," we will dive into the structuring of decision-making problems in ways that are meaningful to assisted analysis and transparent to those in practice (aided by concepts and approaches to visualizing key aspects of these problems). Simplification tactics in managing large sets of data and approaching problem solutions in general are then discussed as a prelude to more sophisticated approaches to leveraging problem structures and available solution technologies. Use of Excel's Solver and Palisade's RISKOptimizer packages will be discussed here, along with the use of XLStat.

In the "Leveraging Dynamic Analysis" section, Chapters 8 through 10 deal with the design and construction of simulations from a number of angles, making use of a variety of available tools. Use of controls to simplify the management of simulations is discussed, as are approaches to simulation optimization as a merger of concepts from past chapter discussions. The high potential value of Macro recordings are introduced, along with how to make the best use of them in conjunction with a range of methods and tools. Approaches to rich visualization of simulations are discussed as well.

In the last section of the text, "Advanced Automation and Interfacing," we deal with work that could not easily be conducted in a spreadsheet interface alone (even one as advanced as Excel's). The Visual Basic developer environment is discussed throughout. Coverage includes topics dealing with Macro editing, function creation, application calls, integrated automation, and advanced interface development. Example spreadsheets referenced throughout the text are available at www.bizbreed.com.

As a reminder to the reader, this is not a textbook designed for an advanced programming course. Nor is it a statistics text, nor a single source dictionary of all things Excel. This is a guide for the sorcerer's apprentice – for those professionals who want to demonstrate their own genius, and need only the right coaching, inspiration, and reinforcement through example to get there. The structure and content are not designed to inundate, but rather to illuminate.

Because readers come to this text at various skill levels, multiple starting points have been built in. Even those looking for uncommon references and keys to unlocking automation and application integration are going to find value here. However, the real hope is that this book will open the world of DSS development to a community otherwise intimidated by software supported analysis. Everyone deserves to know how accessible DSS design can be and the potential it holds. It's time to shatter the wall between the untouchable programmer and the professional in need. It can start here.

2

The Development Environment

This discussion of decision support design starts by jumping into the basics of the Excel development environment. Figure 2.1 provides an annotated view of what people typically see when opening up a new file in Excel. Only a few key elements of this interface are central to our early discussion.

Excel files are called workbooks. They contain any number of worksheets (i.e., spreadsheets) that can be used in tandem. Ninety-five percent of the time, Excel has been relegated to storing information, largely by those who don't know what else Excel can do. Not that storing info in Excel is bad, but there are often better alternatives available for storage, such as databases in the case of very large sets of data. Functionally the storage capability of Excel represents only the bare tip of this technological iceberg.

Regardless, knowing how the cell structure in the spreadsheet works is a good place to start and is essential to our future discussion.

Cells in spreadsheets can contain:

- *Fixed data:* Data you've entered, numerical or otherwise.
- *Formatting:* Background color, border thickness, font type, and so on.
- *Labels:* References other than the standard ColumnRow reference.
- *Comments:* Notes regarding the contents.
- *Formulae:* Can be mathematical/statistical, text based, or a range of other types such as logic based or search oriented.
- *Live data links:* Data that are drawn from an externally linked source, such as a database or the Internet.

2.1 Fixed Data

Data entry in Excel is about as basic as it gets – just click and type. And it's probably the only thing that people universally know how to do in Excel. But Excel makes some kinds of data entry easier in ways that many current users don't realize.

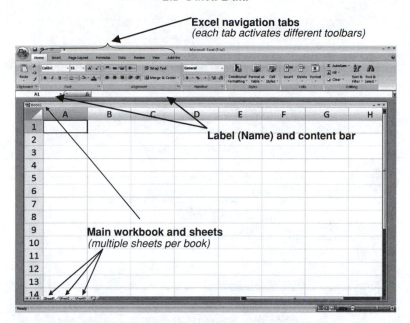

Figure 2.1. Basic front-end elements of the Excel environment.

For example, Excel has an automatic pattern-recognition element that, by default, will *attempt* to aid you in filling in additional cells of data. Although it's not always successfully, it's often convenient.

For example, say I want to enter the number 1 into five cells in row 1. I can start by entering the number 1 in cell A1. This is shown in Figure 2.2.

Note that when cell A1 is selected, its border is bold and a small square appears at the bottom right of the cell. That small square is the copy prompt. If I pull that square either right or down, Excel will attempt to fill in all other cells I highlight with the pattern – in this case, the number 1. By pulling the square to the right and highlighting the next four cells, I get the results shown in Figure 2.3.

At this point, with all five cells selected, I could pull that copy prompt down a couple rows and get the spreadsheet shown in Figure 2.4.

Ascending values and alternating text values are also recognized. For example, take a look at Figure 2.5.

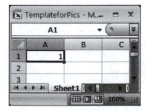

Figure 2.2. Initial entry.

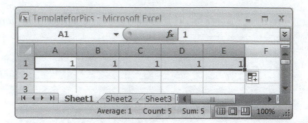

Figure 2.3. After copying across.

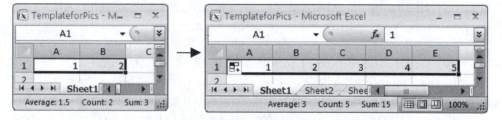

Figure 2.4. After copying the row down.

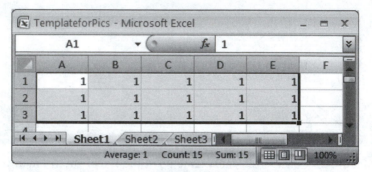

Figure 2.5. Initial sequential entry, followed by copy.

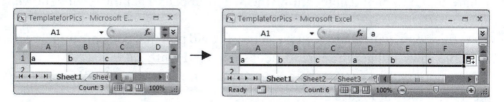

Figure 2.6. Initial text sequential entry, followed by copy.

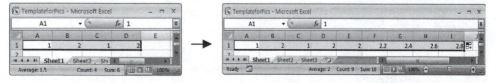

Figure 2.7. Initial switching sequence, followed by copy.

Or consider the copy shown in Figure 2.6.

Although this may not be exactly what we wanted (the alphabet isn't extrapolated here), we are provided with a potentially meaningful sequence based on Excel's existing pattern recognition. Some results of pattern recognition by Excel are a bit less intuitive, however. For example, take a look at Figure 2.7.

Here, as in the previous examples, Excel is trying to figure out exactly what numeric pattern the user is trying to specify. However, not every pattern that may seem natural to us is encoded in these rules, or other mathematical rules may have automatic priority in Excel. There are often a lot of options for trying to recognize and continue numeric patterns; in this case, the option selected just isn't one we expected. Excel has a lot of intelligence built into it, and sometimes it just tries too hard.

There are several simple ways to avoid ending up with an Excel-extrapolated pattern that doesn't fit a user's need. One method is to completely avoid relying on pattern recognition and use some kind of a formula that generates the pattern you want. For example, type $= A1$ into cell E2, press Enter, and use the copy prompt on E2 to pull that entry into all later cells in that row. This would essentially duplicate the pattern in cells A1–D2 for as long as you would want it repeated.

If you would prefer to rely on Excel's pattern-recognition mechanisms, you could also try entering your numbers as text. Excel's options for intelligently identifying and extending text patterns are much more limited and may be more likely to generate unexpected results. To enter numbers as text in any given cell, precede the number with an apostrophe, such as '1 or '2. This will ensure that Excel interprets the entry as text, at least as far as pattern recognition is concerned. Within the spreadsheet Excel will still let you perform mathematical functions using the numbers following that apostrophe, although it is an added step and may create other difficulties in formatting and more advanced use of such data down the line, so this doesn't tend to be an approach that's often used.

Still another mechanism to augment existing pattern-recognition capabilities is made available through the Edit Custom Lists button, found in the Popular tab of the Excel Options dialog box (Figure 2.8 shows the location of the Excel Options button under the Office button drop-down, as well as the appearance of the Popular options dialog once Excel Options is selected).

Click the Edit Custom Lists button to open the Custom Lists dialog box, as seen in Figure 2.9. This functionality allows you to view the existing custom lists, generate new lists, and import other lists that aren't currently being recognized by the workbook.

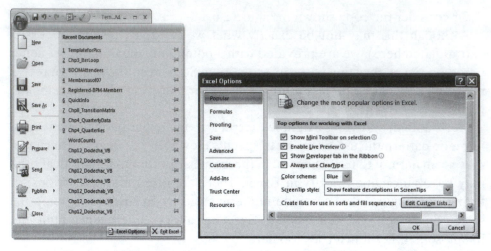

Figure 2.8. Excel option access and access to Edit Custom Lists.

2.2 Formatting

Formatting can be applied to a wide range of elements within Excel. The most common is cell formatting. The following sections explore static and conditional cell formatting.

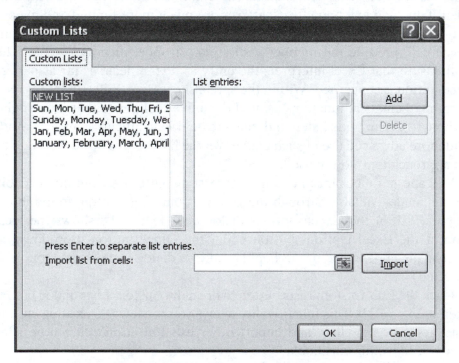

Figure 2.9. Edit Custom Lists dialog box.

Figure 2.10. Accessing cell formatting options.

2.2.1 Static Formatting for Cells

Static formats can be modified in a variety of ways. Access to formatting options is gained by either right-clicking on the desired cell and then selecting Format Cells in the shortcut window that appears (as shown in Figure 2.10), or by selecting Format>Format Cells from the standard toolbar.

Whether choosing Format Cells from the shortcut menu or selecting Format>Format Cells, the Format Cells dialog box displays. The formatting options in this dialog box include:

- *Number:* Allows modification of the type of numeric/text presentation for that cell. For example, this allows numbers representing percentages to be presented as such (i.e., with a % sign), numbers that represent dates to be presented in month-day format, or very large/small numbers to presented in scientific notation (e.g., 3.45E8 instead of 345,000,000, or 3.45E-8 instead of 0.0000000345).
- *Alignment:* Allows changes to horizontal and vertical alignment of contents within cells, as well as whether cells are merged with neighboring cells, and whether or not text within the cell simply keeps running outside the boundaries of the cell or wraps (as it would in a paragraph in MS Word) based on the boundaries of the cell.
- *Font:* Self-explanatory. Pick a font, any font. Not to mention color, bold, italics, underline, etc.

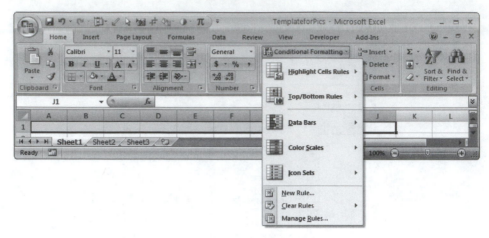

Figure 2.11. Accessing conditional formatting.

- *Border:* Allows changes in the appearance of the cell boundary. Line thickness, color, and line type are options.
- *Fill:* Allows changes in the appearance of the interior background of the cell. Pattern selection (for example, striped or hatched) and color fill are options.
- *Protections:* When accompanied by sheet security options, prevents unauthorized users from modifying the contents or other attributes of the cell.

2.2.2 Conditional Formatting

Unlike static formatting, conditional formatting offers a more dynamic approach to highlighting the contents of cells. Any cell or set of cells subject to conditional formatting will take on a special appearance only when it contains special values. In the current standard versions of Excel, each cell can have up to three conditional formatting rules associated with it, aside from the default cell format.

Click the Conditional Formatting button in the Home tab. A drop-down menu appears with a list of conditional formatting options (shown in Figure 2.11). From here, you can select which type of conditional formatting you want to apply.

If you select the Manage Rules option, the Conditional Formatting Rules Manager opens, and you can add, edit, and delete rules from the same window. Basically, this dialog box allows you to spell out rules or conditions, and specify fonts, borders, and patterns to apply when the cell(s) take on specific values or ranges of values. In the example shown in Figure 2.12, cells subject to the conditional format will take on one colored background pattern when their values are below 0.4, while those with value above 0.6 will take on an alternate pattern.

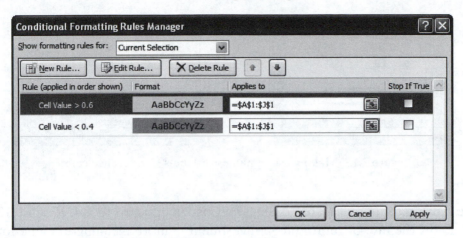

Figure 2.12. Developing conditional formatting rules.

Any other default, such as static formatting, will apply to cells that don't meet either criterion. In this case, the static format of these cells involves no background shading of any kind, so cells with values between 0.4 and 0.6 are unshaded.

There are a couple of points I'd like to make here about formatting multiple cells.

• All static formatting and conditional formatting actions can be applied to multiple cells simultaneously by selecting a group of cells prior to beginning any of the above procedures. A group of adjacent cells can be selected by selecting a cell at a corner of the range desired, holding down the mouse button, and highlighting all other cells in the adjacent range. A group of non-adjacent cells can be selected by holding down the Ctrl key and then clicking on each of the cells in the desired group. When selected, the same access to both static and conditional formatting windows is available.

• If you've already formatted a single cell in a particular way and would like to replicate that format in other cells,, the Format Painter is a handy tool for copying that format to new cells. You can access the Format Painter by clicking the paint brush icon in the Home toolbar of Excel 2007. Select the cell with the appropriate format you want to copy, click the Format Painter icon, and select the set of additional cells where you would like to apply your format.

2.3 Labeling (Naming)

Labels, or names as they are called by standard, provide a way of referencing cells in a meaningful fashion other than the generic A1 or C12. For example, a cell that is consistently used to contain the estimated cost of shipping might

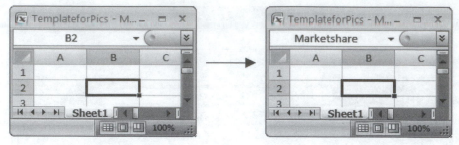

Figure 2.13. Making use of names or labels to reference cells.

be more meaningfully labeled ShippingCost as opposed to G4. If cell H13 contains the rate of return on an investment, a more meaningful name for this cell might be RateofReturn.

Clearly labeled or named cells can be helpful for at least a couple of reasons. Other users can more easily understand what the cell contains. For example, when calculating using a formula, it's beneficial for others to know what terms you are referring to in the calculation. Excel makes it easy to visually associate terms with the data they represent by highlighting cells on a spreadsheet when cells with a formula are selected. Another reason for clear labeling is so that you know what you were thinking after you built a tool (when you might want to modify that tool).

Labels can be assigned to cells by first selecting the desired cell and then entering a new label for that cell in the label box (name box) usually located near the upper-left corner of the spreadsheet.

When unlabeled cells are initially selected, their column-row reference will appear in that label/name box. Click the Label box, enter the new label or name for the cell, and then press Enter. The new name for the cell will display in the label box, such as MarketShare (Figure 2.13).

The cell may then be referenced by either its column-row designation or its new label. More conveniently, however, if at any point the developer wants to move the location of that cell and its contents, the new label will go along with it. This can be very helpful in avoiding confusion when other cells or applications depend on being able to locate the cell's information after such a move.

2.3.1 Handling Label Typos/Changes

If a typographical error in labeling is made, or if the developer later wants to change the name of the cell, the most secure route to correct this issue is to select Name Manager from the Formulas menu to open the Name Manager dialog box. This dialog box enables the user to delete the undesired label and

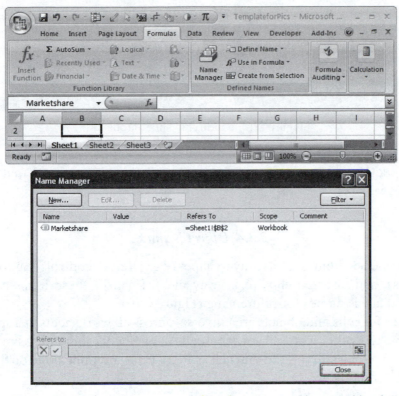

Figure 2.14. Managing names assigned to elements in a workbook.

add others. From the Name Manager all existing labels in a workbook can be modified (Figure 2.14).

2.3.2 Cell Range Labels

As with formatting, multiple cells can be selected simultaneously and assigned a specific label. For example, cells A1:A30 might be labeled Top10Companies if they reference information on the profitability of 10 leading firms. The use of range labels becomes more meaningful in more advanced applications, but they remain extremely useful in helping others to understand the design of a developer's tool.

2.3.3 Worksheet Labels

Referring back to the idea that Excel documents are really workbooks that contain multiple worksheets, each worksheet has a name that can be relabeled as well. Changing the label of a worksheet is extremely straightforward. Just double-click the tab label corresponding to the worksheet of choice

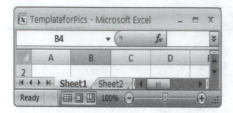 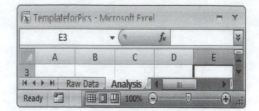

Figure 2.15. Modifying sheet labels.

(e.g., Sheet1 as shown in Figure 2.15), and type in a new name for that sheet (e.g., Raw Data).

2.3.4 Object Names

Objects include items such as drawn shapes (e.g., circles), controls (e.g., option buttons), and inserted clips (e.g., .wav files). Each of these items can be assigned labels/names for referencing (Figure 2.16).

Labels for cells and objects are universal across all worksheets in a specific workbook. In other words, if you label cell A1 on Sheet1 something similar to PRICE, you can still refer to that cell as PRICE for anything done on Sheet2 in that workbook.

2.4 Comments

Along with the labeling of cells to provide better reference mechanisms, comments can be added to specific cells to add greater clarity when needed. For example, aside from labeling a cell Cost, a developer might add the text shown in Figure 2.17 to appear in comment form when the cursor passes above the cell.

Comments are added to selected cells by right-clicking on the cell and then selecting Insert Comment from the shortcut menu. The developer will

Figure 2.16. Assigning names to objects.

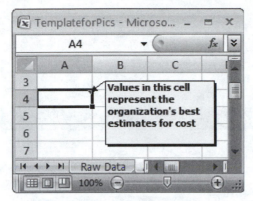

Figure 2.17. Application of a comment to a cell.

then be able to modify the text within the new comment bubble as well as manipulate the height and width of that bubble.

2.5 Hyperlinks

Although hyperlinks (links to Web pages and pages on local drives) can be embedded within cells, they require the cell content to be used entirely for this purpose. So why waste a cell this way when hyperlinks can be assigned to non-cell objects such as drawn circles? Honestly, I've never found a good reason; however, the option is available by either right-clicking and selecting Hyperlink from the shortcut menu or selecting a cell, and then selecting Hyperlink from the Insert tab on the main menu.

2.6 Formulae

Some formulae are basic, such as adding the contents of two cells, dividing the contents of one by another, and then subtracting a third. The syntax of others (such as factorial, power, and natural log) is less obvious.

Excel 2007, when loaded with Palisades software, has more than 500 functions already built in for use within cells. These are probably more than any one person will probably ever want to use, but it's nice to have them available. After you select a cell in which to embed a built-in function, follow the Formulas>Insert Function menu path. The Insert Function dialog box (shown in Figure 2.18) will display.

The great thing about this dialog box is that the functions are organized into a set of about 10 fairly intuitive categories, plus the all-encompassing All category and User Defined items. Even better, this dialog box gives you instructions on the kinds of inputs each function takes, and what it does with

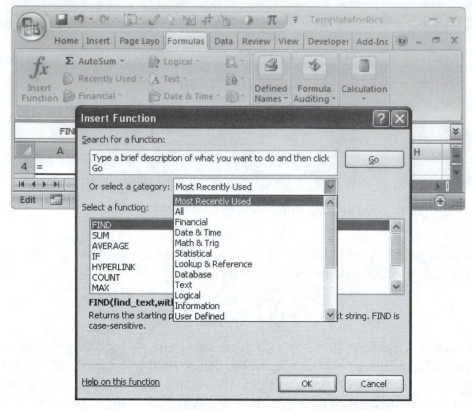

Figure 2.18. Selection of functions for use by category.

those inputs. (I'll show a couple of examples shortly.) The following is a list of some of the options available in the Insert Function dialog box:

- *Financial:* Anything from interest-accrual calculations to net present value (NPV) to yields on T-bills. Useful stuff (makes you wonder why you were ever forced to memorize any formulae in Finance classes).
- *Date & Time:* Getting and working with current date and time representations.
- *Math & Trig:* Common calculations that come up in business models such as sums (Σx), products ($\prod x$), factorials (x!), exponentials(ex), and rounding.
- *Statistical:* Averages, counts, normal distribution (such as z-score) calcs, quartiles, F-tests, and even things like the Poisson distribution.
- *Lookup & Reference:* Some of the neatest and most useful functions are in this category. Sifting through data can be a very frustrating activity for a manager. These functions make the task a lot easier, quicker, and potentially more accurate. An example of a simple reference tool that allows for an alternative means of accessing information elsewhere in a workbook is INDIRECT. Providing a cell reference or cell label/name in quotation marks as the argument of this function will return the value in the corresponding cell. For example, if cell A1 is labeled FirstCell and contains the value 12, the INDIRECT(A1) or INDIRECT(FirstCell) will provide the value of 12 when called.

The Lookup & Reference function is often used in conjunction with other functions in a workbook. For illustration, the following sidebar provides an example of how often some functions (VLOOKUP, MATCH, and OFFSET) might be used in integration.

Sidebar on Formula (Function) use: VLOOKUP, MATCH and OFFSET

In the workbook Chp2_IdentitiesList we have an example of where a class roster is used to look up a fake ID associated with a student's name (B2 re-labeled Name) in a table (StudentInfo). As shown in Figure 2.19, the ID is in the second column of the table. (This function needs the exact spelling of the name.)

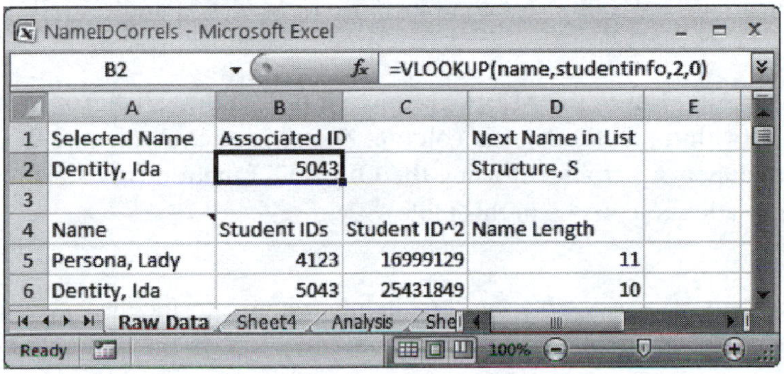

Figure 2.19. Example of VLOOKUP function in use.

Although I may already have an understanding of how to use this (and other functions), Excel won't leave me in the dark if I don't. If I select Insert Function, I'm given a full list of all the parameters associated with the function, some of which may be optional. In the case of OFFSET, for example, the Functions Argument dialog box opens, as shown in Figure 2.20. And as far as an example of integrated use, check out Figure 2.21.

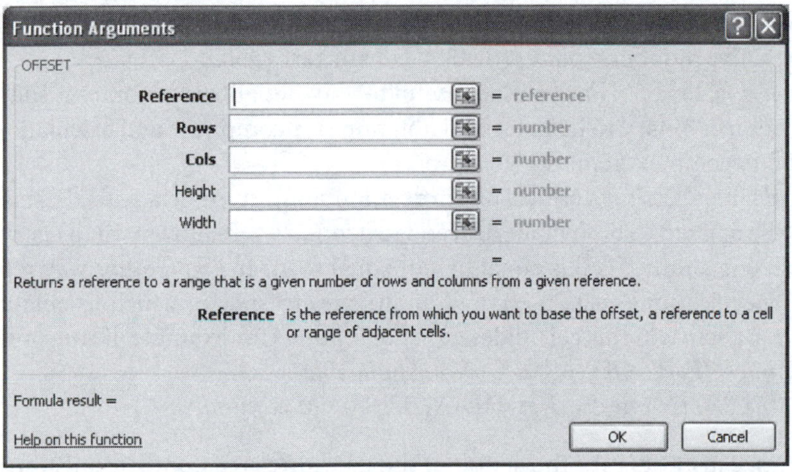

Figure 2.20. Example of assisted field interface for the OFFSET function.

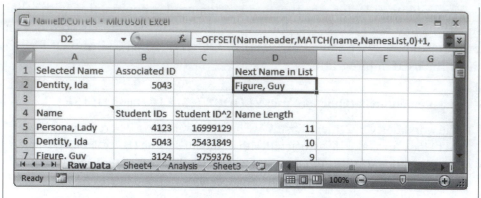

Figure 2.21. Example of combined use of MATCH and OFFSET.

In Figure 2.21, I used the MATCH function to find out which row a student's name is in (within just the Names column, NamesList) and selected the student name that appears just after it using the OFFSET function (my starting base it the Nameheader cell – A4 – in this table).

- *Database:* Not an impressive list, but handy when interfacing Excel with DBs. Provides averages, sums, and other summaries based on the contents of fields in databases.
- *Text:* Functions that allow you to merge text into a single string {such as CON-CATENATE(alien,ate) = alienate}, determine the length of a string {such as LEN(alienate) = 8}, extract a portion of text in a cell {such as MID(alienate,2,4) = lien}, or simply find text within a large text {such as FIND(nate,alienate) = 5 or FIND(nation,alienate)=#VALUE!, which essentially represents an error because *nation* cannot be found anywhere in the text alienate}.
- *Information:* Provides information on the contents on cells, such as whether the number contained is odd, whether it's not a number at all (text), or whether the cell contains an error as an output of the function within it (taking the square root of a negative number would provide the error term #NUM).
- *Engineering:* Probably not all that useful to you, but allows for options such as the translation of binary to hexadecimal notation (for comp sci.) and calculations with imaginary complex numbers (for physics).
- *Logical:* Short list, but a critical one in decision support – specially the IF statement. IF can be applied to both numerical and text inquiries. It allows you to test whether the value in another cell is equal to, not equal to, or in some other way related to other specifications (e.g., >=), and allows you to specify which calculation you want to be active in this cell under either condition (for example, if true or if false).
  - *examples: IF(B2=B3, B3*B3, "Not Applicable")*
  - *IF(OFFSET(Nameslist,1,1)=MAX(B2:B3),"Maximum","–")*

For more insights into the scope of the usefulness of conditional statements in general, see the supplement to this chapter. For those not familiar with the nature of logical statements (perhaps from past philosophy or computer science coursework), this supplement will provide essential insights. Similar ways of thinking will be assumed throughout the later chapters of this text.

2.7 Copying Content and Formats

As shown in use of the copy prompt in copying fixed data across cells, and in doing so making implicit use of Excel's pattern recognition, functions of all kinds as well as cell formats and other attributes can easily be pulled across (or down) ranges of other cells. A few caveats are worth mentioning, however. Cells conditionally formatted relative to a group of other cells (e.g., as available through Excel 2007's group-relative formatting capabilities) may impact the conditional appearance of other cells in the original range. If not expected, this can occasionally prove frustrating, particularly if new cells in the formatted group represent outliers of some kind. They may reduce the apparent distinctiveness of certain cells in the originally formatted group.

Another caveat deals with functions that include cell references (as many do). As cells with such functions are copied, if they use soft-references to cells (e.g., "=MATCH(B3, A1:A20,0)") Excel will automatically change these referenced cells as well (e.g., "=MATCH(B4, A2:A21,0)" if the cell copied to is one row below. Obviously this often not what a user wants. In this case, a user would probably not want the key range A1:A20 to change. To avoid this, the use of cell and cell range labels (names) can do the trick beautifully because Excel will not attempt to alter the use of such labeled ranges as it copied among other cells. Alternatively, one can use hard referencing to prevent any such changes in references as they are copied. A hard-referenced cell in a formula has its column and row each preceded by a dollar sign ($), such as $A$1 or $A$1:$A$20. When typing such a reference into a cell or function within a cell, you can toggle between soft and hard referencing by pressing the F4 key on the keyboard – or more directly, by adding a $ as needed. Partial hard references that allow changes in either row (e.g., $A1) or column (e.g., A$1) but not both can also come in handy, as we'll see in some of the more advanced examples presented throughout this book. Of course, if there are only a handful of cells or cell-ranges that you plan to regularly reference, the best tactic is still to use the cell and range labeling approaches discussed earlier.

2.8 Built-In Tools

Functions are great, but sometimes you need to perform a more sophisticated task that can't be handled easily by a set of functions. Here's where Excel's tools and data manipulation devices come in handy. Generally they are found

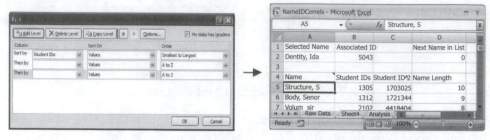

Figure 2.22. Example of the Sort capability in Excel.

on the Data tab. In the interest of time, we'll only go over a few elements found in the Data Tab menus.

We'll start with Sort. As an example, select a range of cells (e.g., the Stu-dentInfo range from the last example); select Data>Sort to open the Sort dialog box. Then select which column you want to sort by (and how). Fig-ure 2.22 shows the result of choosing the StudentID column for sorting:

You can apply a hierarchical sort, by adding "Then by" requirements in the window above (e.g., first sort by "Program" to get all the BBA and LAS students separated, then by "StudentID").

Another nice tool is the Data Filter. This one's pretty handy for tables that you've already constructed. You can select any cell in that table and go to Data→Filter. Excel will automatically convert your table headers into drop-downs that you can use to selectively present only specific records of interest. For example, having used the Autofilter on this table, I have the choice of filtering out all but the LAS students.

Other convenient tools are considered "Add-ins." Many come standard with Excel but are not 'active' until you specify that you want them added to your list of available tools. Other tools (like the cluster analysis that we'll discuss later) don't come with Excel, but can be acquired from other sources (i.e., either freeware or purchased from other sources).

Data Analysis (possible through the "Analysis ToolPak" add-in) actually does come standard with Excel, though again you may have to "add it" to your data menu. To access Excel Add-Ins, click on the Office button in the upper left hand corner of your screen (see Figure 2.23).

Under Excel Options you'll find the option to make additional tools, referred to as add-ins, available to you for use in analysis. Some of the tools that come standard with Excel (and may be particularly useful but may not be formally added into your version) include the Analysis ToolPak and Solver Add-In. To make these available for use, select Excel Add-ins on the lower pull-down tab and then click Go. A new dialog box displays that shows a set of add-ins your system (see Figure 2.24). After the installation process completes, the Data Analysis tool should now be part of the data menu.

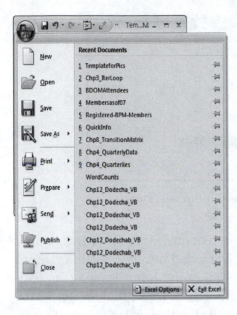

Figure 2.23. Reiteration: Office Button access to Excel Options.

Data Analysis provides access to a range of tools; some are more useful to certain kinds of work than others. For example, let's try it out the Histogram tool using the data on the Analysis sheet of the LookupExample workbook. From the Data Analysis dialog box, select Histogram and then click OK (see Figure 2.25).

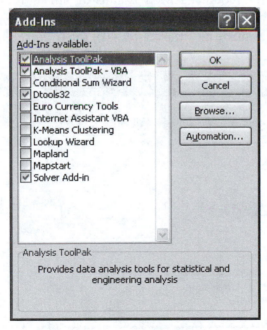

Figure 2.24. Add-ins pop-up interface.

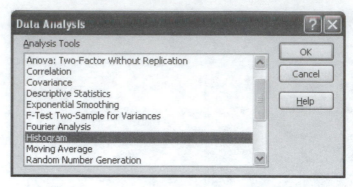

Figure 2.25. Data Analysis pop-up interface.

Imagine that we're interested in a histogram of the length of student names. The Histogram dialog box (Figure 2.26) is divided into two sections: Input and Output Options. In the Input section, fill in the Input Range (the data that you want a histogram on) as well as a Bin Range (the upper limits of each bar in the histogram). I've created a Bin Range within cells $H$8:$H$13 on the example worksheet and I use it here. In the Output Options section, select the Output Range option button to determine where the bin summaries are provided and where a graphical output, if requested, is to be generated. The completed Histogram dialog box is shown in Figure 2.26.

The appropriate information in this particular case provides a listing of the bins specified, the upper cut-off values for each bin, the number of observations falling within it (count), as well as a histogram (as requested).

You could get the same numbers that appear in the new Frequency column by using built-in formulae (see the contents of the Count column to the left of

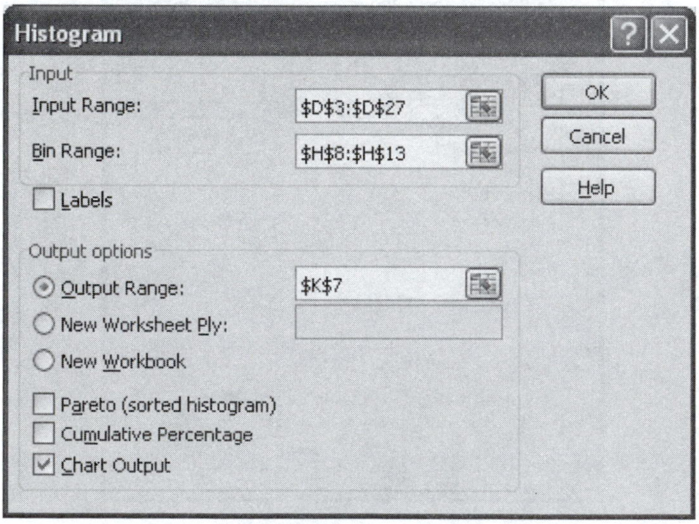

Figure 2.26. Specification of histogram inputs.

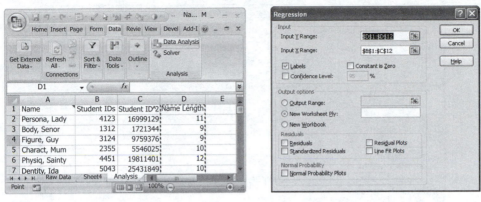

Figure 2.27. Specification of Regression inputs based on structure of spreadsheet.

the new table). Another issue to consider here is the fact that the numbers in the new table are static. In other words, if the calculations behind the original data change (which might shift the data), this table won't change. In contrast, the numbers in the Count column *will* change because they are dynamically linked to the actual data by a function.

Let's consider another tool in the pack: Regression. Choosing that option provides a pop-up screen as shown in Figure 2.27. It allows you to specify a Y variable and any number of X variable that you might want to include in a regression. If we're interested in whether or not student IDs are somehow predictive of the length of student names (we must have hit our heads coming in today), we could include perhaps both the student IDs and the square of those IDs (really hit our heads hard) for example as X variables in the regression. The results provided, shown in Figure 2.28, are admittedly fairly rich from the perspective of the needs of a typical analyst desiring a quick snapshot of possible data relationships.

As with the histogram example, the results here are also static, meaning that they are not responsive to changes in original data. There are other more dynamic capabilities in Excel that allow for similar informational depictions. Beyond this point, and as far as interpretation of the present results are concerned, here the interdependence between the predictive and dependent variables are fairly slight, as would be expected. Keep in mind, however, that a single regression taken alone can indicate patterns even among unrelated random numbers. Be cautious. In general it's always valuable to question the kinds of results that tools provide to you – touch base with reality before you take the output of analysis as infallible.

Chapter 2 Supplement: Logic and Structure in Conditional Statements

In most management settings, decisions that are made at one point in time affect the kinds of decisions that need to be confronted down the road. As

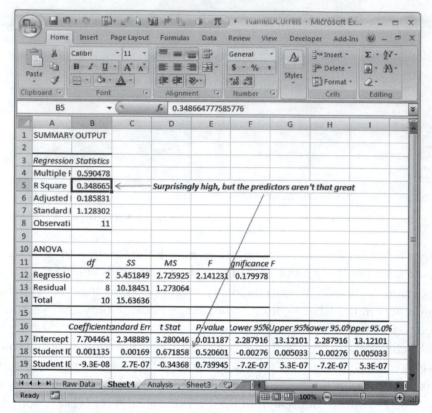

Figure 2.28. Sample annotated output of the Regression tool.

an example, consider the choice to expand the number services offered by a firm to its clients. If an option to expand is rejected, perhaps no additional decisions on the matter need to be made. However, if expansion is the choice, additional questions need to be answered. Should the expansion be targeted toward acquiring new clients, or toward better serving existing clients? If we simply want to better serve existing clients, is our end goal to increase their patronage, or to increase the likelihood of retention? Are we concerned about encouraging mid- or long-term retention?

The structure of these complex multiphase decisions can be mapped out in a straightforward and commonly used framework called a decision tree.

Decision tree structures (shown in Figure 2.29) are useful not only in outlining the course of a decision-making process, but also in outlining the course of a set of questions that might be asked in attempting to assess the specific state of a management scenario. We can draw an analogy here with the common game of 20 Questions with the answers true or false (we stick to this assumed limitation for now).

Different kinds of questions might be relevant when trying to determine what kinds of calculations to make based on the current information available

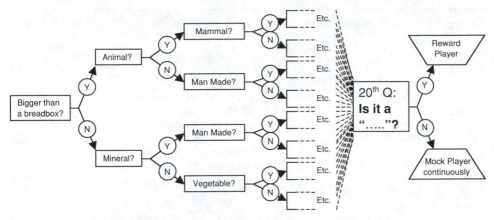

Figure 2.29. Example tree structure for determining identity.

to a business analysis (such as contained in a spreadsheet). For example, let's say that we are a firm that manages large advertising projects for other businesses. We have a facility with a limited number of rooms, and typically assign an individual room to a single advertising project. Other rooms may be used for a variety of other activities that we manage (printing, secretarial, storage, management offices, maintenance offices for on-going campaigns, and so on). Occasionally we may run short of space and need to consider renting additional space. We might like to try to determine the risk of such an event in planning for such rentals. But our calculation of risk may be based on a complex set of issues including the number of projects, past space reserved, managers involved, nature of the projects and clients, and so on.

It wouldn't take much for the calculation of risk, conditional on so many variables, to become complex, but we could consider starting to map it out in a spreadsheet (see Figure 2.30). Let's say that based on the information we've started to lay out, the nature of risk (or uncertainty) we face regarding our need for capacity might be spelled out in a decision tree as shown in Figure 2.31.

Calculating this risk can become convoluted. But no matter how strange or complex the conditions of a work system may be, they shouldn't be ignored; rather, they should be captured as faithfully as possible with regard to their potential impact on decision making and performance.

Similar decision structures, as well as much simpler ones and much more complex ones, are possible in Excel through the use of.

The simplest form of the IF statement has three components:

1) A condition to test for (should be something that can be shown to be either TRUE or FALSE)
2) An affirmative response (what to do if TRUE)
3) A negative response (what to do if FALSE)

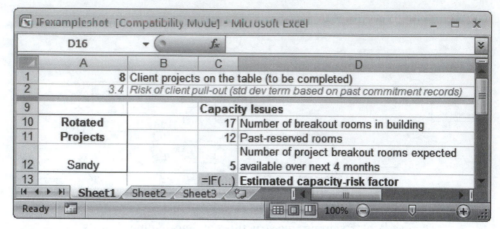

Figure 2.30. Example professional application of a conditional statement.

Using the space rental example, consider a much simpler version of 20 Questions to figure out the risk level facing the firm.

Rather than 20 Questions, this game can be called 1 Question. Basically one question is asked (one condition is tested) and one of two results (either an affirmative or a negative response) will be recorded (in cell C13, shown in Figure 2.32).

We don't have to limit ourselves to games of 1 Question, however, when it comes to using IF statements. In a single cell in a worksheet we may want to ask a sequence of questions that are each appropriate given the result of earlier questions (conditions). We do this using embedded or compound IF statements. Figure 2.33 shows an example using the first three levels of the earlier example (in alternate shades of gray here).

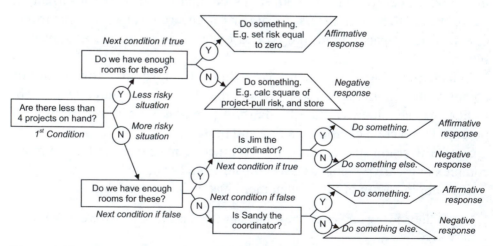

Figure 2.31. Tree structure characteristic of current professional application.
Note: Implied is a different "risk-dynamic" dependent upon projects coordination.

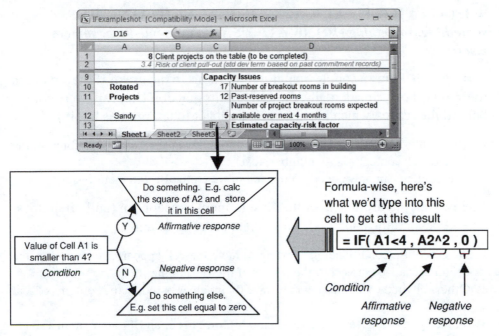

Figure 2.32. Relationship between conceptual tree structures and use of IF statements.

The IF statement that would embody this structure is as follows (gray-shaded to match above). Note what each gray-shaded set of parentheses encloses: always three elements – a condition, an affirmative response, and a negative response.

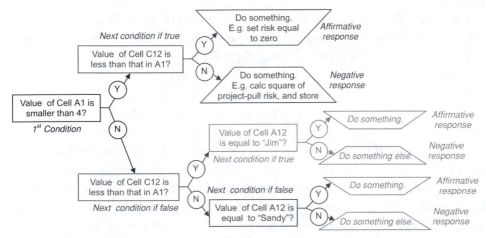

Figure 2.33. Gray-shaded representation of tree structure (specific to content in a spreadsheet).

= IF(A1<4, IF(C12<A1, 0, A2^2), IF(C12<A1, IF(A12="JIM", *something, something else)*, **IF(A12="SANDY",** *something, something else)))*

It's worth noting a couple of major limitations to the use of IF statement in the spreadsheet. (Incidentally, these are limits that don't apply if we're coding behind the scenes, which is something we'll get to later in this book.)

1) The result of an IF statement developed in a spreadsheet can only come in the form of cell content (e.g., a number, text).
2) This content can only appear in the cell in which the IF statement resides.

However, the usefulness of the IF statement concept can (and often does) extend beyond the contents of any single cell. For example:

1) We could use conditional formatting to have the cell appearance change as the contents change (subject to the results of the IF statement).
2) Other cells in the spreadsheet may have their values based on the contents of that cell.
3) Similarly, in recursive use (iteration mode), we can use an IF statement in a single cell to basically serve as an ON/OFF switch for a host of other automated activities in the spreadsheet (such as data record construction, Monte Carlo simulations, and so on).

As a final note on how Excel interprets "conditions" or "logic" statements, it is worth mentioning that whenever we use a statement such as A11>12 as part of an IF statement, it triggers a response in Excel. Excel recognizes it as either TRUE or FALSE.

If you type =(A11>12) into a cell in a spreadsheet, the result that pops out will be either True or False, depending on what value is in cell A11 in this case.

However, Excel also uses numerical representations for True and False. In Excel, True is equal to 1 and False is equal to 0. If you multiply a True times a True, Excel will give you the value 1 (i.e., $1 \times 1 = 1$). If you add a True to two Falses, Excel will give you the value 1 as well ($1 + 0 \times 0 = 1$).

This dual interpretation can come in extremely handy when you want to do quick calculations with existing data that already contains True or False responses.

Say for example you're trying to keep track of the capacity of a network of warehouses. In one column of a spreadsheet you might have records of the storage space for each warehouse. In the adjacent column you might have True or False statements on whether the space is accessible on a given date (perhaps some of these are in regions you can't get to, don't have the capabilities to store what you want to store, or have simply been shut down). You could create a third column that multiplies the first (#) and the second

(True/False) and have a sum at the base of that column to let you know how much space is really available.

PRACTICE PROBLEMS

Practice 2.1

All of the minor methods discussed in this chapter can be used together to get some otherwise tedious work done in a quick but user-friendly way. For example, let's work to develop a threshold table for z-scores.

1) Type the following text into the cells of a new spreadsheet: In cell A1 type z-score, in B1 type Cumulative, in C1 type Density.
2) In the cells below A1, create a list of numbers from –3, –2.9, –2.8, up to 3. Use the copy prompt to do this. Label that full numeric range of cells z-scores.
3) In the cells below B1, use the normsdist function to convert the values in the range z-scores (using the label as your reference, not the column-row designation) into percentages (fixed format them to be viewed as%). Use the copy prompt to copy down the rest of column B. Label that full numeric range of cells Cumulative.
4) In cell C2, type =Cumulative. In cell C3, type =Cumulative-B2. Use the copy prompt to copy the contents of C3 down to the rest of the cells in column C.
5) In D1 type Threshold =, and in D2 type some number between 0 and 0.04. Label D2 threshold.
6) Use conditional formatting to make the background of any cell in column C green if it is greater than that threshold.

Practice 2.2

Select an approximately 200-word paragraph to analyze. This doesn't need to be relevant to your area of expertise; however, it might make this exercise more meaningful to you. Import the paragraph it into a single cell in a new workbook. Using the FIND and MID functions, decompose it into a list (column in Excel) of individual words.

Use the COUNTIF function to create a second column that specifies how many times each word is found in the list you created. Then use conditional formatting to color numbers (in that second column) red if they are greater than 2 and green if they are equal to 1.

3

Getting Data – Acquisition, Linkage, and Generation

Aside from typing information into Excel, there are a number of other ways to get new data into spreadsheets. These methods include opening structured, plain-text files in ways that are meaningful to Excel (for example, rawdata.txt); using other desktop applications as data sources (such as tables in MS Word and tabular results from SPSS); drawing information from structured or nonstructured online sources (such as content from COMPUSTAT or even the whitepages.com); and developing systems that create/simulate large volumes of data with desired characteristics (mainly for use in illustrating or testing the robustness of proposed management policies). In this chapter we'll touch on each of these at some level.

3.1 Text File Imports and Basic Table Transfers

If you have a text file that contains information, such as a survey or database data in text-file format, it can be opened into Excel as a new file. You simply need to specify how data in that file are organized, such as separated by spaces, tabs, commas, and so on.

As an example, imagine a text file titled Chp3_MultRespsFinal.txt. Each record in this file occupies a new row, and the information relating to each record is organized sequentially with each field separated by a comma. This kind of data organization is referred to as comma delimited. Select Home>Open in Excel and then find and select this text document. The Step 1 of the Text Import Wizard opens, as shown in Figure 3.1.

In this case, we have what is referred to as a delimited file. It's relatively easy to import raw files such as these into other programs – certain markers such as commas help designate where a type of data ends and another begins. Most applications are designed to be able to make sense out of data organized this way.

Comma delimitation (or delimitation of some other kind) is specifically designated in the Delimiters section of Step 2 of the Text Import Wizard,

34

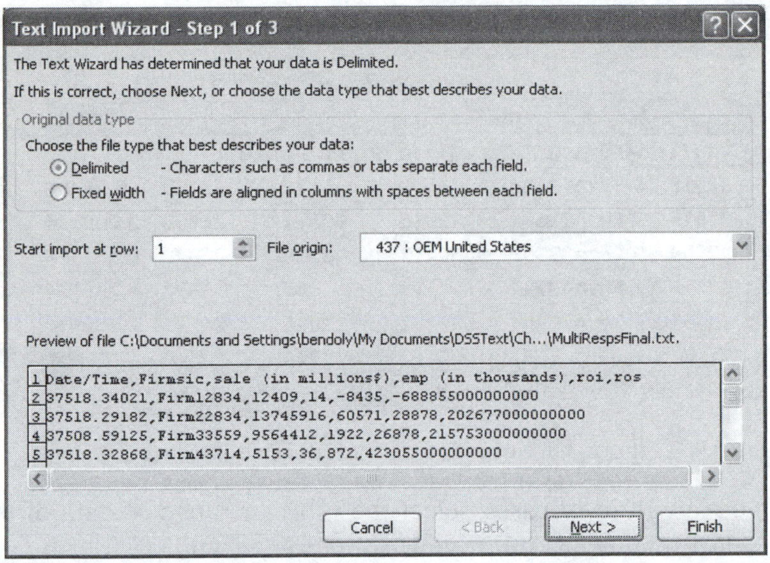

Figure 3.1. Text Import Wizard interface.

shown in Figure 3.2. In this case, selecting Comma provides you with a preview of how the data will appear in the spreadsheet once Finish is selected. What you end up with in the spreadsheet is a relatively intuitively structured display of the contents of that file, if done correctly (Figure 3.3).

Direct imports from other MS office programs (such as tabular data in MS Word) or non-MS programs that use tabular structures (for example, SPSS)

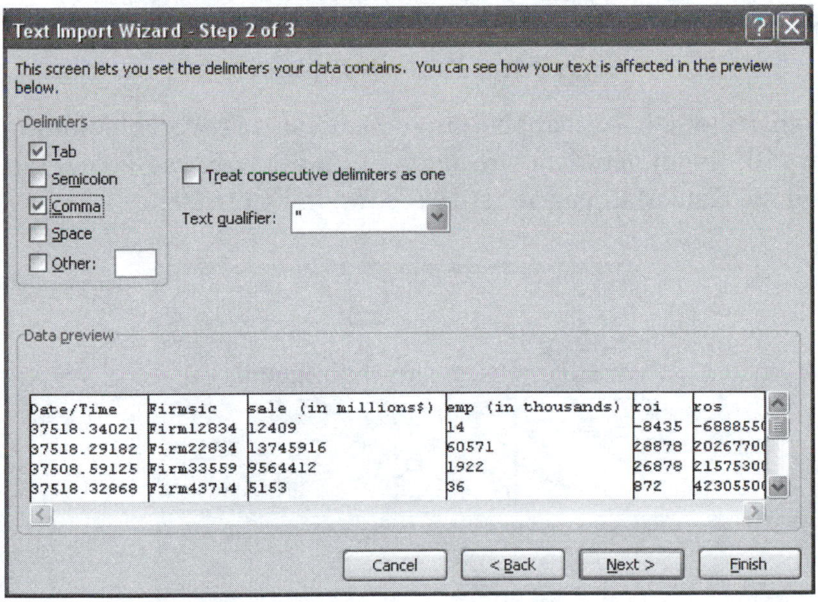

Figure 3.2. Specification of comma delimitation.

	A	B	C	D	E	F
1	Date/Tim	Firmsic	sale (in m	emp (in th	roi	ros
2	37518.34	Firm12834	12409	14	-8435	-6.9E+14
3	37518.29	Firm22834	13745916	60571	28878	2.03E+14
4	37508.59	Firm33559	9564412	1922	26878	2.16E+14
5	37518.33	Firm43714	5153	36	872	4.23E+14
6	37518.3	Firm53559	680401	2056	20171	1.46E+14

Figure 3.3. Spreadsheet content once imported.

are even easier. In most cases, select the table or range of data of interest, copy it, select a starting cell in your spreadsheet, and paste it by pressing Ctrl-P. Alternatively, you can select Edit>Paste and achieve the same result.

3.2 More Sophisticated Application Transfers

Few meaningful corporate decisions can be made without some implied, if not explicit, consideration for the geographical surroundings in which the firm is set (local demand, local labor, environmental regulations, international law, and so on). Fortunately, if we want to account for geography, infrastructure, and demographics, we have a number of resources already available to us. One of those is MS MapPoint, shown in Figure 3.4.

3.2.1 MapPoint Data Sources

MapPoint is more than a mapping program. It's also a geographic information system (GIS) with geo-data already built into it. You can access this data through the Data Mapping Wizard as shown in Figure 3.5.

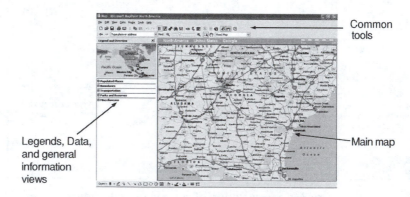

Figure 3.4. Basic front-end elements of the MapPoint environment.

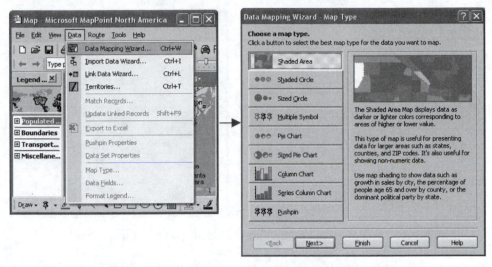

Figure 3.5. Specifying map type for data depiction.

The wizard starts by presenting several different ways to graphically represent this geo-data. After you select a presentation type, you'll need to specify what data you want to present. For example, you might be interested in graphing demographic data relating to specific areas in the United States (Figure 3.6).

MapPoint can then present a host of demographic options specific to your needs (depending on what MapPoint database you have access to). When those data are fully specified, you can then tweak some of the aesthetics of the map you want to generate (see Figure 3.7). Before you know it, you have

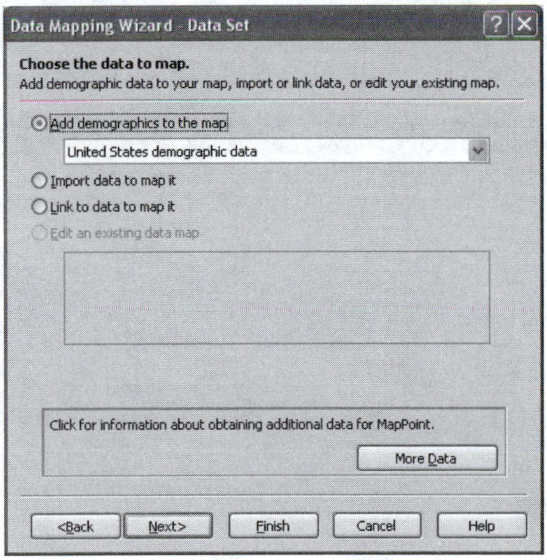

Figure 3.6. Initial data specification.

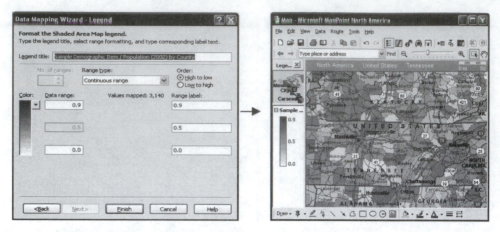

Figure 3.7. Potential demarcation specs and final mapped result.

a geographic representation of data to which you can add information, pan across, and zoom in and out.

These maps are interactive. If you place your cursor over certain areas or features, comment boxes will pop up to provide specific details. With this in

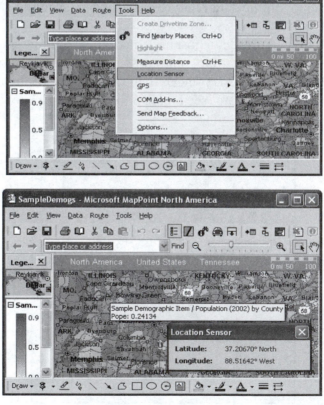

Figure 3.8. Activating and using the location sensor by panning.

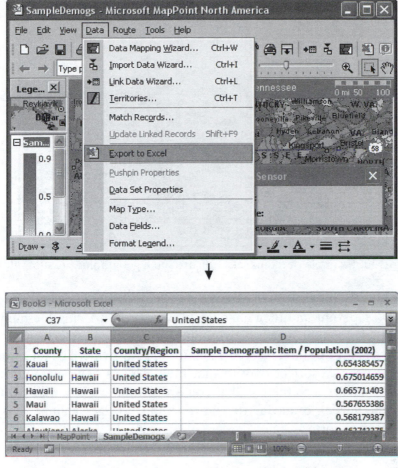

Figure 3.9. Requesting an export to Excel, and spreadsheet generated.

mind, the Location Sensor shown in Figure 3.8 is another tool that might be helpful.

When the Location Sensor is turned on, you can move the cursor over a location (for example, Monroe Heights, VA) and see a summary of the data mapped at that location as well as the longitude and latitude. This could come in handy for some quick approximations of distances between a variety of locations.

3.2.2 From MapPoint to Excel

It is easy to export MapPoint data into Excel where the data can be manipulated. There are several approaches worth going over for those interested in leveraging this data. In MapPoint, the most direct method is Data>Export to Excel, as seen in Figure 3.9.

Figure 3.10. Example of radius selection around a geographic point of interest.

Alternatively, if you want to export a specific geographic region, select that region in MapPoint and then conduct an export only. Using the numerous drawing tools available (such as the radius tool), you can select a geographically relevant area of interest (100 miles around Nashville, TN, for example), and restrict the export of data to that area. This is demonstrated in Figure 3.10. And the nice thing is that you are getting exactly what you want without the burden of having to wait for a much larger volume of data to otherwise be exported.

3.2.3 *From Excel to MapPoint*

Data stored or created in Excel can also be imported into MapPoint; however, the more MapPoint-related data you add to an Excel project, the more time it will take for functions such as zooming, panning, analysis, and so on to work. So, if you are interested in a select set of data, such as associated with a relatively specific geographic area like New York, it's worth avoiding importing and exporting large volumes of unrelated data.

The Link Data Wizard is particularly useful if you want to import update-able data from Excel – for example, data that you might want to eventually change in both Excel and MapPoint. To open the Link Data Wizard, start by selecting Data>Link Data Wizard (Figure 3.11). In the first page of the wizard, choose the Excel spreadsheet from which you want to retrieve the data and then click Next.

The wizard will then ask for a unique reference key to designate each record in the data you want to import. That reference code can be numeric- or text-based, but it has to be unique. In other words, each record must have a value for that key that is not used by another record. This is an important point

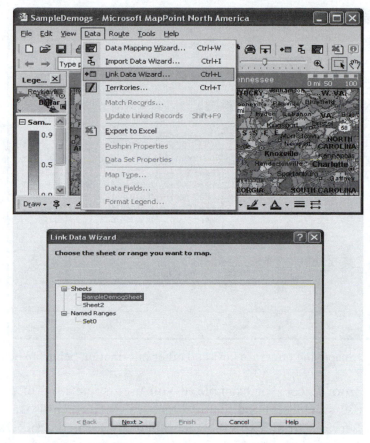

Figure 3.11. Using the Link Data Wizard to tie MapPoint maps to Excel data (refreshable).

to keep in mind with geo-data because many geo-names, such as Springfield, Monroe, Oakville, and so on, are used by many cities in the United States.

After the key is selected, designate what each record attributes matches concepts in MapPoint (See Figure 3.12). For example, MapPoint recognizes geographic areas such as cities, counties, states, and countries, and has additional data for each of these. There may be more data than you would like to import that MapPoint isn't familiar with – and MapPoint will be happy to graph that for you, but that's about all you can expect as far as MapPoint's understanding is concerned.

The Link Data Wizard can update your map without much additional work on your part. As an example, try setting up a data link using the Chp3_ SampleDemogs file. When mapped, edit the data by adding sound or taking the square of the data and copying over the original. Click the scale/legend in MapPoint and select the Update Now option to update your map in MapPoint.

You are not limited to previously exported data that you have simply modified in Excel. You can always pick an entirely new series to export into

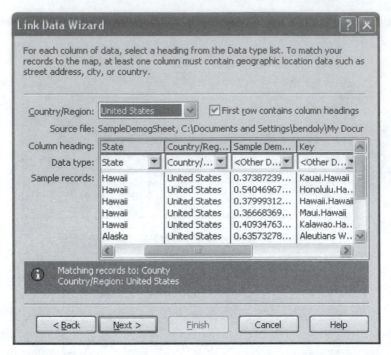

Figure 3.12. Specifying reference keys and other information being linked to a map.

MapPoint from Excel. For example, if you used some kind of marketing model to assess the likelihood that residents of specific census tracts would seek your services from a specific geographically located firm, you might import and graph those newly derived data (Figure 3.13). Or, as shown on the right side of Figure 3.13, if similar analysis helped designate which of a set

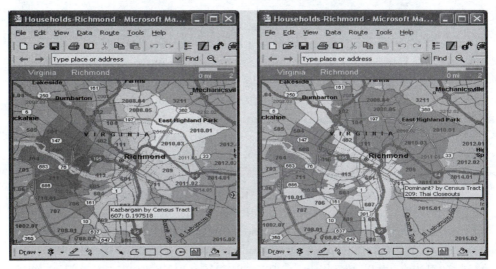

Figure 3.13. Examples of imported data for the same region showing intensity and partitioning.

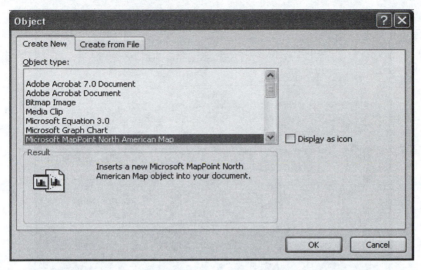

Figure 3.14. Inserting (embedding) a MapPoint map object in Excel.

of competing firms were dominant in a geographic marketspace, you could import and graph that information.

3.2.4 Excel (MapPoint): Embedded Maps

MapPoint objects can also be imported into Excel. To do so, select a cell within the range of data and reference-key designations you want; then select Insert>Object to open the Object dialog box (Figure 3.14). Scroll down to Microsoft MapPoint North America Maps, and click OK to embed a map of the United States into Excel. Double-click the map to activate the MapPoint toolbar in Excel, shown in Figure 3.15.

Click the Link Data Wizard to initiate a series of pop-up windows prompting you to specify where the data are located in the workbook. Browse for your Excel filename (in this example, Chp3_SampleDemogs.xls). From the Link Data Wizard, select the worksheet name where your data are stored. Depending on compatibility, you may need to re-save your Excel file as an Excel 97-2003 worksheet prior to linking, or MapPoint might not recognize it. Otherwise, it's the same procedure as followed when the Link Data Wizard was discussed.

In many cases, Excel may graph your data using a method you might not want (using pushpins rather than colored regions, for example). But, as with all graphs in Excel, this can easily be changed by selecting the map and clicking the Shaded Area button in the Data Mapping Wizard – Map Type page. (See Figure 3.16. Note: This page is available only after a map is embedded.)

In the case of maps embedded in Excel, you might find the updating process more convenient at some level (e.g., if the spreadsheet containing the source

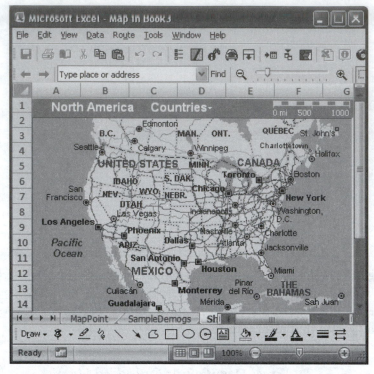

Figure 3.15. Appearance of a MapPoint map embedded in Excel.

data also contains the mapping of that data). Unfortunately, graphical updates are not as dynamic as those with Excel plots. You still need to double-click the map, right-click the legend, and then click Update Now. To perform this update, only Excel needs to be open; you don't have to switch between programs.

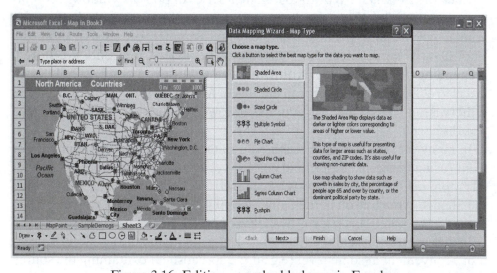

Figure 3.16. Editing an embedded map in Excel.

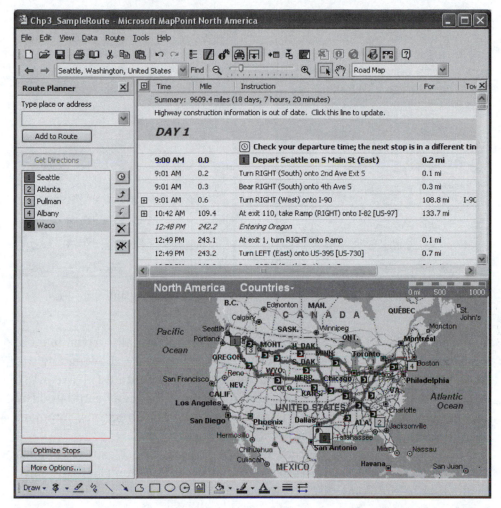

Figure 3.17. Example of route specification, derived directions, and route mapping.

3.2.5 *Routing Information and Insights through MapPoint*

Aside from data storage and visualization, MapPoint's Routing tool provides fairly accurate estimates for travel distance, time, and cost. To activate this tool, select the automobile icon on the main MapPoint toolbar, or choose Route>Route Planner. This provides the opportunity to add any number of sites to a constructed route. Selecting Get Directions will do just that: provide a set of step-by-step directions for carrying out the route in the sequence specified as well as a graphical mapping of that sequenced route. Additional summary measures of the specified sequence also comes in the form of total trip distance, time estimates, and cost (Figure 3.17).

Some sequences specified in routes are less ideal than others. Visual inspection alone would suggest that driving directly to Atlanta first in this example

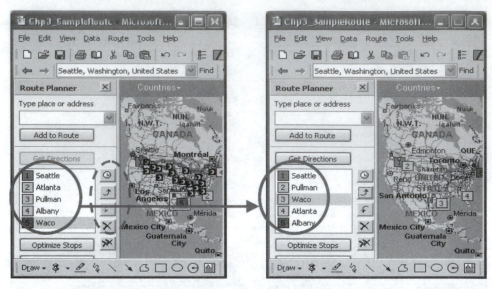

Figure 3.18. Manual editing and resequencing of routes.

might not be ideal. Fortunately, MapPoint makes the visually driven manual manipulation of route sequences fairly straightforward by allowing any site to be selected and shifted in its order of sequence in a route (Figure 3.18). After a sequence is modified, associated route directions can be updated (by clicking Get Directions again) to provide a new set of directions, summary of total route distance, time, and cost (Figure 3.19).

I don't have to do all of that in MapPoint directly. I can accomplish the same thing using a map embedded in Exel (i.e., I don't actually have to deal with MapPoint directly to get this done; however, it often runs faster).

As with everything else, all of these data are subject to export into Excel for further analysis, manipulation, and subsequent feeds back into MapPoint. The key here is that these products can be used in a back-and-forth dialogue to develop meaningful insights that anyone of these applications alone might not provide.

Quick note on re-sequencing: As may already have become obvious, manual re-sequencing with the intention of minimizing costs or distance can be substituted for by MapPoint's built-in route optimization mechanism (Optimize Stops on the Route Planner frame). We will discuss the mechanics of route optimization in Chapter 5 and then again in Chapter 7. The art of route optimization is not a simple one, and there are many approaches that can be taken. Some will be better than others, subject to the specific goals of the analyst or DSS developer. For now it is sufficient to just recognize that whatever method is used, MapPoint continues to provide an excellent mechanism through which to visualize solutions derived.

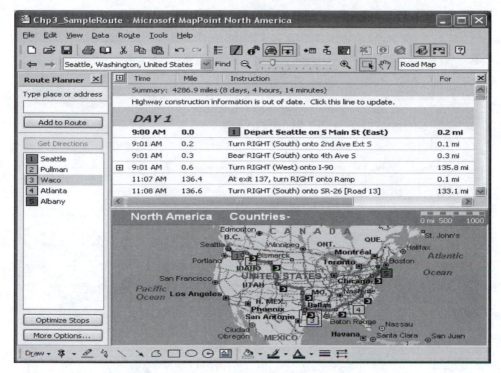

Figure 3.19. Updating directions, graphics, and summaries after route editing.

3.3 Online Data Acquisition

The integration of alternative data-rich applications with Excel has the potential of opening up numerous opportunities for developers and managers who might otherwise be unaware of these convenient resource integrations. At this point, let's look at how we can bring the Internet into this intergration fold.

Many online sources of potentially valuable data are already publicly available and are updated on a regular basis. The number of these sources is on the rise. The implication of this, however, is that what the sources said yesterday may not be relevant to a decision that needs to be made today. In Excel, Web queries are used to draw information from online resources. Similar to data analysis, a Web query is a tool that comes standard in Excel.

Select Data>Web Query to open the New Web Query dialog box. Specify from where the data will be drawn, such as the URL. Figure 3.20 shows an example of the public job site hosted by Microsoft.

Newer versions of Excel, such as Excel 2007, have an updated interface for selecting what you want to import. In the previous example, only the job specification table has been selected (shown as a gray check marked box here, however in a live document it would appear as a green check marked box as

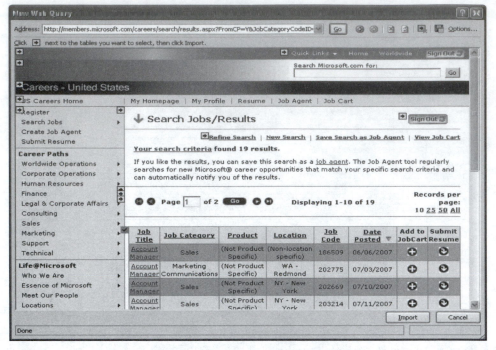

Figure 3.20. Example Web query interface.

opposed to one containing a yellow arrow). You can toggle between selecting and deselecting these elements with the click of the mouse.

Click Import after making the table selections (check marks will appear). You will then be asked where you want the results of the query to be placed in your spreadsheet. Specify the in upper-left corner where you want the input data to start. I usually pick cell A2 for simplicity. After you provide location information, the first importation of data will occur. The data you're interested in will start somewhere to the right of and below the cell you selected, depending on the table structures on that Web page.

So that updates don't overwrite other work on the worksheet, consider doing additional work to the right or below the import space. Losing information can be frustrating, so I recommend saving various versions as you develop your spreadsheet.

After a new Web query is created (or just prior to import), further specifications can be made by selecting Properties from the Data tab. This opens the External Data Range Properties dialog box, as shown in Figure 3.21.

This dialog box enables you to set a number of properties for your Internet-imported data. In this example, I've made additional specifications that the data be updated every 10 minutes, updates do not change the column widths on the spreadsheet, and all formats are preserved. Later in this chapter, we'll take a look at how this might be important when building a tool for collecting Web data over time.

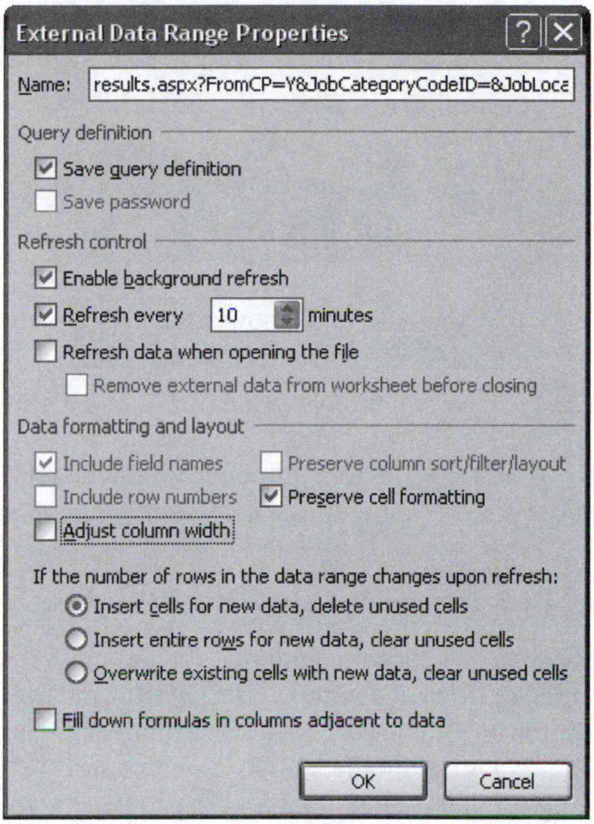

Figure 3.21. Example specifications for Web query.

3.4 Simulating Data: The Basics

When acquired data are not available or do not sufficiently characterize future scenarios, developers often rely on random numbers to portray dynamics. There are many different ways to calculate random numbers in Excel. The following sections discuss some of the more common methods. (For examples, refer to Chp3_RandomNumbers.xls.)

3.4.1 Uniformly Distributed Randoms

These are basically a random values ranging from some minimum value ("a") to some maximum ("b"). To create a random number based on this distribution in Excel, start with the random number generation function Rand(). Rand() automatically gives you a random number between 0 and 1. To change that to a range from "a" to "b," enter the following information into a cell (replacing "a" and "b" with real numbers):

$$= a + \text{Rand()}^*(b - a)$$

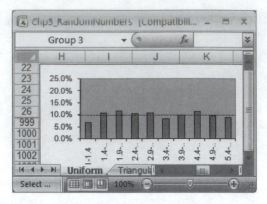

Figure 3.22. Example sample population from uniform distribution.

If a $= 1$ and b $= 5$ for 1,000 random numbers, we might get what's reflected in Figure 3.22. *Note: Press F9 to generate new random numbers.*

3.4.2 Triangularly Distributed Randoms

These distributions also represent random values ranging from some minimum value ("a") to some maximum ("b"). However, unlike uniformly distributed randoms, the chance of picking a number in this range peaks at some value "c", and is essentially zero at both "a" and "b." Excel uses the IF statement along with the Rand() function to provide the following form:

= IF (Rand()<(c-a)/(b-a),   *{for example, is Rand() below the peak?}*
  a+SQRT((b-a)*(c-a)*Rand()),   *{for example, if yes, then use this calc}*
  b-SQRT((b-a)*(b-c)*(1-Rand()))))   *{for example, if no, then use this calc instead}*

If a $= 1$, b $= 5$, and c $= 4$ for 1,000 random numbers, we might get what's reflected in Figure 3.23.

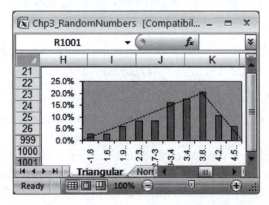

Figure 3.23. Example sample population from triangular distribution.

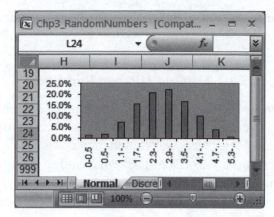

Figure 3.24. Example sample population from normal distribution.

3.4.3 Normally Distributed Randoms

You're probably familiar with this one (at least in theory – i.e., the bell curve). Fortunately, Excel makes this simple:

$$= NORMINV(Rand(), \mu, \sigma)$$

If $\mu = 3$ and $\sigma = 1$ for 1,000 random numbers, we might get what's reflected in Figure 3.24.

Excel's built-in functions allow for several other common distributions to be handled the same way (such as CHIINV() for the χ-dist, FINV() for F-dist, TINV() for t-dist, and so on).

Sometimes it's useful to consider the chances that alternative discrete events occur. For example, a person decides to buy Brand X as opposed to Brand Y; or three people don't show up for hotel room reservations on Friday (as opposed to one person, or two or four peope); or a competing firm decides to build its new facility in Jacksonville instead of Des Moines or Toledo; or items 2 and 17 are dropped from a federal bill outlining tax incentives for small exporters.

Each of these events is discrete – it either happens, or it doesn't. If it does occur, the implication is that alternative events that could have happened in its place didn't, at least for the specific timeframe considered. Sometimes the alternative events are related in an ordinal fashion, for example three people not showing up is more than two people not showing up. Sometimes alternative events are simply nominal – not easily comparable by a single measure, but distinct from each other nevertheless (buying Brand X instead of Brand Y, for example). The consideration of these kinds of variables and their uncertainty are just as important to good decision making as is the consideration of more continuous variables (those that can take on meaningful decimal values).

3.4.4 Uniform Discrete Randoms

These are the simplest of these are variables that describe multiple discrete events, with each event having exactly the same chances of occurring at a given points in time. Regardless of what each event is, it can be represented by some kind of coding such as Event 1, Event 2, and so on, up to Event n. This makes it easy to use Excel to generate random events with equal (uniform) chances of occurring. For n random events, we can use either:

$$= RANDBETWEEN(1,n), \text{ or } =INT(n*RAND()+1)$$

Both will provide equally weighted random integers between 1 and n that can correspond to each of the n events under consideration.

3.4.5 Bernoulli Discrete Randoms

In some circumstances, we are interested in only one of two events taking place, such as a potential customer either signing up or not signing up for an offered service contract. The chances of either event are often not equal. These are called Bernoulli events, and the outcomes are typically coded numerically as 0 (doesn't sign up) or 1 (does). If the probability of the 1 event is p (29%, 73%, 8%, or another percentage), we can generate a 0,1 variable value in Excel by using the following IF-based statement:

$$= IF(RAND()<=p, 1, 0)$$

We could even replace the 0,1 coding directly with meaningful info, such as by continuing the previous example as:

$$= IF(RAND()<=29\%, \text{"Signs up"}, \text{"Doesn't sign up"})$$

3.4.6 Custom Discrete Randoms

In some circumstances, we have multiple (more than two) alternative events, each of which has its own probability of occurring instead of the others. Because these are true alternatives, adding up the chances of each event should give us 100% (all possible outcomes need to be accounted for). We can consider these events and their probabilities in a tabular format. The following is an example from the hotel industry:

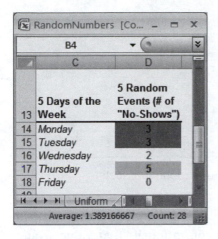

Figure 3.25. Example sample pulls from a discrete distribution.

Past data shows that the following number of no-shows occur by these probabilities regardless of the day of the week:

Number of No-Shows	Probability of that Number of No-Shows Occurring	Cumulative
0	9%	0%
1	12%	9%
2	22%	21%
3	28%	43%
4	19%	71%
5	10%	90%

An easy way to draw random values from this table is to use the VLOOKUP function again with the RAND() function. Specifically, using the last two columns in the previous table, VLOOKUP will return the row with the Cumulative probability <= RAND() (see Figure 3.25) and will return the value in the second of those two columns:

$$= VLOOKUP(RAND(), LastTwoColumns, 2)$$

3.5 Living Data Records: The Basics

The standard calculation mode in Excel is non-iterative automatic, meaning that every time you make a change in the workbook, all cells get updated. But sometimes you want to have more control over your data. The iteration option enables you to gain some of that control.

Iteration allows for actions such as setting the value in cell A1 equal to the value in A1 + 1 (for example, it enables you to enter the A1: "=A1+1"equation into cell). In general, this is referred to as a circular loop

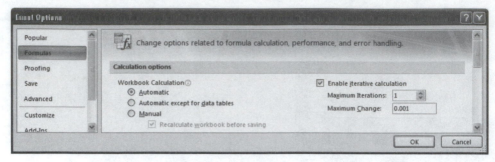

Figure 3.26. Specification of iteration mode in Excel.

because you're asking the computer to base the value of something off of itself. If the computer were told to do this continuously, that value would soon become huge (and would keep growing). When faced with this situation, some software will give you an error message saying something to the effect of "a circular loop has been detected and the value in the cell will not stabilize."

Iteration mode allows developers to say exactly how many times the computer should do the calculation before stopping, thus avoiding problems usually caused by circular loops. To switch into the iteration mode, click the Office button and then select Excel Options>Formulas to open the Excel Options dialog box. Under the Calculation options section, check the Enable iterative calculation checkbox (See Figure 3.26). For most cases, 1 iteration maximum is appropriate. Select that and click OK to enable this setting.

Note: Use iteration mode only when it's your best option. Trying to create other kinds of spreadsheet workbook tools can be tough in this mode, as well as frustrating. Most work is done in the non-iterative mode.

Under the iteration setting, calculations begin with the upper-left cell (such as A1), and then progress through the first row of the spreadsheet from left to right until that row comes to an end (cell IV1). Calculations then resume, starting at the first column of the next row and progressing again from left to right, until all cells containing calculations are handled (see Figure 3.27).

In iteration mode, recalculations are started by pressing the same key used to refresh/generate new random variable values in normal modes. In the specifically single iteration mode, whenever F9 is pressed, if there is a calculation to be made in cell A1, Excel will base that calculation off of all information *currently available* (such as information that *currently* appears in all). If there is subsequent calculation to be made in cell B1, that calculation will take into account all current information as well as the value just calculated for A1. Similarly, any calculation for B2 would involve the updated values for

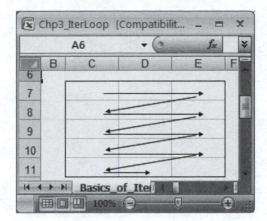

Figure 3.27. Order of refresh calculations under iteration mode.

both A1 and B1. After calculations are made for cells during a single iteration (pressing F9), they will not change until another iteration is started. This
holds true for all mathematical calculations and logical and text functions, as
well as random number generation.

The spreadsheet Chp3_IterLoop.xls contains examples of how the iteration
mode might be applied. The first example is basically the baseline example
that illustrates how a typical circular loop is constructed, and how cell calculations based on it are changed upon each iteration (each time F9 is pressed).

In this example I have set up 14 cells such that the values contained in
13 of them are based on the value of the cell before it. I've depicted this
dependency with dashed lines. (Note that it is in the opposite direction of the
order by which cell calculations are made in the iteration mode – I did that
on purpose.) The value in the 14th cell is calculated by increasing itself by 1
(D18 is set to =D18+1, shown in Figure 3.28).

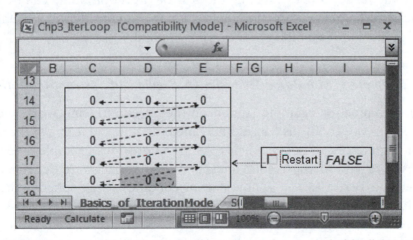

Figure 3.28. Example of living record cell interdependency needed for living records.

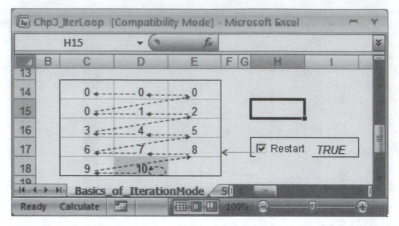

Figure 3.29. Associated result of example living record update.

I've also restricted calculations to only particular situations (here only when the value for a cell labeled Restart is set to True. In the spreadsheet this value can be either modified directly through typing or toggled using the associated check box.

Note: we'll talk about creating check boxes later.

The calculations begin when Restart is True and I press F9. But after the first iteration, the only cell that should change is cell D18 (=0+1=1). All others take on the value of their assigned neighbors (0 to start). After a second iteration, D17 takes on D18's value (1) and D18 becomes 2. After 10 iterations we get what's shown in Figure 3.29.

3.6 Living Records in Practice

To give the reader a better feeling for how the iteration mode can become a critically valuable resource in practice, it's worth considering a couple of more sophisticated examples in which it is applied.

3.6.1 Example 1: Simulated Histories (A Preview of System Simulations)

The first in-practice example (found on the StockoutDemo worksheet of the previous workbook) is considerably more complex in terms of the number and nature of cell dependencies. As in the previous example, I've illustrated where both forward (solid lines) and circular/backward dependencies (dashed lines) exist, as well as how starting conditions are applied (light dotted lines). Also, in this example one of the variables (Units in Stock) is tied to a live data record and associated graph (see Figure 3.30).

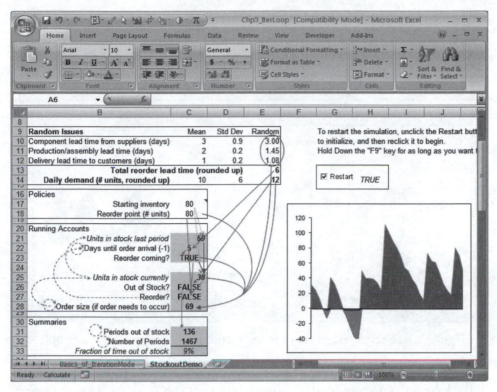

Figure 3.30. Inventory system example of living record use.

This example shows how far an individual might be able to leverage the iteration mode and living records. The live data record that the graph is working off of is no more complex that the previous 14-cell numeric example. Basically, we have one cell at the bottom that continues to update itself (see Figure 3.31). This cell is based off of the most recent value representing units in stock, while cells above it take on values of those below them (i.e., values from the past).

Note: The form of the plot shown is a simple line graph with the x-axis assumed to be time. It is therefore depicting changes in inventory positions as time progresses.

3.6.2 Example 2: Web-Import Histories

Having already discussed the potential of acquiring data from the Web, and given the example of building a living record based on randomly generated data, we now have the basic tools necessary to construct a live data-recording mechanism based on data updates from external sources.

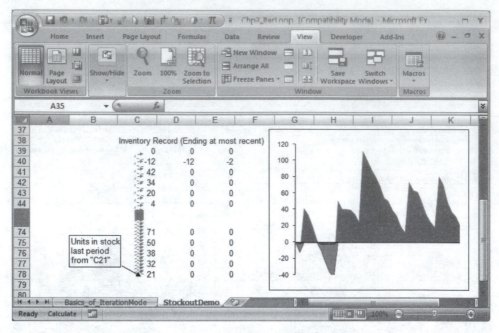

Figure 3.31. Specific structure of living record in inventory system example.

With online data provided by external sources, it often makes sense to only record new data when we're assured that they're different from past data, and to collect the time at which these changes are detected. This way you can get a good idea of how data changes over time without having too much redundant information. In a spreadsheet, that will basically mean selecting two columns in which you want to store records (one column for your imported data, another for the time at which the data are recorded). This approach requires only limited (four, in this case) kinds of cell calculations. In this case, two of these calculations will be repeated throughout most of your data record. A typical spreadsheet layout for this purpose is described in the following clip from Ch3_nrtRecords.xls. It's fully annotated, and duplicates much of the logic we've discussed (see Figure 3.32).

PRACTICE PROBLEMS

Practice 3.1

Select a set of data to map; then select a portion of the map and export that data into Excel. Modify the data to your liking, maybe by replacing some of it with other random values or some simple mathematical function. Click Update Now to see the resulting change in the mapping.

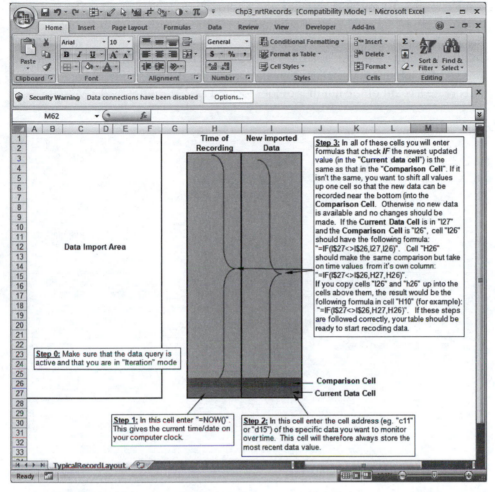

Figure 3.32. Specific structure of living record in Web query example.

Practice 3.2

Create a stock-value generator that picks values of a stock based on a random mechanism for selecting recently observed values of that stock. Create a stock-value collector for an individual company (your choice), using the iterative mode Web query and recording method discussed in this chapter. Run the collector for a two-hour period (start early to make sure you have it working) and then use the collected record and the RAND function to pick values from the list. Use whatever technique you think may be appropriate.

Practice 3.3

Use a Web query to import a page from the *NY Times* job database. Use the following URL stem, and add the last digit of your birth date to it to signify the page number

being referenced: http://jobs.nytimes.com/js.php?qInd=nytcategorymanufacturing&
pp=25&view=2&page= (e.g., if my student ID ended with 0, I'd include a 1 at the
end of the above URL stem). Assume that interest in job locations (state info) is
uniformly distributed (for example, there's a 1 in 50 chance that someone will be
interested a job in a particular given state). Use that info to draw a random state,
and create a count of the number of jobs located at that randomly drawn state.

Section 2

Harvesting Intelligence

4

Structuring Problems and Option Visualization

Decision modeling/representation describes the use of data and logic to clarify the specific nature of a situation for which assistance in the decision-making process may be needed. The hope is that in clarifying such details, the development of meaningful suggestions and solutions may be easier to create.

Most management problems for which decisions are sought can be represented by three standard elements – objectives, decision variables, and constraints.

Objective
Maximize profit
Provide earliest entry into market
Minimize employee discomfort/turnover

Decision variables
Determine what price to use
Determine length of time tests should be run on a new product/service
Determine the responsibilities to assign to each worker

Constraints
Can't charge below cost
Test enough to meet minimum safety regulations
Ensure responsibilities are at most shared by two workers

All of these elements can be visualized graphically often to the benefit of analysis and general insights. Our initial discussion will be limited to objectives and decision variables; we'll discuss constraints later on in this chapter.

In most business scenarios, managers are faced with making a set of decisions that impact a final outcome (objective). This tends to make the decision process more complex, and sometimes the rationale for making specific decisions are difficult to describe.

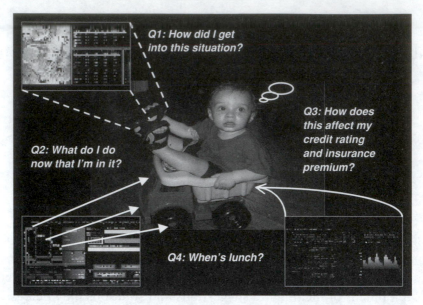

Figure 4.1. Value and limitations in visualization.

4.1 Value of Data Visualization

As the old saying goes, a picture is worth a thousand words (Figure 4.1).

Some pictures are cute, but may say very little to professionals – at least not initially.

Misleading suggestions can throw a decision maker off his or her game. It's the responsibility of individuals charged with providing decision support to clarify what limitations exist in a graphical representation – what to take with a grain of salt, and where consistency and relevance exists.

There are plenty of graphs that can be built through Microsoft Office products, ranging from basic pie and bar charts to more sophisticated plots. For example, geographic mappings such as shown in Figure 4.2 (integrated through MS MapPoint and discussed in the previous chapter) are at one extreme.

Ultimately non-geographic plots can be just as aesthetically sophisticated as mapped data, and are often more directly meaningful. For example, the basic scatter plot can be used to show how a group of publicly traded firms (e.g., by industry) compare along two performance measures or strategic orientations. Figure 4.3 shows a plot of Inventory/Sales (X) and Earnings per Share (EPS), (Y) plots for a set of firms in the chemical and materials fabrication industries.

Figure 4.3 is a time shot that depicts a single instance in time. What can we gather from this plot? If the answer is "not much," we might want to rethink whether or not we are depicting the right kind of information in

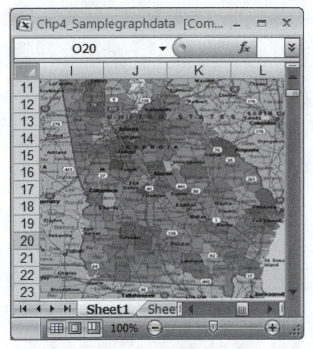

Figure 4.2. Sample map generated by MapPoint embedded in Excel.

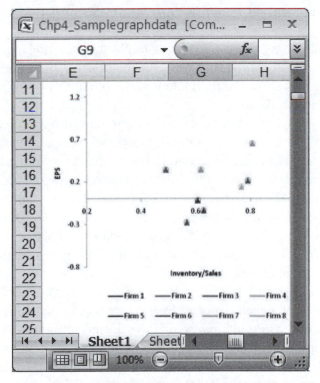

Figure 4.3. First quarter 2004 numbers for a range of Chem/Mat firms.

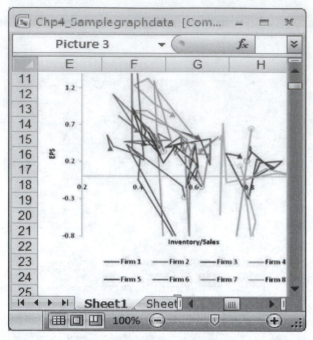

Figure 4.4. All quarters from 2001–2004 linked chronologically per firm.

the right kind of format to either draw inferences or get a particular point across.

Of course if we have more data (for example, data relating to prior periods) we can attempt to show them as well. We might even link together the data for a single firm to show the path taken in the pursuit of changing inventory costs and EPS (Figure 4.4).

Again, however, something is left to be desired in such a depiction. A lot of information is being shown in a potentially meaningful way, but the rendering and the nature of noise incorporated in the graph as a whole is detracting.

But the right mix of info can be informative. As shown in Figure 4.5, only the first quarter 2001 and first quarter 2004 estimates are depicted.

Here the graph starts to become useful. For example, most firms that started with negative EPS levels decreased their average inventory positions (increased turns). Those same firms also significantly increased their EPS into the positive region. Similar observations are made when we limit ourselves to only the average 2001.1-2002.4 values and average 2003.1-2004.4 values.

The critical intelligence depicted by a graph is not only contingent on the selected form of the graph, but also on the selected subset of data presented. Mastery of graphical attributes can only get you so far without an appropriate understanding of the ultimate visualization goal. Fortunately, the basic logic required to create and manipulate any graph in Excel is much the same. Given a selected subset of data to graph, you need to specify how to use

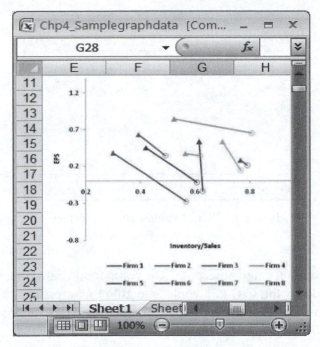

Figure 4.5. First quarters from 2001 and 2004 linked by firm for comparison.

it (e.g., as a label, or as data to be plotted) and then specify the particular aesthetic features of the resulting graphical presentation. For this reason we will review the construction and manipulation of three representative types of graphs – bar charts, scatter plots, and surface graphs – and will devote the rest of our discussion to analytical intelligence and the dynamic enrichment of visualizations.

4.1.1 Bar Charts

Since bar charts represent a fairly expansive range of graphing possibilities, from the simplistic to the highly information-packed, they serve as a useful foil for describing the various options available when developing visuals in Excel. Here we'll start small and build up to much more complex variants of bar chart construction.

4.1.1.1 The Basics

Basic bar charts are useful when you have a small set of categories, each of which describe and compare along a single measure. For example, we might want to chart the efficiency of inventory use for a single firm across each financial quarter starting from 2001 onward (i.e., 20 observed records).

First select the data. The AllData sheet in Chp4_QuarterlyData provides a good starting point. If the categorical data that interests you (year.quarter,

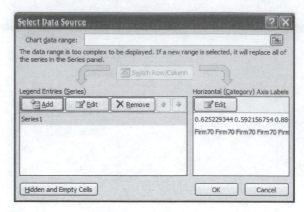

Figure 4.6. Series value editing interface.

for example) is not located adjacent to the comparison data (inventory/sales), we can hold down the Ctrl key while selecting the appropriate cells. When selected, choose the desired chart type from the Insert tab, such as the Column chart type chosen here.

Next, select the type of graph we want (such as the standard graph in the upper left of the options). At this point Excel will attempt to provide us what it thinks we want – and often it's wrong. It's not uncommon for Excel to pick the wrong way to transform selected data into a plot. We might want our categories (X-axis for this kind of graph) to come from cells Z3882:Z3898 and our comparison data from cells T3882:T3898; however, that might not be Excel's first intuitive stab at depicting the data.

Fortunately, we can correct for Excel's initial stumble and ultimately generate exactly what we want. We just need to get comfortable with how to make the necessary requirements clear to Excel.

Once any chart is created in Excel the Chart Tools menu automatically displays at the top of the screen. This menu will allow us to modify any part of the chart, including the messed up data. Clicking on Select Data from the Design tab displays the screen in which both the series of values and the series of labels can be manipulated (i.e., corrected in this case). The value editing interface in this case (again with the initial incorrect configuration) appears as follows (Figure 4.6).

Click on Edit in the left hand pane to select the appropriate series values; in our case we want the data in "AllData!$T$3882:$T$3898" as the series values. The name of this series is defaulted to "Series1" but we could change it at this point as well, for example, by typing in "Inventory/Sales" given our data. Click Edit in the right hand pane to change the category axis labels. We want to choose "=AllData!$Z$3882:$Z$3898" for our horizontal axis labels (Figure 4.7). After making these adjustments, the following chart is

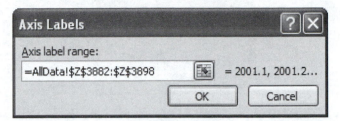

Figure 4.7. Series label editing interface.

displayed with year.quarter along the x-axis and Inventory/Sales along the y-axis (Figure 4.8).

We may now have a chart that will work, but we can probably do better in terms of presentation. We can use the Layout tab of Chart Tools menu (Figure 4.9) to modify axis titles, chart title, legend, data labels, axes, gridlines, or the entire plot area. All of that can be done after the chart is created in Excel. Additionally, we can click on any element in the chart (such as the gridlines or legend) to manipulate it. For example, if we don't want gridlines we can select them and press Delete. We can also add a chart title by selecting Chart Title from the Layout tab.

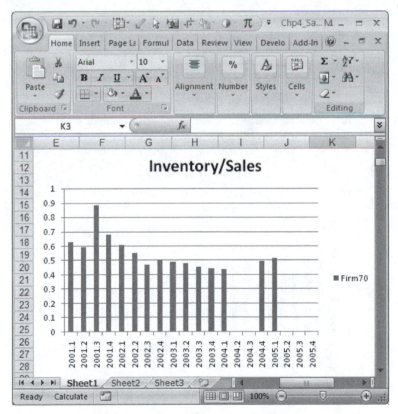

Figure 4.8. Simple bar chart example.

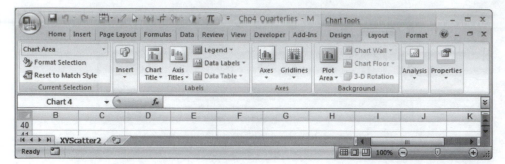

Figure 4.9. Various options for modifying charts.

At this point we can also add additional series of data. For example, perhaps we want to compare Firm70 to another comparable firm in its industry, such as Firm172. We could click the Add Series button and make the appropriate additional specifications based on the location of the series in our spreadsheet. The graph shown in Figure 4.10 displays these modifications.

We could then continue to make additional aesthetic changes to elements such as the bars and background. Click Plot Area>More Plot Area Options>Picture or Texture Fill to open the Format Series dialog box

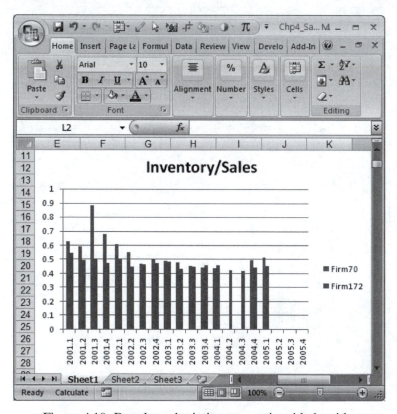

Figure 4.10. Bar chart depicting two series side by side.

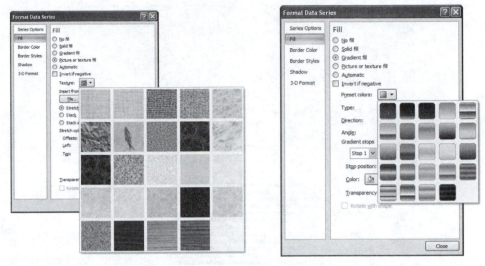

Figure 4.11. Sampling of graphic fill options.

(Figure 4.11). From here, we can replace the existing area-fill or background with something more visually pleasing, such as a marble texture.

Double-click the bars within the graph and then select Format Selection from the Format tab to access graph formatting options. Here, we can modify other elements such as the gaps between the bars and the extent to which they overlap. We can also make color changes to them at this point using features such as gradient fills. The Legend itself can also be transposed (made horizontal rather than vertical) and moved around. Basically we can change anything in the graph that we can click.

4.1.1.2 Compound (Stacked) Bar Charts

Compound bar charts are somewhat more complex. These charts are often used to depict compound concepts. For example, rather then viewing just inventory efficiency, we might want to look at how capital resource costs relative to sales contribute to total expenditures. We'll build this new variable (Plant and Equip Costs/Sales) on the right-most column of the data table, and select the last 20 quarters of a particular firm along with this new variable. In this case the new chart we'll build is called a stacked or compound bar chart. By specifying the correct information for each axis and making some quick modifications to the appearance of the graph, we can generate a chart for a particular firm similar to Figure 4.12.

By copying and pasting this graph, we get a duplicate that we can then edit to develop a comparable graph for yet another set of data. We could even make most of the subsequent plot transparent by selecting None as an area and line coloring option. With a little careful positioning, we could overlay it

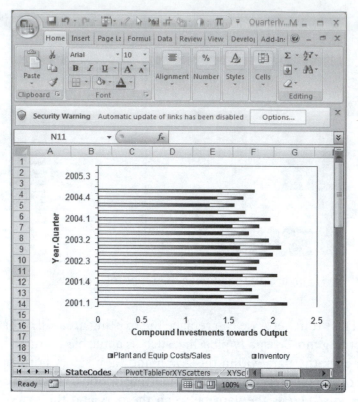

Figure 4.12. Compound (stacked) bar chart example.

on top of the original graph for comparison. Figure 4.13 shows an example of a chart along these lines reflecting data on a couple of firms.

In contrast to the graph in Figure 4.11 that showed only inventory investments for a couple of firms, the compounded graph shows much more information that could be comparatively valuable. In this particular case, the data (drawn from a COMPUSTAT) suggests that Firm B has much less money tied up in capital resources relative to its investments in inventory. This may indicate a greater focus on productivity than on input efficiency (vis-à-vis Firm A). Furthermore, Firm B seems to be gaining ground along this single measure over time as compared to Firm A. This may demonstrate an overall distinguishing strategy in place at Firm B.

Still, we need to be cautious about trying to throw too much into aesthetic features while providing rich detail. I'd argue that the example in Figure 4.13 probably reaches the limit (if not already far over) for overcrowding. When confusion grows faster than insight, it's time to rethink the design and the purpose behind it. The fancy background graphics in Figure 4.13 could definitely be dropped, and higher contrast colors used. The use of gradient fills might also be rethought. Remember that just because you can enhance multiple aspects of graphics doesn't mean you should.

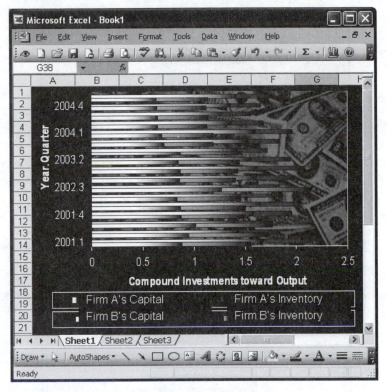

Figure 4.13. Two compound bar chart series side by side.

Note: Gantt charts, popular in project management, are another variety of stacked bar charts. In such cases each of the Y categories (in Figure 4.13 Year.Quarter) could be an individual activity following in chronological sequence in a project. The two series data you would want to use to build a Gantt would be Activity Start Time and Activity Duration. By coloring the Activity Start Time bar portions as transparent, or the same color as the background, the Activity Duration bars gain the appearance of hanging in place – in thin air, so to speak.

4.1.2 Scatter Plots

Scatter plots are commonly used graphical forms for data presentation and analysis, and are often used to demonstrate the relationship (or lack thereof) between two variables depicted along the x and y axes, respectively. To construct a scatter plot, select any data available on your spreadsheet (e.g., on Chp4_QuarterlyData.xls, PullFromPivot2 sheet) relating to two variables of interest. For example:

1) Average inventory/sales figures for companies in the Industrial Equipment industry as the X variable
2) Average earnings per share for those same companies as the Y variable

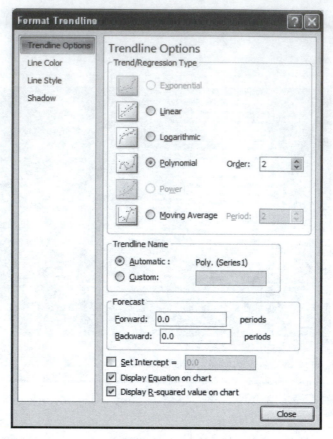

Figure 4.14. Trendline options for scatter.

From the Insert tab, select Scatter and then select the desired scatter type. Select the first type of scatter plot (unconnected points) unless you have reason to believe that the data to be plotted represent a sequence of observations (e.g., x-y pairs changing over time).

Of course a lack of direct connections between points in a series doesn't preclude the ability to depict an underlying relationship embedded in the data. Such a relationship might very well be described by a line, straight or otherwise, just not based on the current sequence and probably greatly muddied by the existence of multiple sources of variation in the data. Because of this, scatter plots are often designed to consist of not only individual points, but also general trendlines (e.g., regression lines) that attempt to depict relationships not always immediately obvious.

4.1.2.1 Adding in Trendlines and Their Stats

Right-click any data set on a scatter plot to be presented with the option of adding a trendline – a best fit, based on the kind of relationship you believe might exist, such as linear, quadratic (parabolic), and so on (Figure 4.14). You

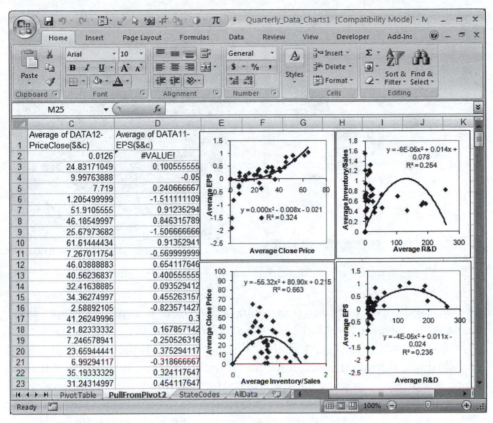

Figure 4.15. Example use of plot-embedded line fits and equations (live).

have the option of also specifying what summary numbers for that best fit should appear on that graph, such as regression coefficients, R^2 values, and so on.

In contrast to the detailed results provided by the data analysis regression, trendline fits to a data set in a graph do remain live. This means the fit coefficients and R^2 value will change as the data points change. This can be handy when different data sets or when different levels of simulated variation in data might be worth considering. It's also handy when you want to duplicate graphs for alternate variable combinations – just cut, paste, and change the source data to which the graph is referring. The regression equations will automatically adjust for you (Figure 4.15).

4.1.2.2 Kicking Up Scatter Plot Graphics

Scatter plots aren't just used to depict association. They can also be used to describe general closeness or proximity among comparable observations. For example, we could compare multiple firms with respect to the dimensions of Cost (x) and Quality (y) to see which firms seem to dominate various positions, and which seem to lag behind. Or we might want to simply show

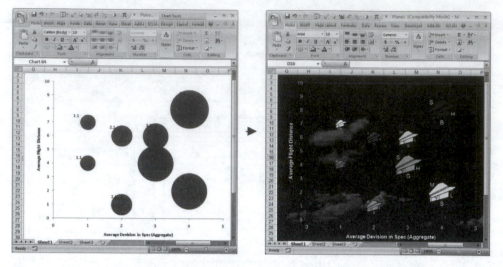

Figure 4.16. Swapping basic data points for more intuitive images.

how various firms are located relative to one another in some geographically meaningful space, such as Latitude (x) and Longitude (y).

If we we're interested in comparing distinct entities rather than estimating relationships, we might want more meaningful depictions of those entities. In other words, we might want to pick something other than a dot to depict these entities; maybe a picture of a paper airplane, for example (Figure 4.16).

These kinds of graphic substitutions are amazingly simple in Excel. If you have a particular picture in mind, you can import it into Excel by choosing Insert>Picture>From File to open the My Pictures dialog box. Choose the picture you want to insert into Excel and then click OK. After your picture appears in in Excel, you can make it smaller, combine it with a text box, adjust color contrasts or transparency, and more. You can also copy it (right-click and choose Copy), select any individual point in the scatter plot (or all of the points simultaneously), and paste it (right-click and choose Paste) on that point. The picture will then respond to any changes in the graph and associated data the same way than any traditional point would.

4.1.3 3-D Surface Templates and Plots

Aside from looking cool, surface templates and plots are useful when you want to depict the relationship among three variables. For now, we'll talk about the generic structure of surface plots and what you need to create them. Later on in the chapter we'll present an example that directly relates to options faced by management decision makers.

You first need a set of X and Y values that occur multiple times, or can be roughly categorized into a set of discrete values that seem to be meaningful multiple times across the data set as a whole. These can still be ordinal

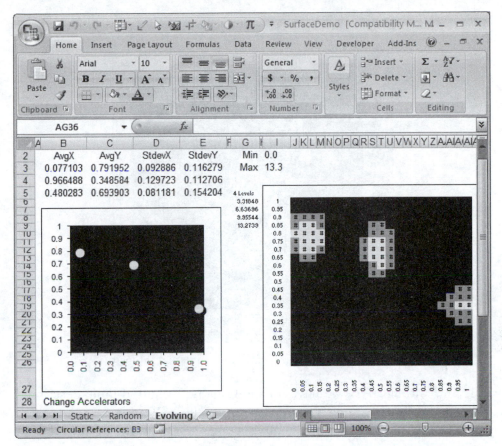

Figure 4.17. Example using conditional formatting to develop intensity pseudographs.

categories (e.g., increasing whole numbers, or equidistant fractions such as 0.25, 0.50, 0.75, 1.0, 1.25). The more X and Y categories you choose, the more complex your plot, but potentially the more informative as well.

For generalization, let's assume we have three entities; they could be firms, machines, patents, or consumer populations. Each has two distinct attributes – X and Y. X might be the entity's value in the marketplace, and Y might be some measure of associated liability. Both the X and Y attribute have a central value (a mean), and can be described as having a certain amount of variation over time (i.e., standard deviation). If these attributes are normally distributed, we can describe the probability of both X and Y taking on specific values and show how those probabilities (or intensities) decrease farther away from central (average) attribute levels.

A simple way to describe this might be with a table that includes various X and Y values and associated intensity levels (i.e., a third variable that might be dependent on the other two). We could even use conditional formatting to color cells in that table to add emphasis to the variations in intensity (probability) levels for differing levels of X and Y. Shown in Figure 4.17,

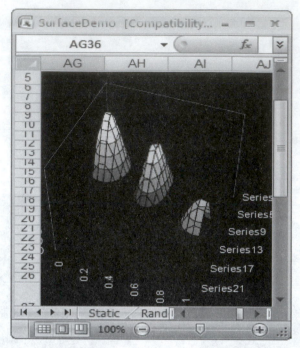

Figure 4.18. Example surface plot to depict intensity.

in rows J through AE, we have a conditionally formatted table describing intensity levels depending on where we are in the X-Y grid.

This could be cool and informative, depending on what we're trying to make sense of.

On the other hand, we have all the elements we need to develop a 3-D surface map – specific X and Y values and values of a third associate variable (in this case probability or intensity). If we select the data in the conditionally formatted (colored) and relatively large table shown in Figure 4.17 and then select the 3-D surface graph option, we generate a rough form of a 3-D image (Figure 4.18) that we can format and edit in the same way we have other graphs.

Note: Incidentally, these graphs don't need to be static. If we believe that values change over time according to some meaningful dynamic or process, we could build that into the parameters on which the graph was originally based. All of these graphs are ostensibly live and ready for updating based on our needs. In this case a simply press of the F9 key advances the random number generation that lends to a living appearance of our graphs. We'll get into the details of dynamic visualization in Chapter 10.

4.2 Selective Pruning for Presentation and Analysis

We've already breezed over filtering, which is one way to limit data presentation in Excel. But the Filtering tool can be somewhat limiting.

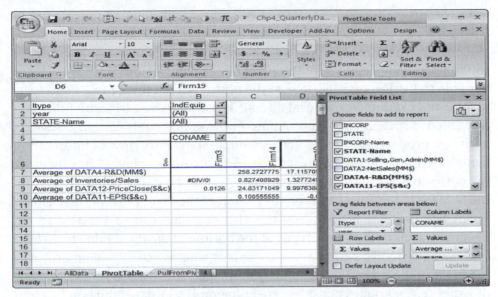

Figure 4.19. General nature of a PivotTable interface.

If you plan to filter along one categorical variable, it only allows you to pick a single value of that variable to filter along. For example, if filtering along the variable Industry, you might select chemical, consumer electronics, or aerospace, but never all but Chemical. If filtering along a variable such as year, you can filter along 2003 or 2006, but not just 2003 and 2006. Also, filtering doesn't provide much insight into summary data relating to how multiple categorical variables jointly impact other issues of interest.

Filtering also doesn't have a standard mechanism for summarizing data that takes on numerous values for the same filterable categories. For example, if you have a categorical variable such as Industry and a large number of firms that fall into each of it's categories, it might be more useful to present the average calculated across the selected set of firms on a specific year, as opposed to every observation separately. Standard filtering won't give that to you. To attempt to make up for these deficits, Excel provides PivotTables, which are alternative filtering and data presentation tools.

4.2.1 How to Build and Modify PivotTables

Consider the PivotTable that already exists on the PivotTable sheet of the Chp4_QuarterlyData workbook. Click on the table to view available options, shown in Figure 4.19.

The following describes the three mechanisms you can use to prune presentation and analysis data using PivotTables.

Pages (global filters): These allow you to restrict the data presented in the table as a whole to only certain cases (e.g., firms in the industrial equipment industry and nothing else, students at the Junior rank and nothing else). Add a page filter by using the cursor to drag and drop a variable (e.g., firm type, or student type) from the field list (e.g., shown in the right portion of Figure 4.19) to the Page Fields box above the PivotTable. You can also drag and drop a variable to the Report Filter box at the bottom of the PivotTable Field List.

Row and Column filters (local filters): These allow you to restrict the data presented in specific rows and columns of the table to only certain cases (e.g. each row provides summaries across a single state. Fifty rows of information would then supposedly be presented). Add a row or column filter by using the cursor to drag and drop a variable (e.g., firm type or student type) from the field list to the Row Fields box at the left of the PivotTable or the Column Fields box on table header. You can also drag and drop a variable to the Column Labels or Row Labels box at the bottom of the PivotTable Field List.

Data elements: These allow you to restrict what is actually summarized in the meat of the table. For example, you might want to see how any number of issues (e.g., earnings per share, spending on R&D, depending on location and size of firms). If you divide your table by placing location categories (e.g., state) in the Row Field box, the size categories (e.g., 100–999 employees, 1,000–9,999 employees) in the Column Field box, and earnings per share (or spending on R&D) in the Data Items box at the center of the table, you would be able to see such comparisons.

By default, Excel's PivotTables tend to pull data in as counts (i.e., how many pieces of data exist for the row-column combination as opposed to averages in the data selected for that combination). If you are summarizing a single variable in the data field, you can double-click on the data header that appears in the upper left corner of the table, and switch to average or any other summary you want. You can change this by right-clicking on any header and selecting Value Field Settings. You'll have the option to specify what kind of data summary pops up at that point.

In a PivotTable you can also generate cross-summaries for multiple variables at the same time (i.e., multiple variables in the Data field). Unfortunately, the task of requesting an alternative form of the data other than the default count becomes less intuitive here; however, it can still be done by selecting Value Field Settings from the Values box shown in Figure 4.20, or by right-clicking on the Data column and selecting Value Field Settings. A dialog box permitting choice of average, max, variance, and so on will display.

4.2.2 Selective Pruning by Row and Column

Aside from limiting the entirety of the data viewed in PivotTables by what you put in the Data Fields and Page Fields boxes, you also have the opportunity to limit the number of rows and columns for which data are shown. For example,

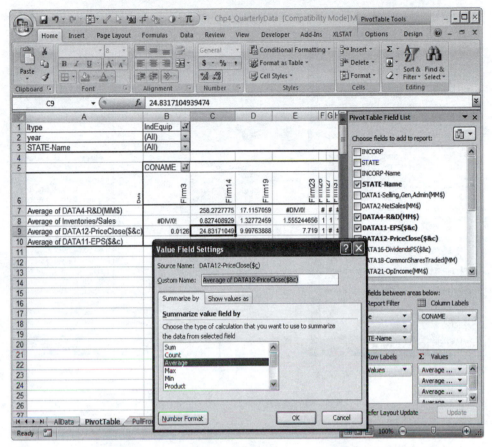

Figure 4.20. Modifying field settings in PivotTables (e.g., pruning by general data content).

if you have placed a location category (e.g., state) in the Rows Field and are only interested in comparing specific locations (e.g., California, Oregon, and Washington, as opposed to all 50 states) you have the ability to do so fairly easily in a PivotTable. Such selective pruning of presented data can greatly increase the clarity of the points you may be trying to make with the data. Click on the category listing you want (e.g., STATE-Name) and then check off the items for which you want data displayed (e.g., California). This is shown in Figure 4.21.

4.2.3 Building PivotCharts

Anything created in a PivotTable can be transferred into a graphical form using the built-in PivotChart function. With a PivotChart, you ultimately are given a graphical interface with which to directly prune the kind of graphical data being presented (often in bar chart form).

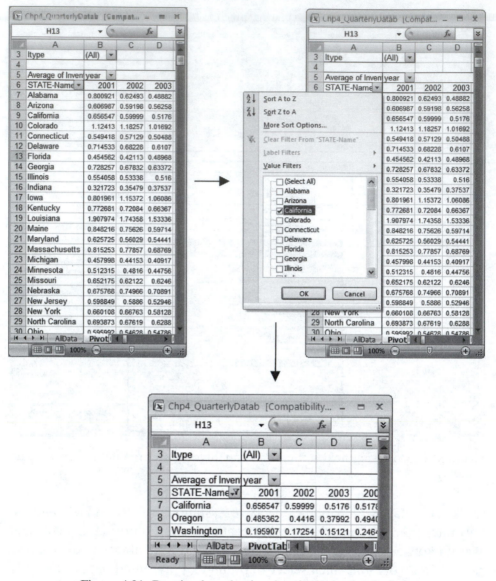

Figure 4.21. Pruning by selective data inclusion/exclusion.

I personally find PivotCharts fairly limiting because they allow only certain presentation styles (such as bar charts, but not scatter plots). I usually create a separate page that duplicates the PivotTable data and develop my own graphs based from those duplicates.

4.3 Visualizing Constraints

Up to this point, we have just been fiddling with good ways to demo the possible impacts of one variable on another (or differences in dynamics of

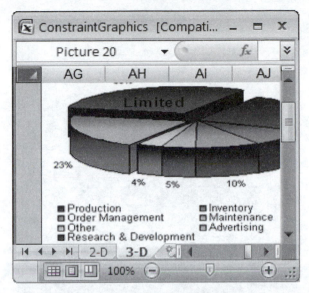

Figure 4.22. 3-D pie chart depicting allocation constraints.

certain elements of a system, e.g., restaurant). Unfortunately, all of that can be misleading if we don't account for unavoidable limitations in the decisions we make and the performance we attain. We also need to be familiar with methods by which to graphically depict constraints.

Constraints come in the form of rules like:

Can't charge below cost.
Must test enough to meet minimum safety regulations.
Must make sure responsibilities are at most shared by two workers.

Constraints can range from financially based considerations, as shown in Figure 4.22. They can also come from geographically based considerations (Figure 4.23).

Sometimes constraints are even more sophisticated and require us to recognize dependent relationships between various decisions and variables relevant. For example:

As the price goes up by $X, expected demand will fall Y%.
Additional product tests will need additional specialists to be assigned to assessment.
The more new responsibilities we create, the less focused our workforce may become, and the less productive they may become in existing duties.

These get to the heart of the tradeoff aspect of constraints. Specifically when constraints are active, and we always have something constraining us, we need to consider the costs and benefits of picking specific decisions over

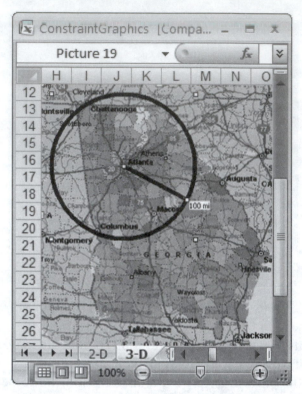

Figure 4.23. MapPoint-generated embedded graph, depicting constraints.

others. In other words, constraints ensure that we can't have it all, so to speak.

The overall impact of multiple constraints and relationships may be hard to put into a few words, which is why we often rely again on visualization in the early phases of complex decision making. Visualization is equally important when we first get our hands on a set of data that we believe is relevant to our decision making.

For example, consider the classic economic trade-off example of guns vs. butter (most people who took basic economics courses in the last 20 years are familiar with this one). The constraint here is a relational one. We have fixed resources and can devote them to either activity, but we can only assign more resources to one manufacturing activity by pulling from another (Figure 4.24).

More complex relational constraints can also be depicted using surface graphs. For instance, in a restaurant example, the number of barstools, two-seat tables, and four-seat tables may each be individual decisions planners might have to make, but given limited floorspace, the managers might want to visually depict the tradeoffs of increasing one of these kinds of seating elements over the others. Figure 4.25 shows two views (top down and center in)

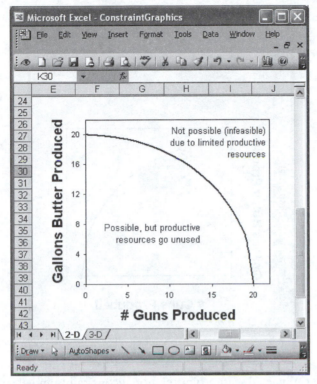

Figure 4.24. Connected scatter plot relational constraints.

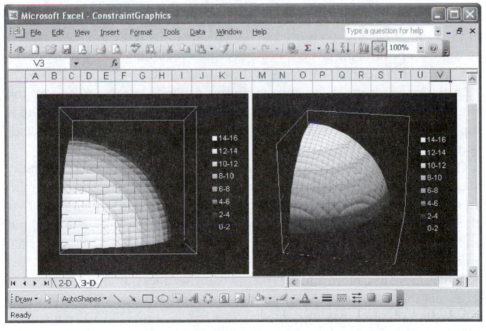

Figure 4.25. Surface plot depictions of 3-D relational constraints.

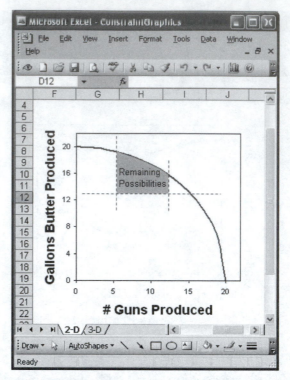

Figure 4.26. Connected scatter plot relational constraints and absolute limits.

of a hypothetical feasibility plot for the space use at a restaurant. The legend to the right of each graph is used to demark quantity (e.g., four-seat tables) possible for positioning given specific decisions regarding the quantity of the other two variables (e.g. barstools and two-seat tables).

In the classic form of the guns vs. butter economic problem, any option along the production possibilities frontier make full use of resources, and is superior to more interior points (at least from a resource utilization stand-point).

On the other hand, there may be additional constraints that limit our ability to consider certain production options. For example, there may be some min-imally required level of gun and butter production needed to maintain other elements of the society. Furthermore, regulations might place an upper limit on the number of guns manufactured (probably a good thing). As additional limits continue to build up, our ability to choose from a variety of alternatives becomes more and more limited (Figure 4.26), as does our ability to excel in terms of other performance measures (e.g., police force readiness, NRA self-esteem, international baking contests). Figure 4.27 shows the 3-D equivalent of Figure 4.26.

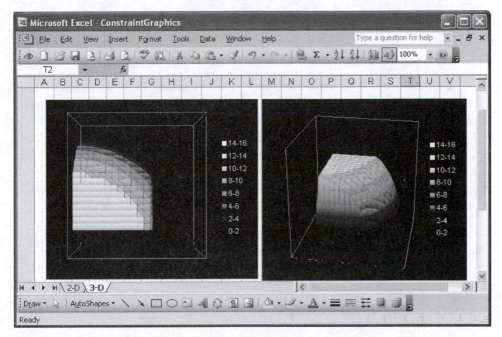

Figure 4.27. Surface plot depictions of both relational constraints and absolute limits.

PRACTICE PROBLEMS

Practice 4.1

Develop two scatter plots based on the data in Chp4_Samplegraphdata.

  1st plot – A on the X-axis; C along the Y-axis
  2nd plot – B on the X-axis; C along the Y-axis

Add best-fit parabolas (also knowns as second-order polynomial firs) to each plot.

Practice 4.2

If we assume A and B both independently impact C, what would a plot of C as a function of both A and B look like? (Graph it using a 3-D surface plot.)

Practice 4.3

Create two columns of numbers. The first column should contain integers from 0 to 20. Label this Apples. The second column should contain the following formula:

  = SQRT(20^2 – {*Whatever # of Apples are in the adjacent cell*} ^2)

Call that second column Oranges. Create a line-connected scatter plot of the two, and call the plot Production Frontier.

Pick one cell in the sheet and label it Location. Label the cell to the right of it Direction. Use the following to define the value inside Location:

= Location + Direction

Use an IF statement within the Direction cell that makes Direction equal to 1 if Location is 0, or equal to −1 if Location is equal to 20, or remains unchanged at all levels in between. (I'll let you figure that out.)

Use a lookup to set two additional cells in the sheet (below the Location cell) equal to the number of apples and number of oranges that are given in the row corresponding to the value of Location (e.g., the 0th row, the 1st row, the 20th row). Add that X-Y data point as a new series to your plot. In iteration mode, F9 should move that point back and forth along the production frontier you've plotted.

Note: You may want to include an IF statement in the "Location" cell tied to a "Restart" (or "Toggle") cell so that you can make sure that things start the way you want them to (i.e., at Location=0) when the iterations begin.

5

Simplification Tactics

There is a clear truism in George Box's 1979 statement that "all models are wrong, some models are useful." We attempt to model reality to see how changes can affect it – hopefully for the better. But models of reality are, by their very nature, incomplete depictions and tend to be misleading. Still worse can be models and associated solutions that faithfully attempt to do justice to reality by incorporating many facets of reality into their structures. Unfortunately, a common result is an overemphasis of certain issues in decision making that, although perhaps interesting, are far less practically relevant to effective decisions than other issues that haven't been taken into account.

Ultimately, any approach to decision making is a balancing act between an appropriate accounting of relevant reality (i.e., the objectives, decision variables, and constraints as discussed in Chapter 4) and not getting bogged down in details that only obscure or mislead. When we attempt to rationalize all of the factors that might go into a decision-making process as well as possible solutions that might be practically viable, we often "satisfice," a term used to describe making a decision about a set of alternatives that respects the limitations of human time and knowledge.

Of course, there are some decision makers who are extremely effective at coming up with quick effective solutions to otherwise complex problems, whereas others are less so. The difference often comes down to a familiarity with tried and true rules of thumb, applied either consciously or unconsciously, that fit specific settings or that simply help decision makers consolidate knowledge regardless of settings. Fast and frugal heuristics (codified approaches to developing ideas/decisions/solutions) embody this by employing a minimum of time, knowledge, and computation to make adaptive choices in real environments. (The interjection Eureka! derives from the same Latin stem as heuristics.) Fast and frugal heuristics are characterized by consolidations and simplifications of solution-search procedures.

To the surprise of many managers and practitioners in many fields, the simplest models and solutions are often some of the best.

5.1 Heuristics in Decision-Making Practice

Given this introduction to the general benefits of simplification in decision making it is worth providing an overview of some of the simplest and most commonly used rules of thumb that exist in practice.

5.1.1 The Recognition Heuristic

One of the simplest examples of an effective fast and frugal heuristic is the Recognition heuristic. Rather than assuming that people act as unboundedly rationale individuals (strangely, a common assumption in much of academic literature to date), the recognition heuristic assumes that human ignorance not only exists, but is an important factor in determining the strength of specific decision options. In fact, the foundation of this heuristic relies on at least some level of human ignorance to develop good solutions to problems.

As an example, consider a study performed by Borges, et al. (1999) relating to the ability of lay individuals to develop high-performing stock portfolios based on their personal, albeit limited, exposure to corporate information.

Objective: Develop a portfolio with consistently high returns relative to the market average.

Decision variables: Which publicly traded firms should be bought/shorted?

Constraints: In the case of the heuristic, the ability of individuals to recognize companies in domestic and foreign markets (obviously differs by expertise).

Certain United States companies are widely recognized by career financial workers and lay people overseas. Likewise, we in the United States recognize only a relative handful of foreign companies by name. Does that signify anything? The assumption of the Recognition heuristic is: Yes. That recognition probably indicates the ability of a brand name to penetrate foreign markets, as well as the resiliency of the reputation it has developed within those markets. In most cases, we'd assume that resilient reputation to be positive because companies with negative reputations don't last very long, thus aren't resilient.

But can something as simple as name recognition by lay individuals provide performance even close to the level of highly sophisticated financial techniques? More sophisticated approaches, aside from being vastly more complex, are often proprietary in nature (not so publicly accessible); however, more alarmingly, they often don't do that well. In fact, the history of major U.S. investment management and mutual companies suggest that the selections of many highly experienced financial professionals perform worse than the market as a whole. This suggested that sophistication and experience might bias professionals toward misleading decision-making approaches – perhaps less sophistication and experience might avoid such biases, at least in some cases.

To compare the Recognition heuristic to more sophisticated and expert solutions, a research team asked average people in the United States as well as experts in financial careers to specify from a list those companies in Germany that they recognized. They did the same thing in Germany with a list of U.S. companies. How well did the ten most-recognized U.S. stocks do, chosen on the basis of German recognition?

Those top ten German choices (again, based on the Recognition Heuristic) beat the Dow 30 by about 10 percent along with a number of funds supposedly based on sophisticated intelligence. They did much better than a random portfolio method. Granted, sophisticated methods of field experts showed better performance against random portfolio assembly as well (but, of course, it costs to hire such professionals – one might question the value of the incremental gain against the Recognition heuristic here). Even better was the top-ten portfolio based on U.S. recognition of German firms. The average Joe was able to outperform the Dax 30 by 23 percent over the 6-month test period, and similarly over subsequent periods studied.

In subsequent studies, this phenomenon has been retested with mixed results, largely by those financial professionals who have a clear interest in suggesting that simple techniques have limitations relative to proprietary expertise. This may be true in some cases, but these and other related results certainly cast critical doubt on what it means to be a financial *expert*. This is not to suggest that there may be very successful sophisticated selection procedures developed in the future to consistently beat lay recognition; however, perhaps the best approach would be to incorporate such simplistic rules into such models.

5.1.2 Nearest Next – A Routing Heuristic

Another well-established fast and frugal heuristic can be taken from the history of the shipping and transportation industry. Before computing power was abundant, shippers relied on professional planners to use their own modes of judgment to develop shipping routes and schedules that economized on cost but still met the service levels their clients expected. The types of problems about which these planners had to make decisions were highly complex.

Imagine a central facility, a single vehicle, and seven locations to which we need to make deliveries. Obviously, it might be in our best interest to find the most time- and cost-effective route to carry off those deliveries. Basically, what we want is a good sequence of stops. But how many ways can

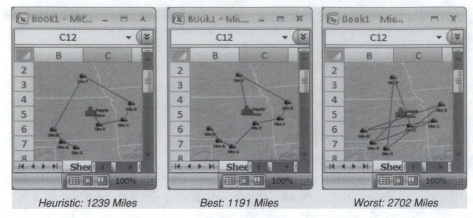

Heuristic: 1239 Miles   Best: 1191 Miles   Worst: 2702 Miles

Figure 5.1. Heuristic versus best and worst routing solutions.

we sequence seven stops? As it turns out, quite a few (7*6*5*4*3*2*1=5040). Do we really want to compare 5,040 stops to find the best one, and do that every time we need to find a new route? The Nearest Next heuristic provides a shortcut. Its rule is: "Go to the closest site next," and repeat this rule from there until all sites are visited.

> *Objective:* Minimize total time or cost of transit.
> *Decision Variables:* Sequence of sites to be visited in turn.
> *Constraints:* Visit each site once, and in the case of the heuristic, the next site visited is the next closest site available.

Figure 5.1 shows an example comparing the heuristic solution to the absolute worst and absolute best options. It doesn't quite hit the best solution, but it's closer to the best solution than it is to the worst.

The number of calculations (actually just searches) needed to determine the Nearest Next solution is only 7+6+5+4+3+2+1 (28). In general, Nearest Next needs $n*(n+1)/2$ searches (where n is the number of sites) whereas a comprehensive search for the absolute best needs n! (i.e., n factorial) searches (assuming no other ancillary heuristics are applied). So if we needed to find a decent solution for n=15 sites, the Nearest Next would give a solution after 30 searches, while a complete review of all possible solutions would require 1.3 trillion. Not a trivial task for many computers. Is it worth it? What if n=30 sites?

Routing applications today tend to use a mixture of simple heuristics and complex, large-scale analysis to arrive at highly effective solutions. We continue to see improvements made in these applications with increases in computing power (i.e., speed and memory), hence more and more elements of reality are able to be practically included without an abandonment of fundamentally crucial aspects of reality. Some of the most recent additions to routing applications now attempt to account for the human aspects of shipping, such as individual psychology, relationships between drivers and clients, and morale. Fast and frugal heuristics continue to have their place in these applications. Furthermore, for managers who need to make decisions on the fly (e.g., immediate re-routing responses to real-time road closures), such heuristics continue to provide benefit.

5.1.3 MinSlack and SPT – Two Project Management Heuristics

Resources (e.g., workers, machines) often constrain the processes managed by an organization. This is common in the management of projects, regardless of industry context. The process of deciding which activities will be given access to potentially limited personnel first is a critical one in these settings – and these decisions need to be made quickly. For that reason, a large number of fast and frugal heuristics have been developed by managers in an attempt to make these decisions simple.

Two common fast and frugal heuristics are MinSlack and SPT (Shortest Processing Time). MinSlack assigns resources and starts competing activities based on which activities appear to be most costly/problematic to project completion times if otherwise delayed. The idea here is that specific activities should be addressed as soon as possible so they don't delay subsequent activities. SPT (Shortest Processing Time) assigns resources and starts competing activities based on which activities can be completed quickest. If you can get these activities done quickly, you can free up resources and assign them elsewhere while allowing other activities to start that might not need those resources.

5.1.4 The Punchline: Relevance to DSS Designs

I could keep giving examples of heuristics that have been used in practice to make quick decisions in complex decision-making settings, but that's not really the goal here. Some may be of the mindset that they don't want a simple approach; they want the best solution. Aside from the perception that a single best solution to all management settings exists, this mindset seems to assume that simple approaches cannot be as effective as ones that require several tools used together to deliver ideal solutions.

Each of the example heuristics I've provided represents a structured set of rules that somebody came up with because they made sense in a specific setting. For people who develop decision support systems, there are at least three reasons to provide structured rules that are backed by explanations of the logic behind them.

- By definition, they tend to be both easy to apply and informative.
- They can offer a great starting place for more sophisticated support.

• Perhaps most importantly, they can offer a performance benchmark with which to gauge more sophisticated solutions, in turn helping to convince users of the support system that the system is providing added benefit to them. The effectiveness of decision support system designs comes largely from selling the effectiveness of the support they are designed to provide.

For DSS designers, the question of the practical application of heuristics comes down to how much is gained and lost through the use of such techniques, and, perhaps more fundamentally, can these techniques be automated for integration with other techniques useful in the DSS design. Supplement A discusses an example of a rough approach to automating the Nearest Next heuristic, although we will see that there are much better ways to implant simple decision-making rules behind the scenes for DSS designs.

5.2 Heuristics Applied to Data Rationalization

Whereas the application of simple rules for developing solutions can be critical, another discussion of simplification relates to the nature of the data used to define both the kinds of management problems we face and the solutions provided. Increasingly, professionals are bogged down in vast amounts of available data. The seemingly basic task of selecting which data should be used to develop solutions often becomes a stumbling block, and slows the development of meaningful analysis and solutions. The overwhelming nature of large amounts of data applies to all aspects of decision making, in particular to the ability to apply logically designed heuristics to solution development. Can the concept behind heuristics (i.e., easily applied rules for simplification) be applied to the rationalization of data as well?

Experience (even for lay persons) leads us to recognize that what to leave in or what to take out isn't always obvious. Fortunately, both DSS designers and users don't have to limit themselves to omitting data and issues in their attempts to clarify the decision-making processes. They also have the option of consolidation.

There are basically two general perspectives relevant to considering data consolidation. The first approach is to select a set of attributes that represent similar or associated issues, and somehow consolidate them into a smaller set of representative characteristics for each data record. Here we are grouping together attributes (elements that describe records of people, places, and things), and the consolidated result should have the same number of individual data observations but a consolidated number of characteristic attributes (Figure 5.2).

One common form of this consolidation approach is referred to as Principle Components Analysis (PCA), and is often preferred as a method for data

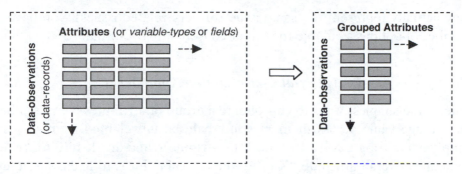

Figure 5.2. Consolidating attributes of large data sets.

reduction. (Note other related methods such as Principle Factor Analysis are also discussed in more complex structural analysis, but a discussion of PCA will be sufficient here.)

The other approach, as you might guess, deals with grouping together data observations (i.e., people, places, or things) of similar kind to reduce the noise that may be inherent across individual observations. A simple example would be to designate groups of students (e.g., by year, or major, or fraternity) and create averages of the attributes by which they are characterized (e.g., GPA, starting salary, summers spent as interns). What we would be left with is a set of consolidated data with the same number of attributes, but with much fewer observations (Figure 5.3).

Ultimately we could do both – again attempting to reduce the complexity of the decision-making task – while avoiding the actual elimination of specific kinds of data or descriptors.

5.3 Attribute Grouping Approaches

If you think you simply have way too many attributes describing the people, places, or things that you have data on and feel that several of those attributes

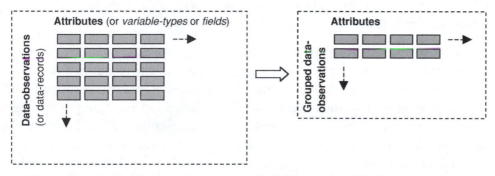

Figure 5.3. Consolidating observations (individual records) of large data sets.

may actually represent the same issue (or very related issues), you have a number of options available to you for consolidating your data.

5.3.1 Trivial Consolidation Approaches

One of the simplest ways to consolidate a group of attributes is by creating an average value across them. If you create an unweighted average (i.e., simply add attribute X + attribute Y + attribute Z and divide by 3 to create some new overall attribute "XYZ"), the critical point is to make sure they are similar in units and scale so that the calculation actually makes sense. For example, it might make sense to average the three student attributes *grade in BUS330*, *grade in BUS331*, and *grade in BUS432* to create something general (perhaps referring to it as "average Organization and Management area grade"). It would probably make much less sense to average "score on 330 final," "bowling score," and "score on breathalyzer test" (different scales and hopefully unrelated issues).

Alternative ways to consolidate attributes may be to take advantage of other standard functions in Excel. For example, if it makes more sense to create something similar to "max performance in Organization and Management," you might use the MAX function to consolidate all final grades in organization and management classes into a single, best attribute. Similarly, if you're interested less in the overall performance of students and more in their tendency to perform inconsistently in a particular discipline, you might calculate the STDEV across related scores. Maybe those who tend to perform more inconsistently in a discipline are doing so for a particular reason that might be meaningful to you.

These are examples that hit close to home for a typical management student, but the same kind of simplified attribute grouping techniques is used in the marketplace:

- Maybe we don't care what consumers spend on individual items, but rather what they spend on groups such as all perishables, electronics, and so on.
- Maybe we don't care about how much all stocks vary on an hourly basis, but are concerned with their before-noon and afternoon averages.

In any case, the methods suggested put the responsibility of consolidation decisions entirely on the shoulders of individual decision makers or DSS designers. They are assumed to be entirely conscious of why certain attributes should be grouped together, and why either unweighted averaging or the use of other summary measures is appropriate. Furthermore, an unmentioned assumption in these examples is that the these schemes are applicable regardless of the nature of the sample population as a whole (i.e., they would provide the same summary results per record, regardless of how many records are involved).

5.3.2 Consolidations Using Statistically Derived Weightings

Sometimes we don't really have a strong feeling about how attributes should be consolidated, only that there's probably some redundancy in the information they provide and that our decision process would be easier if we could crunch them down to more generalized (yet still meaningful) groupings. Fortunately for us, someone has already done the work here. Again, one of the popular methods freely available to us is PCA. As mentioned earlier in this chapter, PCA is a statistical technique that attempts to create a reduced subset of attributes based on a larger set of potentially highly related (perhaps redundant) attributes. It is not constrained to the assumption that all attributes have equivalent relevance in such consolidation, but it does base its statistical approach to the development of weighting schemes on the entire sample of data as a whole (and hence can be sensitive to the size and constituency of that sample).

As an example of the kind of results that might be derived through PCA consolidation, consider the case of Dodecha Solutions, Ltd. Dodecha is a small consulting firm that manages a number of information technology implementation projects over the course of a year. It has been collecting both pre-project selection and post-implementation data for several years, and now wants to base its consideration of future client requests on that data.

Dodecha had the foresight early on to recognize that many pre-project characteristics could not be assessed by anything but subjective (opinionated) reports of their own consultants. They developed a highly structured set of evaluation questions for their consultants to fill out every time they were given a potential client project request to consider. They specifically designed multiple questions aimed at revealing similar higher-level issues (e.g., potential problems with client participation in projects, uncertainty relating to specific technologies), knowing that the use of only a handful of potentially biased questions could provide an extremely misleading view of project potential. Table 5.1 provides the full list of the higher-level issues (left column) and the associated more specific set of items/question (right column) their consultants were asked to answer for each client project proposed.

For each of Dodecha's 115 past projects, prior to making the decision to accept the proposed projects, managers evaluated each of these 33 questions on a scale from 1 to 7 (1 indicating strong disagreement with the statement, and 7 indicating strong agreement with the statement). The full

Table 5.1. *Items Thought to Reflect Higher-Level Management Issues for Dodecha*

Higher-Level Issues	Row	Specific Items/Questions
Ops Fit Issues	A1 :	Will require redesign of many processes
	A2 :	Will require elimination of many processes
	A3 :	Will require resequencing of many processes
	A4 :	Will require addition of many processes
	A5 :	Will require changes in work assignments
Industry Instability	B1 :	Tech capabilities in client industry change frequently
	B2 :	Process capabilities in client industry change frequently
	B3 :	Market of client industry changes frequently
Inter-Org Concerns	C1 :	Client demonstrates poor information sharing
	C2 :	Client demonstrates lack of interest in involvement
	C3 :	Client demonstrates poor worker-resource sharing
	C4 :	Client requires fairly limited time windows for system access/change
	C5 :	Client requires fairly restricted access to stakeholders
New Tech Concerns	D1 :	New technology untested by related firms
	D2 :	We lack familiarity with the nuances of the tech
	D3 :	Patches to new technology are forthcoming
	D4 :	Value of new technology to market still uncertain
Expertise Issues	E1 :	Will require new training for our project staff
	E2 :	Will require work outsourcing to experts
	E3 :	Will require repeated contacts with vendor
Legacy Concerns	F1 :	Much data stored in legacy systems to be replaced
	F2 :	Much data formatting based on noncompliant standards
	F3 :	Culture of use/championship of legacy system
	F4 :	User skills highly tuned to legacy system need changing
	F5 :	Many ties to external systems customized to legacy
Client Issues	G1 :	Client has demonstrated process design and control problems
	G2 :	Client has demonstrated managerial leadership problems
	G3 :	Client has demonstrated poor technical know-how
Org Complexity	H1 :	Involves many separate facilities of client
	H2 :	Involves many functional groups of client
	H3 :	Involves many decision makers at client
	H4 :	Involves many stakeholders at client

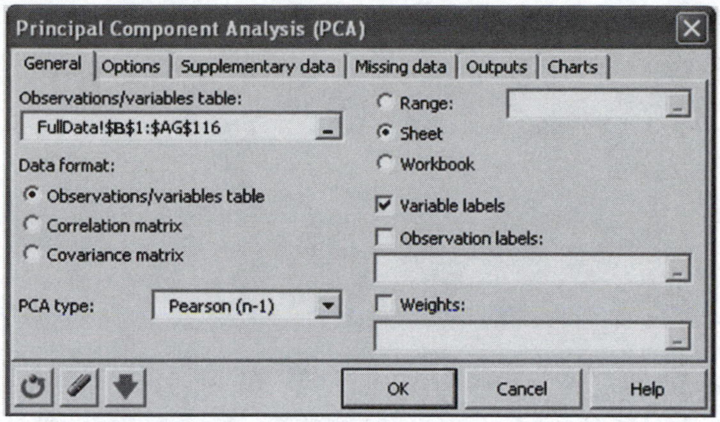

Figure 5.4. Specifying data ranges to be analyzed through PCA with XLStat.

data set along with the complete set of analysis to follow is provided in the Chp5_DodechaSolutions workbook.

Again, aware that any one of these items alone might provide a misleading impression of how managers viewed these projects prior to signing on, Dodecha went back to the full data set and attempted to consolidate it into the original eight factors the management highlighted as being useful in later categorization and analysis. In doing so, they would be reducing their analysis set from essentially 115*33 (3680) pieces of data into what they view a more meaningful set of 115*8 (920). To do this they plan to use PCA.

To demonstrate the use of the PCA consolidation technique (as well as other data simplification tactics), we'll be relying on another tool that goes beyond the typical boundaries of Excel functionality: XLStat (available at www.xlstat.com). XLStat has become one of the industry standards for extended spreadsheet analysis, and is particularly useful for our discussions given the range of tools it makes available as well as the flexibility that it provides to DSS developers (as we will see in Chapter 12).

When installed, XLStat functions similar to any other add-in in Excel. In this particular case, we're interested in making use its PCA function, which is located under Add-ins>XLStat>Analyzing Data>Principle Components Analysis (PCA). This opens the Principle Components Analysis (PCA) dialog box.

The application of the PCA tool can be fairly straightforward. The critical step required by the dialog box is the selection of the data set to be consolidated and some impression of how to consolidate the selected attributes (e.g., into eight components/factors). Although numerous options are made available for professional use, and professional users of this technique are certainly encouraged to investigate their benefits, a demonstration of the basic kinds of results to be expected is sufficient for discussion here. Figures 5.4

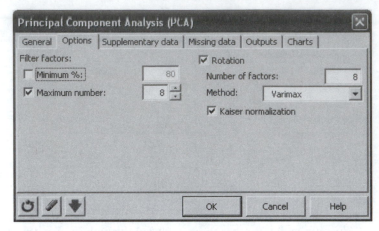

Figure 5.5. Target factor specification for PCA with XLStat.

and 5.5 provide images relating to the specific settings used in the Dodecha case.

The next steps happen largely behind the scenes; however, the output provided by XLStat is extremely rich (beyond the scope of this text). In the most familiar terms for our purposes, the task the PCA algorithm faces can be viewed as the following:

Objective: Construct new factors based on the existing set of attributes such that the new factors are as uniquely distinct from one another (e.g., uncorrelated) as possible.

Decision Variables: The extent to which each attribute contributes to each new factor (e.g., coefficients in each factor equation).

Constraints: Construct exactly eight new factors based on 32 original attributes (in the Dodecha Solutions, Ltd., case).

Figure 5.6 provides an annotated version of the XLStat PCA results in this case. Assisted by a little conditional formatting, we see an output table of what are referred to as component scores, which are higher the more each item relates to one of the eight factors derived from analysis.

Although there is no guarantee that individual attributes will naturally group into the kinds of factors originally conceived of by the designers of the questions (i.e., the eight factors conceptualized in the early table), in this case there does seem to be some correspondence between what was originally conceptualized and the PCA results. It is also clear, as is usually the case, that the items don't load purely on one factor alone, i.e., some attributes provide information that is helpful in forming other factors as well. The specific values of these coefficients are far from immediately intuitive. This is clearly not an equal-weighting scheme as might be derived through a simple averaging approach to attribute consolidation, and not one that could simply be guessed.

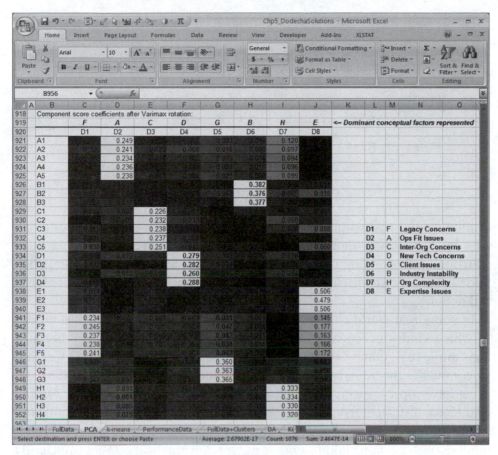

Figure 5.6. Example PCA results (color coded through added conditional formatting).

Regardless, the major conceptual breakouts do seem to be well represented overall, suggesting it might be reasonable to apply the original eight factor labels to the results. In the end, Dodecha can have some faith in the interpretability of the PCA data simplification. In end, the real product of PCA is the consolidated statistically weighted factor scores as shown in Figure 5.7. These will form the bases of further analysis by Dodecha.

	F	A	C	D	G	B	H	E			
	D1	D2	D3	D4	D5	D6	D7	D8	← Dominant conceptual factors represented		
Obs1	0.104	-0.447	1.911	-1.070	0.775	-0.588	-0.481	-0.898	D1	F	Legacy Concerns
Obs2	1.277	0.983	-1.454	0.004	-1.046	0.402	0.946	-1.086	D2	A	Ops Fit Issues
Obs3	-0.995	-1.056	-1.799	0.193	0.032	0.057	0.509	0.748	D3	C	Inter-Org Concerns
Obs4	-1.019	-1.572	0.763	1.049	-0.641	-0.583	-1.312	-1.057	D4	D	New Tech Concerns
Obs5	-0.976	1.133	0.911	-1.473	-0.746	-0.372	-1.441	-0.815	D5	G	Client Issues

Figure 5.7. The eight factor scores for each observation involved in the PCA analysis.

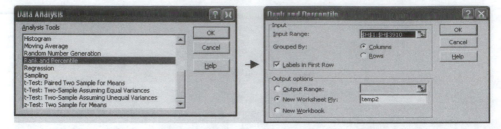

Figure 5.8. Rank and percentile analysis for observation grouping.

5.4 Data Grouping Approaches

Similar to the discussion of grouping attributes, we can start this discussion by considering approaches that might be relevant, provided we have a strong understanding of how we should group based on simple statistics, and then proceed to discuss approaches where such group structures are fairly unknown.

In some real world cases, decision makers already have a logical notion of which kinds of records should be similar enough to group together as a subsample (e.g., maybe we have a reason for grouping student data by major, or companies by industry, or projects by technology type). If this is the case, if we have a pre-existing and well-reasoned structure for grouping. On the one hand, if this categorization scheme sufficiently reduces the complexity of our decision process, we're set and can then move on to other forms of analysis and decision making. On the other hand maybe it doesn't sufficiently reduce complexity. Or maybe we don't have sufficient reason for grouping our data by some prespecified category. Or maybe we just want to group by some numerically driven scheme such as a ranking where we divide our data based on whether it ranks in the top quarter, bottom quarter, or one of the quartiles in between. We can do that easily in Excel.

5.4.1 Quantile-based Categorization

Relevant here is one of the many additional features of the Analysis tool box (brought up in Chapter 2): the Rank and Percentile tool (Figure 5.8). The tool asks you for a set of observations (e.g., 3909 quarterly EPS figures for various firms in a spreadsheet) and the location of the relative ranking of the observations based on that single attribute. As would be expected, the more data you have, the longer the ranking process.

As an example of how to use this tool in a consolidation effort, I've done a simple ranking based on no other criteria other than quarterly sales across all quarters for which we had data in the previous QuarterlyData spreadsheet (see Chapter 4). Figure 5.9 shows an example of the results the Ranking

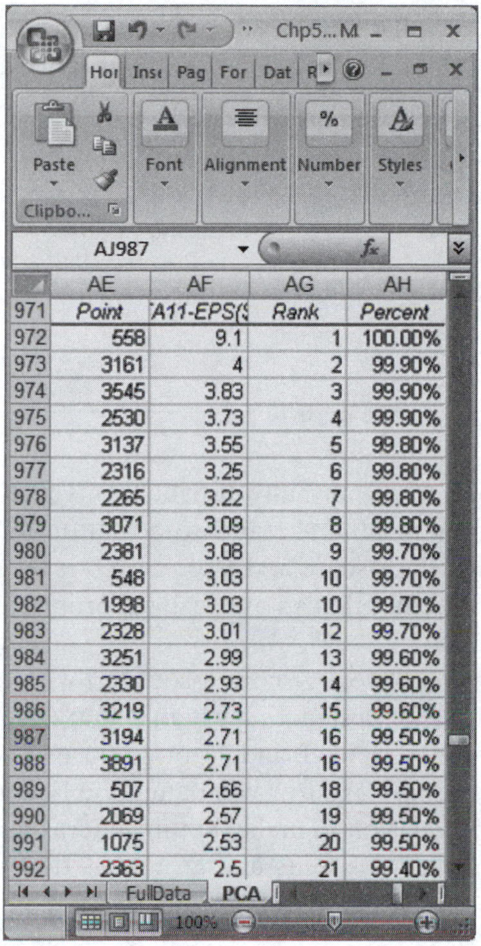

	AE	AF	AG	AH
971	Point	A11-EPS($	Rank	Percent
972	558	9.1	1	100.00%
973	3161	4	2	99.90%
974	3545	3.83	3	99.90%
975	2530	3.73	4	99.90%
976	3137	3.55	5	99.80%
977	2316	3.25	6	99.80%
978	2265	3.22	7	99.80%
979	3071	3.09	8	99.80%
980	2381	3.08	9	99.70%
981	548	3.03	10	99.70%
982	1998	3.03	10	99.70%
983	2328	3.01	12	99.70%
984	3251	2.99	13	99.60%
985	2330	2.93	14	99.60%
986	3219	2.73	15	99.60%
987	3194	2.71	16	99.50%
988	3891	2.71	16	99.50%
989	507	2.66	18	99.50%
990	2069	2.57	19	99.50%
991	1075	2.53	20	99.50%
992	2363	2.5	21	99.40%

Figure 5.9. Example output of rank and percentile analysis.

and Percentile tool kicks out. Note that the data had already been ranked in ascending order prior to using the tool.

A few things to note:

Look at the rankings. Notice that some ranking numbers (e.g., 10, 16) are repeated whereas others (e.g., 11, 17) are absent. What does that mean?

Regarding the previous point, why might this be different than simply selecting the 1st, 2nd, 3rd, and 4th sets of 25 records out of a total of 100 originals?

We could use these rankings to help group data into those in the top 25%, bottom 25%, and so on. How could we use an IF statement to automatically generate such groupings at this point?

5.4.2 p-level/z-score-based Categorization

Measures of standard deviation from the mean provide other meaningful and related approaches to grouping (provided you believe the issue you are

Table 5.2. *Example Structure of Quartile Cross-Binning*

		EPS (earnings per share)			
		Bottom	3rd 25%	2nd 25%	Top 25%
R&D Investment	Bottom				
	3rd 25%		*Cross-tab summaries of other measures (eg. profitability) for firms that fall into each cross-bin*		
	2nd 25%				
	Top 25%				

grouping along is, by nature, normally distributed). There's nothing stopping you from calculating a mean and standard deviation for the set of values, and determining what the z-score and associated p-level of that observation would be; however, whether that's statistically appropriate for the given data set is another question,

Regardless, after you have a z-score associated with each data observation, you have the basis of designating whether that observation is a typical (e.g., z-scores of say between −1 and 1) or (+/−) outlaying (e.g., z-scores greater that 2 or less than −2). How you define the bounds of the outlaying region is yet another decision to make, but in general can be as meaningful (or more so) as the kinds of splits and groupings derived from a ranking procedure.

5.4.3 Multidimensional Bins

If you think that there may be multiple, independent, non-categorical measures that could meaningfully distinguish subsets of your data, make use of them.

Imagine you believe that certain firms, such as those that are simultaneously on the fringes of both (a) EPS performance and (b) research and development (R&D) investment, are relatively unique with regard to other aspects of their operations or financial performance. You have the ability to designate such groups independently, so do that and then use a tool like a PivotTable to create cross-tabs (a table of summary measures, e.g., averages for each grouping combination, shown in Table 5.2).

These can provide a great deal of insight into the effects of multiple factors on additional performance measures. Such insight might suggest further investigations into specific regions of the data (e.g., those firms in the 3rd 25% in R&D but the top 25% in EPS).

Table 5.3. *Example Sub-Populations Associated with Quartile Cross-Binning*

		EPS (earnings per share)			
		Bottom	3rd 25%	2nd 25%	Top 25%
R&D Investmentment	Bottom	2	8	9	5
	3rd 25%	4	5	7	9
	2nd 25%	8	6	5	6
	Top 25%	11	6	4	4

It is also worth noting, however, that although the number of data records that fall into each of the four categories for either the EPS or R&D splits may be equal, there's nothing that will guarantee the number of observations in each cell of a cross-tab will be similar. Consider the example in Table 5.3, where I've entered the number of records that fall into each cross-bin.

There are big differences in the sizes of these bins. Do they make it more difficult to compare other performance measures based on some of the smaller groups?

5.4.4 Cluster Analysis for Multidimensional Splits

You might have the belief that your data are split across multiple dimensions, but in ways that can't necessarily be described by post-hoc combination of independent splits (as done with cross-tabs). That is, maybe there are more complex relationships among the attributes of your data records that tend to group observations in weird though nevertheless potentially informative ways.

To try to illustrate this, consider a bunch of points characterized by three attributes – x, y, and z. In that 3-D space, upon visual inspection, you might think that they tend to cluster into four rough groups. Maybe you could even draw some dividing planes to emphasize those separations. But what if their clustering was less clear? What if there were more points or multiple ways to subjectively split them up? (See Figure 5.10.)

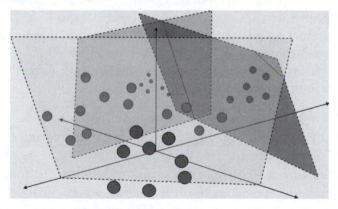

Figure 5.10. Multidimensional complexity in group distinction.

Consolidating observations through non-obvious (although perhaps statistically supported and ultimately managerially meaningful) divisions of their attribute space usually falls into the realm of what is called cluster analysis. This technique for grouping data is actually popular in marketing, where firms attempt to classify specific groups of customers based on a wide ranges of characteristics (attributes).

But how would a somewhat complex and unintuitive approach to classifying data be useful to a manager?

Suppose you collect data on individual entities such as:

• Customers of a business
• Stores of a retail chain
• Students of a university
• IT implementation projects (as in the Dodecha case)

And let's say those individual entities can be characterized by a range of specific attributes, or even higher-level factors such as:

• For customers – age, monthly income, loyalty, tech savvy
• For stores – geo location, sales, market presence, efficiency
• For students – grades in different courses, determination
• For projects – anticipated costs, inter-organizational concerns

To make these data useful, a decision maker/manager might want to identify smaller groups of individuals based on their similarities to one another (i.e., the similarity of their attributes) and then make separate policy decisions for each group, rather than trying to come up with one all-encompassing-yet-perfect solution for everyone.

What kinds of distinct policy decisions might be realistic?

• Designing and deploying different marketing campaigns for different market segments of customers characterized by distinct interests
• Designing and deploying different business and operating strategies to promote sales in different groups of stores facing differing challenges
• Designing different courses, programs of study, or sources of assistance based on strengths and weaknesses of different groups of students
• Designing response plans for dealing with (or rejecting) specific projects requested by existing or future clients

The key to applying customized strategies is in being able to know for whom or what you are customizing (i.e., what is the nature and distinction of the group). Conceptually, the decision maker/analyst must be able to make these distinctions, more often than not, prior to designing customized policies. This conceptual goal translates into the following analytical task of cluster analysis.

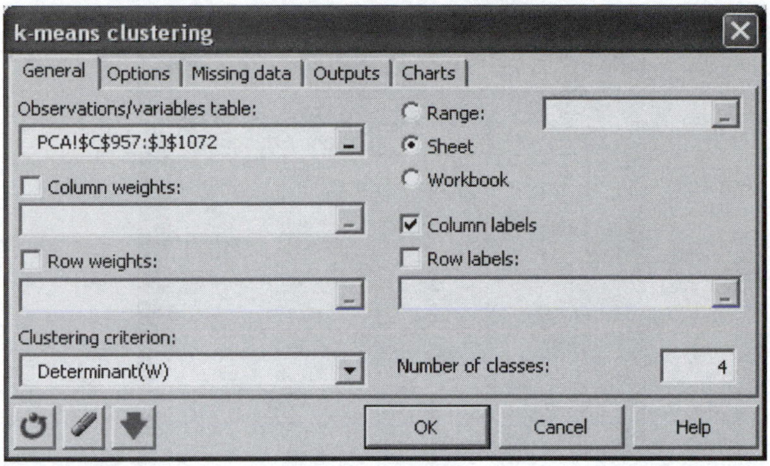

Figure 5.11. Specifying K-means clustering inputs and parameters for evaluation by XLStat.

Objective: Identify a set of fairly distinct groups of entities (records) in the data set, based on some measure of group separation (e.g., minimizing the ratio of within-group to between-group variation, with variation of the entire sample based on the full set of record attributes used for grouping).

Decision Variables: Which entities/records should belong to which group.

Constraints: Often some criteria for limiting the number of groups that might be formed (e.g., limit to the formation of four clusters of projects in the Dodecha Solutions, Ltd., case).

That is, the algorithms used in cluster analysis are designed to locate clusters of data records that possess similar characteristics (whatever those attributes might be), that are distinguishable from other clusters, and ideally that have very few records in between (where group membership is less clear).

Returning to the Dodecha example used to illustrate attribute consolidation (PCA application), we might consider how a tool like XLStat could be used to provide a consolidation of records (projects in this case) into more generalized groupings through the use of cluster analysis. Again, we'll be making use of the Analyzing Data functionality under XLStat and specifically the Cluster Analysis tool.

Again I'm going to specify a few points before letting the analysis run, specifically the range of data; in this case, the eight factor scores for all 115 projects derived earlier from PCA, and a request for the algorithm to limit itself to the formation of four groups (see Figure 5.11).

As with PCA, many other options exist and those professionals who are interested in the use of clustering are encouraged to look into these.

However, a critical point to stress here is that there are many possible combinations for a clustering algorithm to consider. In this case, with 115

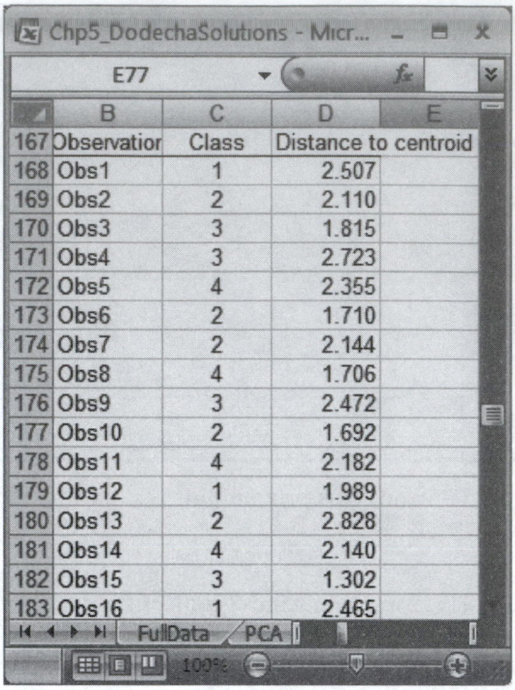

B	C	D	E
167 Observation	Class	Distance to centroid	
168 Obs1	1	2.507	
169 Obs2	2	2.110	
170 Obs3	3	1.815	
171 Obs4	3	2.723	
172 Obs5	4	2.355	
173 Obs6	2	1.710	
174 Obs7	2	2.144	
175 Obs8	4	1.706	
176 Obs9	3	2.472	
177 Obs10	2	1.692	
178 Obs11	4	2.182	
179 Obs12	1	1.989	
180 Obs13	2	2.828	
181 Obs14	4	2.140	
182 Obs15	3	1.302	
183 Obs16	1	2.465	

Figure 5.12. Clustering results (classes/groups assigned) from K-means approach.

projects and four groups of projects, we're talking about $1.72544*10^{69}$ for a comprehensive search. That's basically a 2 followed by 69 zeros – a huge number that makes a routing example involving 15 or even 30 sites seem like child's play. Clustering algorithms are not going to be conducting comprehensive searches; instead, they have their own heuristics built into them, driven in part by statistical cues and in part by random guesses. For that reason, clustering results even on the same data set are subject to variation. For professionals faced with the realizations that results may be somewhat subject to the luck of the draw, the best possible solution is to look at multiple runs of a cluster analysis to see if some consistent group formations are apparent and give greater credence to those group formations that do seem to stand up to a variety of clustering runs.

In any event, the main take-away of cluster analysis will be the derived group constituencies. These are what policy makers are looking for. In the results outlined in Figure 5.12, the Observations represent each of the 115 projects that have been grouped.

Clustering results are only as good as the intelligence brought to bear in their use. Assuming the clusters themselves are fairly robust to other clustering methods that could have been applied, at least two sets of immediate implications typically come into consideration:

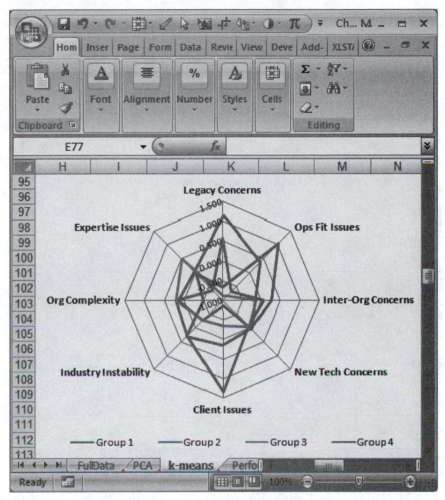

Figure 5.13. Radial plot of group distinctiveness across all factors considered by K-means.

How do the groups differ across the set of factors upon which they were based? Are only some of these factors critical in distinguishing these groups?

At first look, we might try to represent such differences visually. A common visualization tool used in cluster analysis is that of a radar plot. Fortunately, Excel again comes to our aid because radar plots are yet another type of graph made available for representing data. Figure 5.13 shows two versions of radar plots created for the present example.

Not all of the eight factors seem to have been very helpful in distinguishing these groups – for example, look at the New Tech Concerns factor. Unfortunately, the existence of less distinguishing factors tends to de-emphasize the distinctiveness of the derived groups as depicted by measures such as the ratio of within- to between-group variance levels. (This ratio will tend to

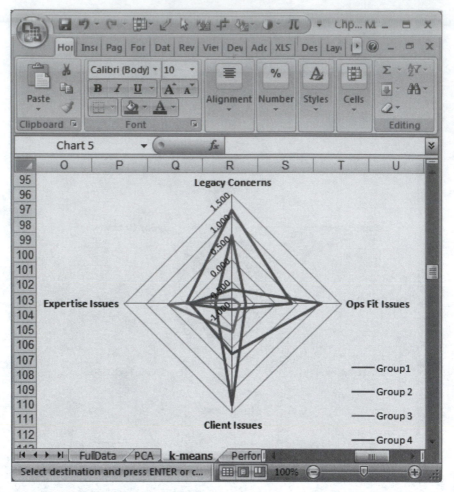

Figure 5.14. Radial plot of group characteristics across four seemingly key distinguishing factors.

go up as more factors are included that don't contribute to group distinction.)

However, we don't need to be thrown by a single measure taken out of context. Our focus should be on any distinctions that seem particularly apparent in the data set. For example, consider a few key factors along which the greatest differences exist. Use a similar radar plot approach to visualization (Figure 5.14).

Although it may be that no one factor could easily distinguish each of these groups (e.g., each of the four factors describing Group 2 reflected in Figure 5.14 seem to be similar to at least one other group), it does appear that a multifactor story could be told relating to differentiation extracted by the clustering protocol.

But even more relevantly, we don't necessarily need to limit our consideration of group distinctiveness to pre-project data. After all, these are completed projects. Post-project performance data would not be available for categorizing future projects into such groups, but Dodecha would surely be interested in knowing how these groups ultimately might differ in performance as well. Which leads to the natural follow-up question for analysis: How do the groups differ across other related outcome or performance measures that might be of interest to managers?

For the purpose of motivating this discussion, the same workbook (Chp5_DodechaSolutions) also includes performance data on the 115 projects analyzed, including ROI (%), Time-to-Completion (in weeks), and two subjective scales reporting on overall customer satisfaction and perceptions of knowledge gained by project team members. Figure 5.15 shows a variant of high-low-close plots (common to Excel) used to summarize how each of the four derived groups differ along these performance measures.

What kind of a story might this tell in general?

1) It seems as if projects that are deemed particularly problematic with regard to client issues (Group 1 projects) also may be slightly more likely to perform poorly with regards to Dodecha's ROI, take a particularly long time to complete, not provide much in terms of customer satisfaction, and certainly don't appear to add to the general knowledge of Dodecha's teams. It might be worthwhile to avoid such projects in the future.

2) Projects that lack client issues but pose concerns with regards to legacy and operational fit issues (Group 2) nevertheless tend to provide decent ROI ranges and team-learning opportunities while potentially facing risks with customer satisfaction. If customer satisfaction isn't an issue for a particular client (e.g., he would tend to complain regardless), perhaps such projects present valuable opportunities, though the issue of customer satisfaction would certainly need to be carefully considered on a client-by-client basis.

3) Projects whose primary distinctive concern surrounds expertise issues (Group 3) provide an interesting opportunity for shoring up expertise through knowledge gains. They tend to be conducted in fairly short time windows, and don't have major shortcomings with regards to customer satisfaction. These may be quick opportunities to gain knowledge relatively free of risk.

4) Regarding Group 4 projects, these are also quick ones, but there is not nearly as much knowledge to be gained as with Group 3; however, there is some potential as far as customer satisfaction and potential word of mouth is concerned. This may all be due to a naiveté on the part of the client with regards to what he truly needs and how to get some basic tasks done, but regardless these projects could be handy in a pinch if testimonials are needed for marketing purposes. A more cynical view might be that these projects are the kinds that other less-scrupulous consulting firms might take advantage of, and perhaps represent an opportunity for Dodecha to play an important interventional role from a market-citizenship perspective.

These are just some sample views of what Dodecha may be thinking based on the results at this point.

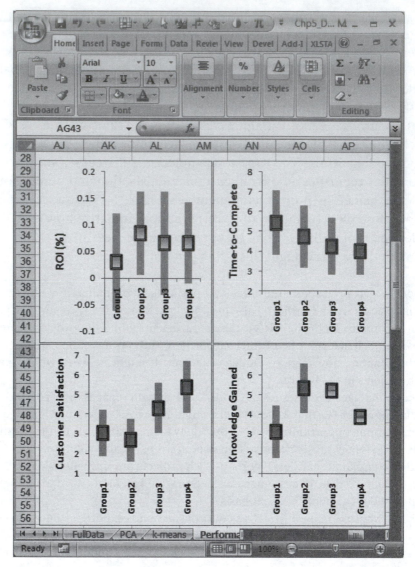

Figure 5.15. Spread charts used to further consider distinction in variance as well as group means.

5.5 Giving Form to Future Categorization

As much as past analysis might be interesting, the focus is still on the past. To truly leverage the findings from the use of consolidation processes such as PCA and cluster analysis, it will be particularly helpful to know if there was some simple way to use future pre-project data to help identify where a new project might fall, and subsequently whether it should be pursued. It would be even more helpful if some basic rules of thumb could be developed to quickly categorize ideal project opportunities.

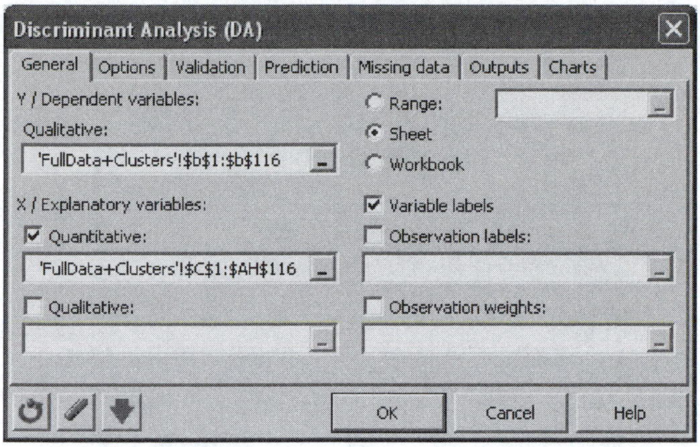

Figure 5.16. Discriminant Analysis parameterization through XLStat.

To close this discussion with an eye on future applications of these results, we'll introduce yet another statistical tool made available by XLStat and the work structure available in the Chp5_DodechSolutions workbook: Discriminant Analysis. The aim of Discriminant Analysis is to make use of a select set of predictive attributes to attempt to create some simple formulation that places specific records/entities (characterized by those attributes) into groups to which they are thought to belong. In this sense, Discriminant Analysis is a nice complement to clustering, which developed group membership based on a set of attributes/factors but typically does not provide a functional form or equation that would formally predict such membership. As with all other XLStat tools discussed thus far, the Discriminant Analysis option is found under the Analyzing Data menu.

On the FullData+Clusters worksheet in the Chp5_DodechaSolutions workbook, we can find the full set of the original 32 items along with the designations into which each derived cluster project has been placed. The hope is that Discriminant Analysis can make use of this or some subset of this original attribute data to come up with a consistent categorization scheme for future projects. Let's first consider what it would come up with given the full set of attributes (expecting some to be much less useful than others). Figure 5.16 shows the settings I'll be using, specifying the qualitative data to predict (i.e., the groups, in this case) and the quantitative data on which I want prediction equations based.

The task of the DA algorithm will be something like this:

Objective: Generate a set of equations that makes use of the predictive data (attributes) to attempt to identify which of the pre-established groups each observation already belongs to at a high level of accuracy.

Decision Variables: Coefficients of the predictive equations.

Simplification Tactics

	B	C	D	E	F
586	Classification functions:				
587					
588		1	2	3	4
589	Intercept	-97.493	-78.720	-59.137	-71.414
590	A1	-4.738	-4.521	-5.250	-4.049
591	A2	-0.851	2.190	2.544	2.458
592	A3	-0.706	-2.556	0.025	-0.918
593	A4	3.884	5.581	2.684	5.760
594	A5	4.318	3.392	1.267	1.247
595	B1	7.464	6.623	4.915	6.120
596	B2	-2.619	-2.159	-2.323	-0.875
597	B3	4.037	1.049	3.274	1.968
598	C1	-4.744	-0.682	-0.232	0.088
599	C2	-4.174	-2.213	-2.931	-2.246
600	C3	-0.452	-0.905	-1.082	-1.266
601	C4	5.262	2.596	4.094	3.259
602	C5	5.488	3.735	3.571	3.753
603	D1	-4.882	-3.399	-3.764	-2.964
604	D2	-0.035	0.127	0.451	0.478
605	D3	3.277	4.156	3.432	4.390
606	D4	6.669	4.402	4.026	2.784
607	E1	-8.146	-7.020	-4.250	-4.229
608	E2	0.571	3.499	2.407	0.823
609	E3	7.493	5.892	4.836	5.015
610	F1	6.483	7.476	6.097	5.324
611	F2	-2.675	-2.234	-1.053	-1.653
612	F3	11.214	6.783	3.579	5.914
613	F4	-8.258	-4.417	-6.419	-6.622
614	F5	-0.413	0.774	0.686	0.638
615	G1	7.667	5.491	4.750	5.367
616	G2	5.919	-0.405	2.604	1.893
617	G3	-2.578	-1.719	-2.667	-2.230
618	H1	-0.752	1.419	0.941	1.992
619	H2	-4.419	-3.760	-4.054	-4.594
620	H3	13.393	7.088	8.695	9.097
621	H4	-4.156	-0.838	-1.266	-2.944

Figure 5.17. Classification function showing individual item roles on cluster prediction.

Constraints: Only the specified predictive variables (could be the whole set or a subset) should be used in the equations formed.

Figure 5.17 show what the analysis provides in this case.

These are essentially a set of coefficients for four equations (one for each group), one coefficient for each of 32 predicting variables (attributes) in this case, plus an intercept. Same kind of thing you'd see as an output to a

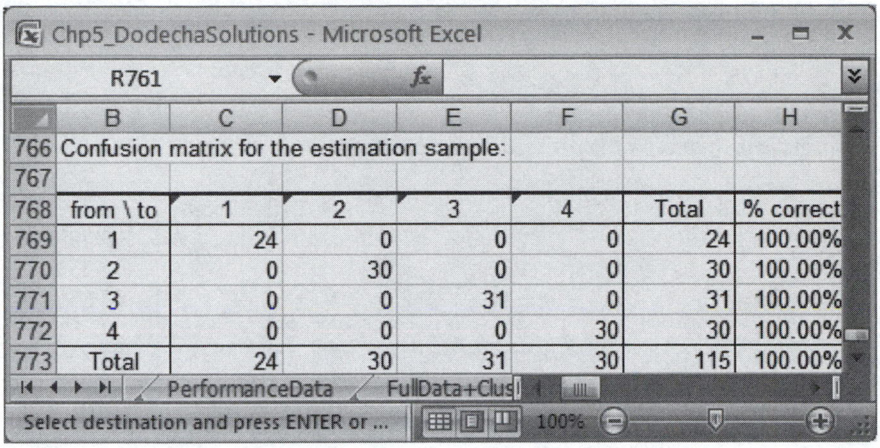

Chp5_DodechaSolutions - Microsoft Excel							

R761				f_x			

	B	C	D	E	F	G	H
766	Confusion matrix for the estimation sample:						
767							
768	from \ to	1	2	3	4	Total	% correct
769	1	24	0	0	0	24	100.00%
770	2	0	30	0	0	30	100.00%
771	3	0	0	31	0	31	100.00%
772	4	0	0	0	30	30	100.00%
773	Total	24	30	31	30	115	100.00%

PerformanceData / FullData+Clus

Select destination and press ENTER or ... 100%

Figure 5.18. Overview of ability of all items to categorize observations in developed groups.

regression analysis. How are these equations used in group-membership prediction? For any record/entity (i.e., each of the 115 projects in this case), and for any of the four discriminant functions (in this case), simply multiply coefficients to their associated attribute values and create a sum of these multiples that includes the intercepts. Formulaically:

$$\text{Value of function "k" for record "n"} = Intercept_k + \sum_{i}^{\#attributes} \beta_{k,i} \cdot x_{n,i}$$

The results of the four functions (again in this case) for a single record/entity (project) are then compared. If the first function provides the highest sum, that record/entity is classified into the first group. If the second function is the highest of the set, the record/entity is classified into the second group, etc. As is often the case with regression analysis, the hope is that a set of equations able to accurately classify pre-existing data will also be able to accurately classify future data. Looking at Figure 5.18, how well do the functions based on the 32 attributes classify?

Perfectly. So the next question is: Do we really need all of these to provide for a decent guess as to where (i.e., into what clusters) new projects might fall? It would certainly be nice to rely on only a few key questions to figure out where it's worth playing ball with a client request or not.

Let's consider the top five of these items based solely on something as simple as the range of their role in the classification function (going with the top five in terms of overall impact might be a better approach, but we'll use this just for demonstration purposes).

C1 (*under Inter-org Concerns*): Client demonstrates poor information sharing
E1 (*under Expertise Issues*): Will require new training for our project staff

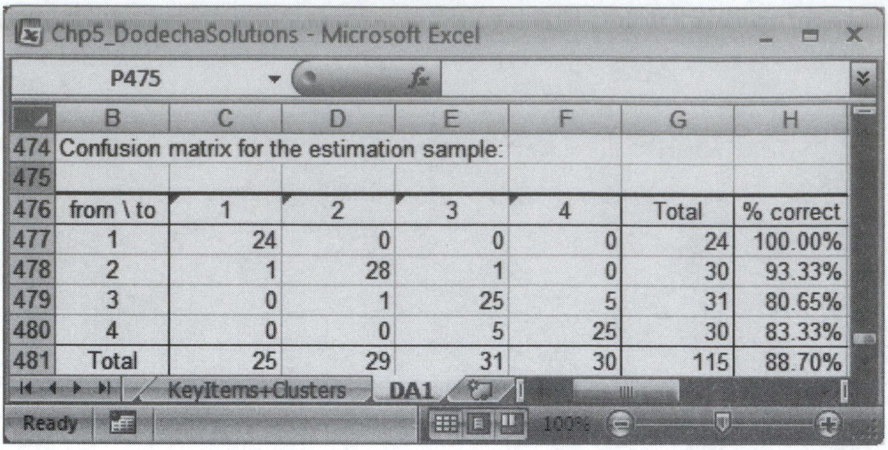

Confusion matrix for the estimation sample:

from \ to	1	2	3	4	Total	% correct
1	24	0	0	0	24	100.00%
2	1	28	1	0	30	93.33%
3	0	1	25	5	31	80.65%
4	0	0	5	25	30	83.33%
Total	25	29	31	30	115	88.70%

Figure 5.19. Ability of only five select items to categorize observations in developed groups.

F3 (*under Legacy Concerns*): Culture of use/championship of legacy system
G2 (*under Client Issues*): Client has demonstrated managerial leadership problems
H3 (*under Org Complexity*): Involves many decision makers at client

Running an almost identical analysis except for greater constraints on the range of attributes available to the discriminant functions, we get the summary of classification strength shown in Figure 5.19.

Not bad for a using a five-question approach rather than 32. If this was an acceptable level of accuracy, it might make type-assessments and subsequent strategies/tactics for handling a heck of a lot easier and quicker.

Cited References

Borges, B., Goldstaeing, DG., Ortmann, A., Gigerenzer, "Can Ignorance Beat the Stock Market?" in G. Gigerenzer, P. M. Todd, and the ABC Research Group (eds.) *Simple Heuristics that Make Use Smart*, Oxford University Press, 1999.

Box, G. E. P., "Robustness in the strategy of scientific model building," in *Robustness in Statistics*, R. L. Launer and G. N. Wilkinson, Editors. 1979, Academic Press: New York.

Chapter 5 Supplement: Making Heuristics Automatic (the Non-Elegant Way)

One of the key advantages to information technologies is that they allow you to automate rules and processes that you would otherwise not want to perform manually, even if you could explain how to actually perform the rule and/or process to the computer.

In decision support systems, the ability to automate tasks such as fast and frugal heuristics can be considerably helpful, especially because it eliminates the need to explain the heuristics to others as well as eliminating the need

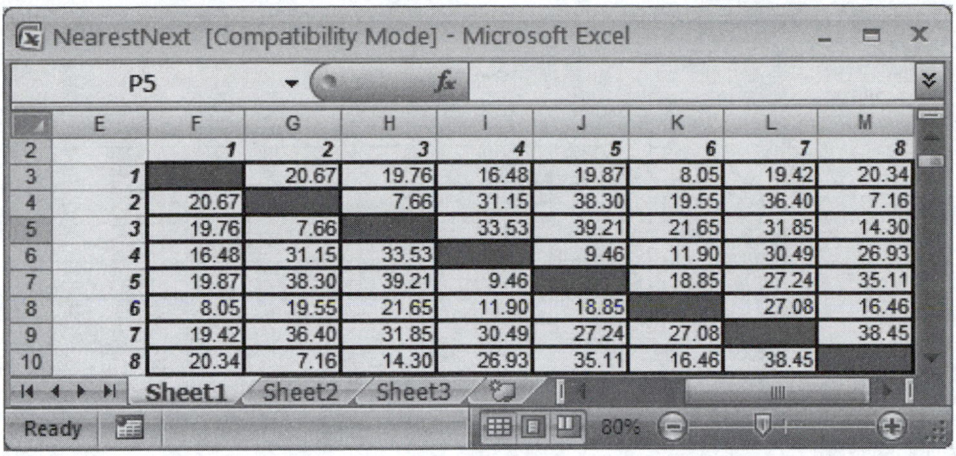

	E	F	G	H	I	J	K	L	M
2		1	2	3	4	5	6	7	8
3	1		20.67	19.76	16.48	19.87	8.05	19.42	20.34
4	2	20.67		7.66	31.15	38.30	19.55	36.40	7.16
5	3	19.76	7.66		33.53	39.21	21.65	31.85	14.30
6	4	16.48	31.15	33.53		9.46	11.90	30.49	26.93
7	5	19.87	38.30	39.21	9.46		18.85	27.24	35.11
8	6	8.05	19.55	21.65	11.90	18.85		27.08	16.46
9	7	19.42	36.40	31.85	30.49	27.24	27.08		38.45
10	8	20.34	7.16	14.30	26.93	35.11	16.46	38.45	

Figure 5.20. Starting set of inter-site distances defining the problem.

to run through them manually (which may be a relatively time-consuming and error-prone approach). Some heuristics are best automated through the use of computer programming, although others can be handled at some level purely through the design of data and cell linkages within a spreadsheet. These automations often do not appear as elegant as their programming equivalents, but they have the advantage of being something that non-programmers can create and understand.

Let's go over how we might automate one of the heuristics discussed earlier in this chapter: The Nearest-Next Heuristic (as might be applied to vehicle routing).

Figure 5.20 is a matrix that shows the distance between any two sites, with the starting point represented by site #1. So the distance from site #1 (row) to site #5 (column) equals 19.87 miles.

Visually, we can tell that the site closest to our starting point (site #1) is actually site #6 (8.05 miles). But we could also use the MIN and HLOOKUP functions to get that result from Excel, provided we tell it to look for the MIN value in the row of our starting point (site #1).

Figure 5.21 shows that same matrix with a few items added to it.

So in the end I have the first step in this heuristic solved (i.e., first go to site #6). If I change the distance numbers in this matrix, my solution might change (automatically).

Now, let's create a second matrix of similar form just below it. In this one, I'm no longer concerned about dealing with site #1 (been there, done that). All I care about is moving on from the last pick (site #6) to the next site closest to it. So I want to eliminate site #1 from consideration, as shown in Figure 5.22.

Most of the structure here is the same as in Figure 5.21. I'm feeding the value of the last pick (6) into the associated new start cell, but I've also

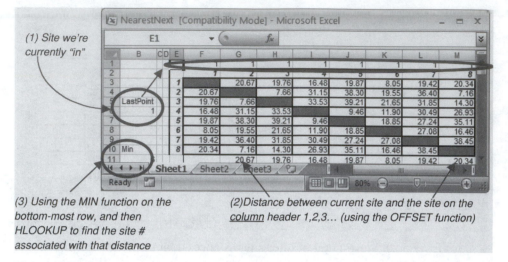

(1) Site we're currently "in"

(3) Using the MIN function on the bottom-most row, and then HLOOKUP to find the site # associated with that distance

(2)Distance between current site and the site on the column header 1,2,3... (using the OFFSET function)

Figure 5.21. Mechanism for assessing set of possible next distances (to find nearest).

excluded everything about site #1. (I've filled it's cells with spaces; not 0s because that would be misleading.) I'm doing it automatically using an IF statement that basically says, "if the row or column header is equal to the LastPoint designated in the previous step (i.e., site #1), put a space in this cell; otherwise, copy the value from the previous table." As seen in Figure 5.23, more of the same is repeated throughout the spreadsheet (essentially duplicated n times; where n is the number of total sites under consideration).

Admittedly, there are more elegant ways to approach this, and this demonstrated method takes up some space (especially if the number of sites increases considerably), but in the end what we have here is a completed

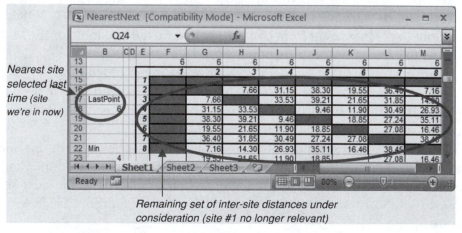

Nearest site selected last time (site we're in now)

Remaining set of inter-site distances under consideration (site #1 no longer relevant)

Figure 5.22. Second stage of the Nearest-Next heuristic automated.

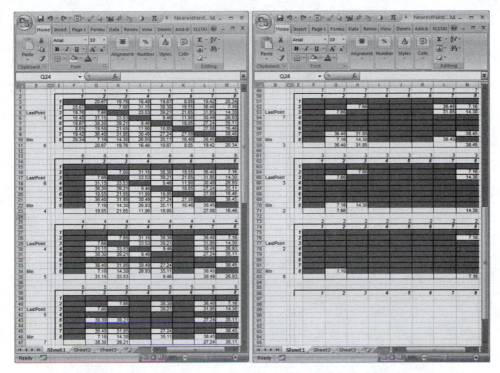

Figure 5.23. Full multistage implementation and derived solution.

routing solution that will change any time we update the original distances. The solution itself is a decent one at that, without the need for an exhaustive search or any formal programming. Relying on code rather than the spreadsheet to crank out this answer would be much more elegant and efficient, but it's worth showing that there's more than one way to accomplish this task, and it doesn't always mean relying on programming skills.

PRACTICE PROBLEMS

Practice 5.1

The file Chp5_PractPCAClust.xls contains earnings-per-share data for 144 firms in three broad industry classifications. It also contains ratings provided by managers that describe the extent to which they invest in each of several research and development activities (e.g., logistics research through customer testing).

1) Use all Research and Testing variables in a Principal Components Analysis to consolidate those attributes into two composite measures. How well do the ratings seem to match expectations with regard to interpretations of the two factors? Does there appear to be some conceptual consistency?

2) Use those two measures to form four clusters of your data records (remember to account for the bug in the cluster labeling part of that program). Discard any

Table 5.4. *Classic Prisoner's Dilemma*

| | | Prisoner 2 Squeals? | |
		Yes	No
Prisoner 1 squeals?	Yes	2, 2	0, 3
	No	3, 0	1, 1

clusters of size fewer than eight. Attempt to generate labels for these groups based on how they may distinguish themselves along the two factors.

3) Use your clustering results to create a PivotTable that shows the average EPS of for firms falling into specific Industry (as your row headers) and R&D-type clusters (as column headers). What do the summaries in the PivotTable suggest regarding R&D strategies (clusters) for specific industries?

4) Use Discriminant Analysis subsets of the original items to attempt to determine whether a small number of questions can provide the similar classifications, and hence predictive capabilities as far as EPS is concerned.

Practice 5.2

If performance differences are so critical, one might ask, "Why not just group by performance to begin with and then see what premeasures might be useful in predicting membership in such performance groups?" Aside from getting into issues relating to potential robustness in the results derived from such an approach, the fact is that such seemingly straightforward approaches, as simple as they may be, often don't yield very strong mechanisms for future prediction (and may turn out to be not all that useful).

Using the existing Dodecha Solutions data set, give this a try. What are the apparent differences in predictive capabilities? Outline both the pros and cons in the predictive capabilities of this approach relative to the one reviewed in this chapter.

Practice 5.3 (Challenge)

A common mechanism for attempting to model the choices that potentially competitive entities may make when faced with a variety of alternative options is provided in the area of what has become called Game Theory (popular in sociology, poly sci, and management).

Table 5.5. *Dominance Applied to Prisoner's Dilemma*

| | | Prisoner 2 Squeals? | |
		Yes	No
Prisoner 1 squeals?	Yes	2, 2	0, 3
	No	3, 0	1, 1

Table 5.6. *Dominance in Gaming Example*

		Player 2's Options				
		1	2	3	4	5
Player 1's Options	1	5, 4	3, 7	3, 4	5, 4	4, 5
	2	4, 3	2, 6	2, 3	5, 6	3, 2
	3	3, 2	1, 7	3, 3	5, 6	2, 2
	4	3, 1	2, 4	3, 6	5, 1	4, 1
	5	4, 2	2, 8	4, 4	5, 5	6, 2

Game Theory assumes that parties competing against each other have at least partial (if not complete) information regarding the payoff structures that each other faces – payoff structures that are dependent not only on their own decisions, but also on the decision of those with whom they are competing. This means that although they may be able to understand where their best outcomes may be, they may have no means of securing those outcomes if they are not able to form prior agreements with their competitors (often the case).

A classic example often discussed in Game Theory is the Prisoner's Dilemma. In Table 5.4, we present the number of years each will get depending on what each crook does. Obviously, the best each could do is no years of time. The worst is three. A perhaps acceptable compromise might be one year each. But how do the players choose the action that will benefit each the most, given that they can't actually communicate on the issue?

The suggested solution is to follow what might be called the Dominance heuristic. Each individual, not knowing what the other might do, tries to figure out if there is one best policy that will do well regardless of what the other individual decides to do, as shown in Table 5.5.

A quick assessment suggests that the dominant policy for each party is to squeal. If Prisoner 1 follows this policy and Prisoner 2 keeps his mouth shut, Prisoner 1 will do not time. If Prisoner 2 follows this heuristic as well, he will do two years instead of three. Of course, both results are worse for Prisoner 2 than would be one year of time, but again that's the nature of heuristics: They're very simple, and they usually provide semi-decent outcomes – but they're often not the best.

Your Task: Use a method similar to that presented in the discussion of automating the Nearest-Next heuristic to automate instances of the Dominance heuristic. Table 5.6 shows a sample matrix from which to base your structure and perform testing.

6

The Analytics of Optimization

Excel gives us a great tool that might help us determine what specific decisions (i.e., values of our decision variables) should be used to obtain our objectives subject to the issues that constrain us. This tool is Solver. Generally Solver can be accessed under the Data tab in the Analysis section (Figure 6.1).

If you do not find Solver in your Excel Data tab, it means that either Solver was not selected for installation at the time your copy of Excel was installed, or it is currently not activated. To activate Solver, click Office > Excel Options > Add-Ins. Select Excel Add-Ins on the Manage drop-down and then click Go. The Add-Ins dialog box opens, enabling you to choose Solver Add-In (Figure 6.2).

6.1 Optimization with Solver

The general structure of Solver fits perfectly with the Chapter 4 description of the three key elements of decision representation/structuring – objective, decision variables, and constraint (Figure 6.3).

Solver is designed to provide the best solutions it can based on the info we give it. It has its limits (it breaks down with extremely complex or large problems), but for smaller problems that still present challenges to decision makers, it does a nice job.

Rather than talk about the theory and math behind simple optimization, we'll take a page from some of the most successful texts on teaching the value and use of this tool by diving right into a few examples in depth. (We'll pick up on how Solver succeeds or, in some cases, fails in its work in Chapter 7.)

6.1.1 Example #1: Atlanta Professional Training

Atlanta has been an up-and-coming hot spot for young professionals over the past few years. As more 20-somethings migrate to Atlanta, they are finding

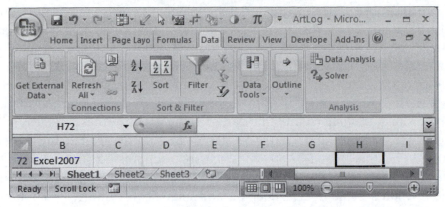

Figure 6.1. Locating Solver in the Excel menu interface.

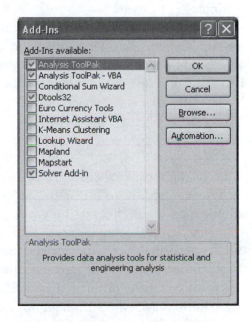

Figure 6.2. Adding-in Solver.

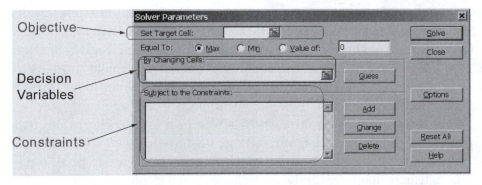

Figure 6.3. Objective, decision, and constraint specification fields in Solver.

it more and more difficult to land that dream job. Extensive market research with the major employers in the area indicate that these job seekers are lacking one of two key job skills – substance (analytics, number crunching, data analysis, etc.) or style (communication, poise, etiquette, etc.).

Dorian McAnderstein, a recent MBA graduate, jumped at the opportunity to spread his expertise in both of these areas. To do so, Dorian founded a professional training facility that caters to the needs of these clueless individuals. He has decided to charge $3,500 for each substance-lacking student (termed "beatnik"), and $2,800 for each style-suppressed student (termed "geek"). There are two professional training boot camps: Beatnik students need 14 hours of number crunching and analytical training, and 7 hours of communication and etiquette training; geeks need only 6 hours of number crunching and analytical, but 11 hours of communication and etiquette training.

Dorian teaches the style courses, and he can work up to 114 hours per month. Dorian's partner handles the substance sessions and can work up to 107 hours per month. In addition, Dorian does not feel that the students benefit from class sizes smaller than nine students per month.

The question is: What mix of geek and beatnik students should Dorian admit?

6.1.1.1 Structuring Models for Optimization

One of the most challenging tasks for those new to optimization methods is figuring out how to translate a story problem into something a computer application (e.g., Solver in this case) can make sense of and assist in solving. The three critical components to all business problems – objectives, decisions, and constraints – are critical to the use of Solver.

Beginners need to get into the practice of asking what falls into each of these bins for every problem they tackle. In the professional training example, what's the objective? Although not explicitly stated, one assumption might be that Dorian is interested in finding a mix of students that maximizes total profit. In lieu of cost figures, we might assume the maximization of revenue to be an adequate proxy. Of course if Dorian has other issues in mind, such as market growth, quality, or even civic virtue, such an objective might be shortsighted. For the benefit of discussion at this point, let's remain shortsighted and go with revenue maximization as our objective. The formulaic form of the revenue function might look like #beatniks*$3500 + #geeks*$2800.

What about the decision variables? These appear to be fairly obvious here. Specifically, a set of decision variables needs to be defined so that we can clearly identify how many beatniks and how many geeks are to be admitted. Although there may be several approaches to this, it is true that there are often better (i.e., more effective) approaches and worse (i.e., more misleading) approaches that might be applied. For example, we could define our decisions directly as the number of beatniks admitted, and the number of geeks admitted.

In contrast, a less effective way to define the decisions would be how many students total, and what percentage should be geeks. However, if our objective function can be defined as the simple linear combination outlined a few sentences earlier, it would require a bit of multiplication among these latter two variables to get to a similar definition. Unfortunately, Solver often has difficulties when objectives are not linear functions of decision variables; therefore, such a definition might provide for undesirable (i.e., sub-optimal) results. We'll talk more about these complications in Chapter 7, but the basic rule for structuring the mathematical forms of story problems for the purpose of optimization is "Keep it simple" (often translating into "Keep it linear").

Regarding constraints, again we'll try to keep things as direct as possible. We know Dorian and his partner have a limited number of hours to devote to the students, and that student training requires time. The total amount of time required for substantive training (#beatniks*14hrs + #geeks*6hrs) must be less than or equal to the amount of time available from Dorian's associate (107 hrs). A similar constraint relates the enrollment numbers to the maximum hours available by Dorian's sidekick. A third constraint ensures that total enrollment (#beatniks + #geeks) does not get below 9. As with decision variables, the "Keep it simple" ("Keep it linear") rule often serves the analyst best.

In Chp6_Examples, I've put all of the information (and the mathematical structure just outlined) from that story problem into some meaningful order on a spreadsheet. I've also added some graphics, but more importantly I've provided sufficient annotation to let you know exactly what each of the numbers on this page refers to. I've also labeled relevant cells and cell ranges with names (e.g., TotRevenue, NofEachStudent) for easier reference (see Figure 6.4).

6.1.1.2 Getting to the Solution

If we didn't have any additional decision support mechanisms to help us at this point, we might start by trying out various values of our decision variables to attempt to meet our objectives without violating any of our constraints:

If I enter 3 Geeks and 3 Beatniks, I get total revenue of $27K

If I enter 5 Geeks students and 3 Beatniks, I get total revenue of $45K (better)

If I enter 7 Geeks students and 7 Beatniks, I get total revenue of $63K; however, that would require more hours than either instructor has available.

Obviously a manual search for a good solution even in this case could take some time. Solver makes it easy for us (Figure 6.5).

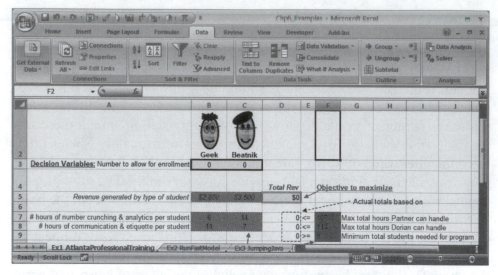

Figure 6.4. Structuring the enrollment decision for APT.

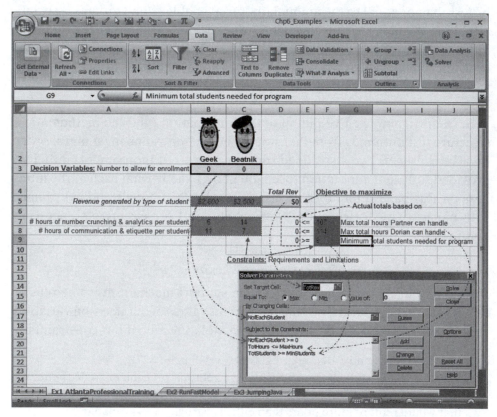

Figure 6.5. Specifying the problem structure for APT in Solver.

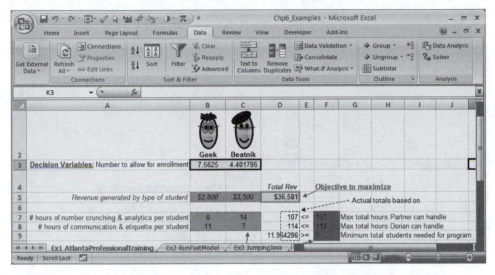

Figure 6.6. Example solution to one specification of constraints for APT.

Because all of the information is entered in some intelligent fashion into the spreadsheet, with decisions linked to both the objective and the issues that are subject to constraint, we're already set up for Solver to help us with this one.

Note how the objective, decision variables, and constraints correspond between the spreadsheet and fields in Solver. One solution is shown in Figure 6.6.

Are 7.56 or 4.40 students reasonable options in this problem? If partial students are not acceptable, we'll need to add another constraint limiting our solution to integer-only options, as shown in Figure 6.7. A more reasonable solution for Atlanta Professional Training is shown in Figure 6.8.

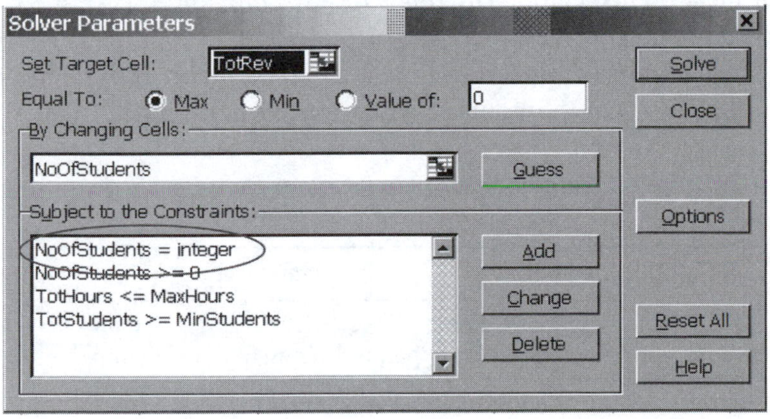

Figure 6.7. Respecification including integer constraints.

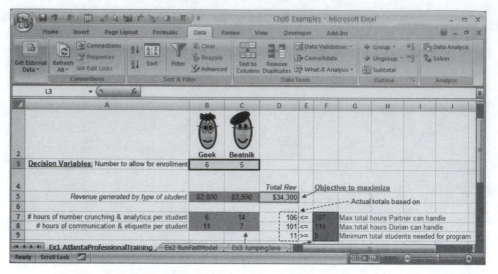

Figure 6.8. Solution associated with addition of integer constraints.

6.1.2 Example #2: RunFast, Inc.

RunFast manufacturers running shoes used to supply specialty running retailers throughout the Southeast. RunFast currently produces three types of running shoes: basic, track, and trail. RunFast wants to determine how many pairs of each type to produce next month. The process of assembling each pair is highly automated, followed by manual inspection of each individual pair to ensure it meets the high quality standards set by RunFast. Each component of the shoe (sole, laces, air wick, insole, and so on) is placed onto a belt that feeds through an assembly machine called the Blazer620. After the shoe is assembled, it passes onto the manual inspection line where it is quality checked and tested.

Each of the three types of shoes must be processed on the Blazer620, and each pair must be inspected. The times required for these two processes for each shoe type are specified in Table 6.1.

There are 90 hours of Blazer620 time available for assembly of these shoes next month. Not all of the hours must be used, but no more than 90 can be

Table 6.1. *Requirements Specifications for a Production Planning Example*

	Shoe Type		
Production Method	Basic (min/pair)	Track (min/pair)	Trail (min/pair)
Blazer620	6.75	4.80	6.00
Inspection Area	15.30	17.40	14.25

Table 6.2. *Cost and Revenue Details for a Production Planning Example*

	Shoe Type		
	Basic ($/pair)	Track ($/pair)	Trail ($/pair)
Revenue	23.85	19.88	18.00
Material cost	7.80	7.34	6.30
Direct production cost	3.03	3.14	2.79
Profit Margin	13.02	9.41	8.91

used. The inspection team has 125 hours available for testing these products next month.

The accounting department at RunFast has provided the production cost per hour of $9.75 for using the Blazer620. This cost should be considered in this decision. Likewise, the direct labor cost for the inspection team is $0.23 per minute. The revenue and overall profit that each pair generates and the cost of the materials used in each pair are specified in Table 6.2.

RunFast is known for its high-quality products and special testing of each pair of shoes. RunFast faces tremendous demand for its products, and is confident it can sell every pair at the given prices. There is one catch: One of RunFast's largest customers has already placed an order for 30 pairs of the track shoes to be delivered next month.

The marketing department wants to ensure that RunFast maintains a full product line to stave off the competition from encroaching on its territory, and has requested that at least one pair of trail shoes be produced for every 10 basic pairs that are produced next month. We now formally state the decision problem confronting RunFast:

Determine a production plan that specifies how many basic, trail, and track running shoes to produce next month in order to maximize total monthly profit.

What constraints do we face?

a) Don't use more than 90 hours of Blazer620 time.
b) Don't use more than 120 hours of inspection time.
c) Do produce at least 30 pairs of track shoes.
d) Do produce at least one pair of trail shoes for every 10 basic pairs.

Figure 6.9 shows a structure that we might use to outline our decision variables, and how they relate to the objectives and constraints we're faced with. Given the appropriate labeling of cells and cell ranges for reference purposes, Figure 6.10 shows how we'd convey that information to Solver. The solution Solver gives us is shown in Figure 6.11.

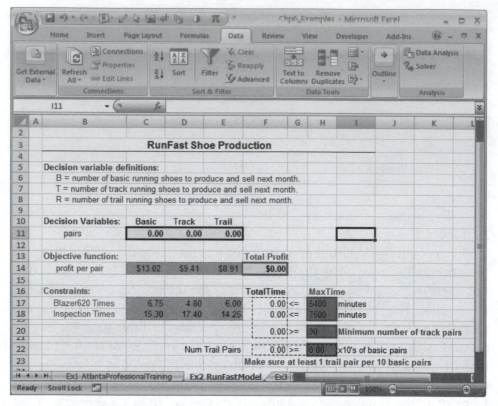

Figure 6.9. Structuring the production decision.

6.1.3 Example #3: Jumping Java, a Worker Staffing Problem

The Jumping Java coffee shop located on a local college campus is open 24 hours per day. The Jumping Java employs mostly students who enjoy the flexibility of 4 hours shifts (6 per day). All shifts start at 4-hour intervals

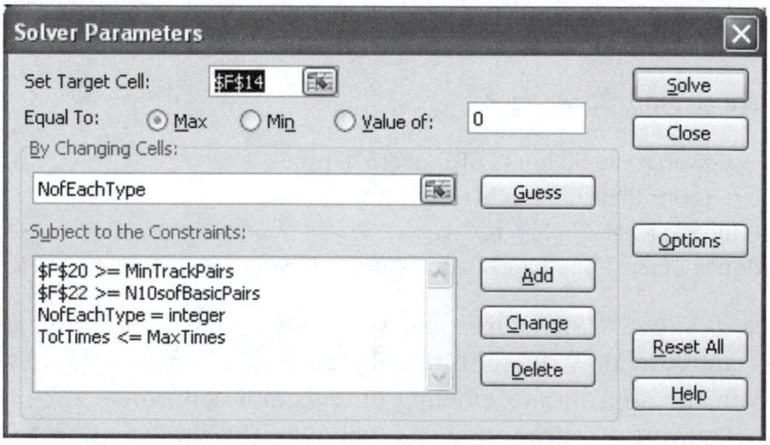

Figure 6.10. Specification of the production objective, decisions, and constraints.

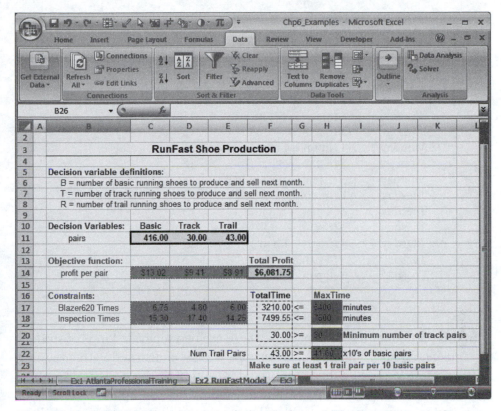

Figure 6.11. Solver's suggested optimal production solution based on specification.

beginning at midnight. The minimum number of employees required in each time interval over the 2-day cycle is given in Table 6.3. The table gives a sample of the staffing requirements for 2 consecutive days (e.g., Monday and Tuesday).

Note: In this example, we are assuming that these staffing requirements repeat every two days. This is a major simplification, but useful to sufficiently demonstrate the structure of the logic and overall nature of the model used. In reality, each day of the week may have different staffing requirements.

Staff members can work either a 4- or 8-hour shift. Employees choosing to work an 8-hour shift receive $13.50 per hour. Those working only a 4-hour shift receive $12.75 per hour. The coffee shop also incurs an overhead cost of $7.50 per person working either shift. Therefore, the total cost of having one person work for 8 hours is $(8 \times 13.50) + 7.50 = \$115.50$. The total cost of having one person work one 4-hour shift is $(4 \times 12.75) + 7.50 = \$58.50$. So the question is: How many employees should be working in each time period on each day to minimize total staffing costs (subject to minimum staffing requirements)?

Table 6.3. *Details for an Employee Staffing Example*

Day	Shift Time	Minimum Number of Employees Needed
Monday	1 (midnight – 4 a.m.)	4
Monday	2 (4 a.m. – 8 a.m.)	11
Monday	3 (8 a.m. – noon)	16
Monday	4 (noon – 4 p.m.)	21
Monday	5 (4 p.m. – 8 p.m.)	18
Monday	6 (8 p.m. – midnight)	8
Tuesday	1 (midnight – 4 a.m.)	3
Tuesday	2 (4 a.m. – 8 a.m.)	13
Tuesday	3 (8 a.m. – noon)	17
Tuesday	4 (noon – 4 p.m.)	22
Tuesday	5 (4 p.m. – 8 p.m.)	15
Tuesday	6 (8 p.m. – midnight)	11

In this particular problem, because there are two separate kinds of staffers (4- and 8-hour-shift people), and because we are concerned with assigning those staffers to specific time slots, the description of the decision variables might seem a little more complex than in the previous examples. It would help if we could design decision variables that would simplify the model regardless of whether we were using a manual search or Solver.

The most straightforward definition might at first seem to be just deciding on and keeping track of the number of people working in each of the time intervals for each day. Unfortunately, if we only know the total number of people (of a given shift type) working from midnight to 8 a.m., we don't know how many of these people are 8-hour employees and how many are four-hour employees. Even if we kept track of 4- and 8-hour shift workers separately for each time interval, we would not know how many 8-hour shift workers were ending as opposed to beginning their shifts in that interval. We could easily get confused in our policy using that approach.

To clarify the schedule and avoid this problem, we define variables that tell us how many people of each type simply *begin* their shift in each time interval. With this information, we can compute total employment costs as well as determine the total number of people working in each of the 12 4-hour time intervals.

Figure 6.12 shows how we might structure the problem in a spreadsheet and in Solver. Figure 6.13 show what Solver gives us. Consider trying to come to this solution through a manual trial-and-error approach. It's nice to have Solver.

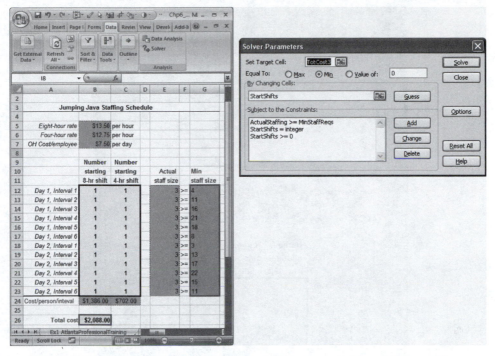

Figure 6.12. Spreadsheet construction and Solver set up for staffing problem.

6.2 Deeper Insights into Optimization Solutions

Although Solver can give us an optimal solution to a problem spelled out in math form, often the specific details that we provide have some uncertainty associated with them. Sometimes the fact is that the parameters we use in specifying the problem are more like estimates than hard fact. To make a problem simpler to solve, we sometimes exclude the possibility that we could modify these parameters (albeit at some additional cost). Sometimes situations are simply subject to change – we might want to consider the implications of such changes to the parameters assumed.

For example, in a hypothetical routing or facility location problem, on one hand, we could start with an assumption that we have only four cities to work with; but on the other hand we might assume we have the opportunity to consider a six-city scenario to solve this problem if we're willing to add in further cost structure. In a different management problem, we could assume workers work at a particular pace; or we could assume the possibility of increasing that pace (at cost) and see how Solver's solution to our problem changes. All of this might alter obstacles that could be preventing us from doing better in our objective, that is, altering certain constraints of the problem can have a significant impact on how well we do.

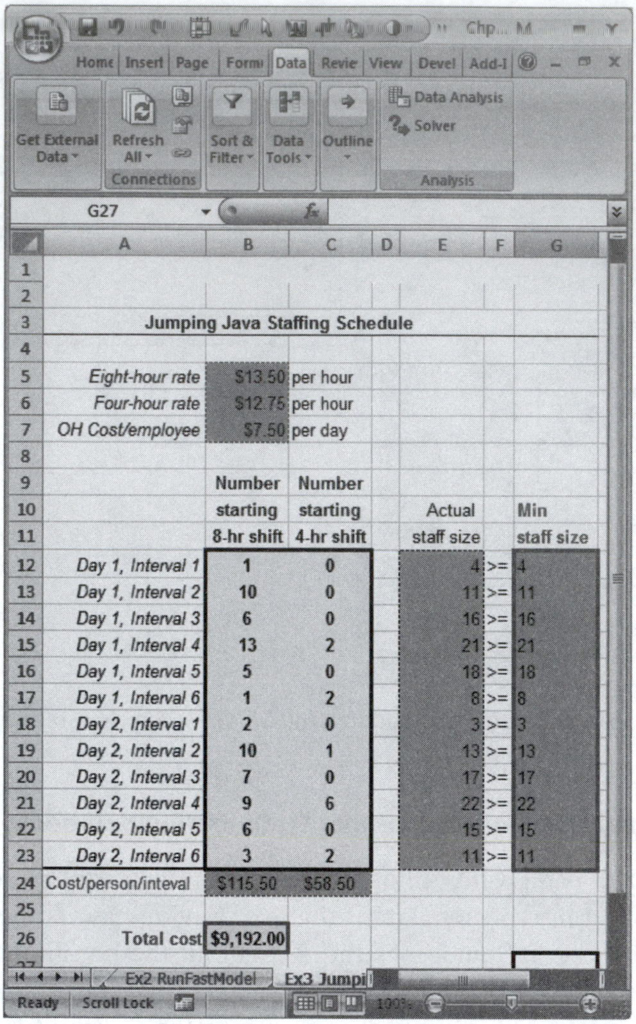

	A	B	C	D	E	F	G
1							
2							
3	**Jumping Java Staffing Schedule**						
4							
5	*Eight-hour rate*	$13.50	per hour				
6	*Four-hour rate*	$12.75	per hour				
7	*OH Cost/employee*	$7.50	per day				
8							
9		**Number**	**Number**				
10		**starting**	**starting**		Actual		Min
11		**8-hr shift**	**4-hr shift**		staff size		staff size
12	*Day 1, Interval 1*	1	0		4	>=	4
13	*Day 1, Interval 2*	10	0		11	>=	11
14	*Day 1, Interval 3*	6	0		16	>=	16
15	*Day 1, Interval 4*	13	2		21	>=	21
16	*Day 1, Interval 5*	5	0		18	>=	18
17	*Day 1, Interval 6*	1	2		8	>=	8
18	*Day 2, Interval 1*	2	0		3	>=	3
19	*Day 2, Interval 2*	10	1		13	>=	13
20	*Day 2, Interval 3*	7	0		17	>=	17
21	*Day 2, Interval 4*	9	6		22	>=	22
22	*Day 2, Interval 5*	6	0		15	>=	15
23	*Day 2, Interval 6*	3	2		11	>=	11
24	Cost/person/inteval	$115.50	$58.50				
25							
26	**Total cost**	**$9,192.00**					

Figure 6.13. Staffing solution suggested by Solver.

But not all issues listed as constraints end up having a major impact on the solution that Solver provides. Those that do are referred to as binding constraints. Those rules that are active but are less severe than binding constraints, and therefore don't actually hold us back, are called non-binding. The concept of a binding constraint is analogous to the concept of a bottleneck in operations management. Bottlenecks are always the key elements that hold us back, even if other rules simultaneously apply. Managers are (or at least should be) always trying to find ways to break down bottlenecks, and find new ones to tackle. When bottlenecks (binding constraints) are broken, we expect other limitations (originally non-binding constraints) to take their place (i.e., essentially become binding in turn). Make sense?

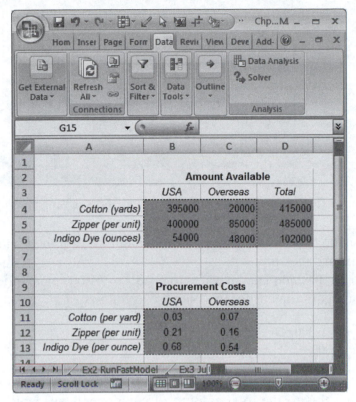

Figure 6.14. Facts relevant to the Fashion Denim case.

Solver provides a few handy mechanisms for describing which specific constraints in a problem are binding, how much they can be modified (presumably at some cost) before becoming non-binding, and to what degree other currently non-binding constraints can be modified (often at some marketable gain) before becoming binding themselves. We're going to focus on the interpretation of the most straightforward tool: Answer Reports.

Answer Reports from Solver specifically tell us which constraints are binding. It does so by reporting specifically on cell references involved in the problem, that is, cells containing decision variables (and implied decisions based on those) and the cells that contain the limits to which those decisions are subject.

6.2.1 Example #4: Fashion Denim, Inc.

Fashion Denim is a designer jeans manufacturer that currently produces all of their goods in the United States. To cut costs, Fashion Denim is considering sourcing some of its materials from overseas for next month's production. Three of the major raw materials used in jeans manufacturing (cotton, zippers, dye) as well as how much of each material is available is shown in Figure 6.14.

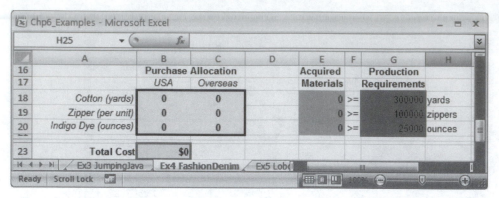

Figure 6.15. Possible spreadsheet structuring of purchasing problem.

In addition, the procurement costs of each material from the United States and overseas are shown.

Next month, Fashion Denim wants to produce 100,000 pairs of jeans. The raw material requirements for this plan are as follows:

Cotton (yards): 300,000
Zippers: 100,000
Indigo dye (ounces): 25,000

Comparing this to the total amount of components available, this goal seems generally achievable. However, given high import tariffs on certain goods purchased overseas, Fashion Denim needs to limit the quantity of zippers and dye imported to 50,000 and 1,500 respectively.

What portion of materials should Fashion Denim acquire from the United States and overseas to minimize the total cost, meet production requirements, and limit import tariffs? To find the answer, we might set up the problem as shown in Figure 6.15. Solver gives us the solution shown in Figure 6.16 (when specified appropriately). But before it does it also asks us what kinds

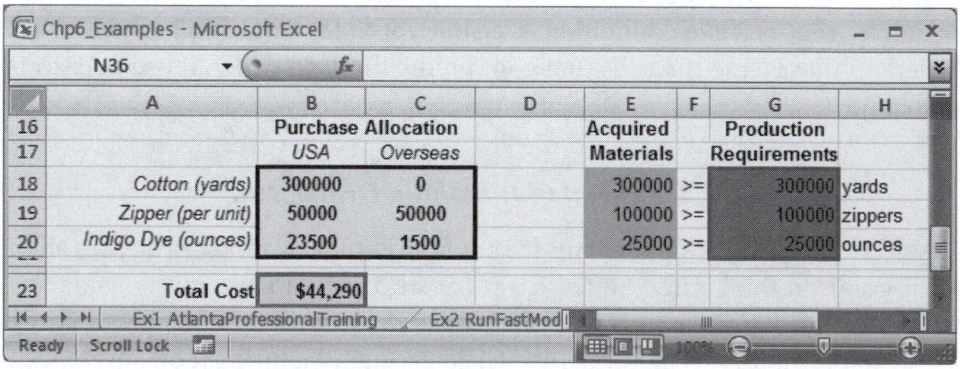

Figure 6.16. Solution to purchasing problem by Solver.

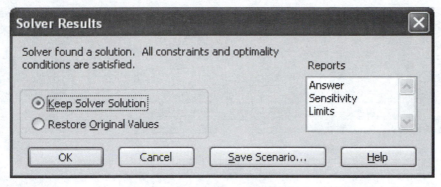

Figure 6.17. The Answer Report option.

of reports we might be interested in. Figure 6.17 shows what happens if we select Answer in the Report scroll box. Figure 6.18 shows what we'd get on a separate tab.

We could figure most of this information from the solution provided, but it's explicit in the report. Solver is basically telling us the only potentially alterable constraints that critically bind our decision. Keep in mind that integer constraints are always binding. We might ask what the situation would be if import tariffs were eased on zippers (which would essentially break the binding nature of this constraint).

If we eliminated that constraint entirely Figure 6.16 shows what we'd get. This is good news because our total cost drops to $41,790.

Sometimes binding constraints are only slightly more severe than the non-binding constraints that exist below them. Real added gains often require the consideration of a series of calculated changes.

6.2.2 Example #5: Lobo's Cantina Layout Design

Lobo's Cantina is considering a redesign of its current layout with the interest of generating a higher profit margin while still catering to desires of its target market. It currently has a total area of 30 feet by 60 feet (1,800 square feet) to work with. The owner realizes that for everything to work together, he will need to consider a variety of implied service and operating requirements in making a decision. The space needs to house its dining area, bar, kitchen, wash area, restrooms, storage, and host stations that include both the greeting station and the rear cashiers.

While the owner has considerable freedom in terms of how to specifically layout each area to provide for an aesthetic look, he does have to follow some rational rules in making the initial space division decisions. For example, if he plans to devote a large area of the floor to dining, he will want to make sure that he has enough kitchen and wash capacity to meet the implied demands

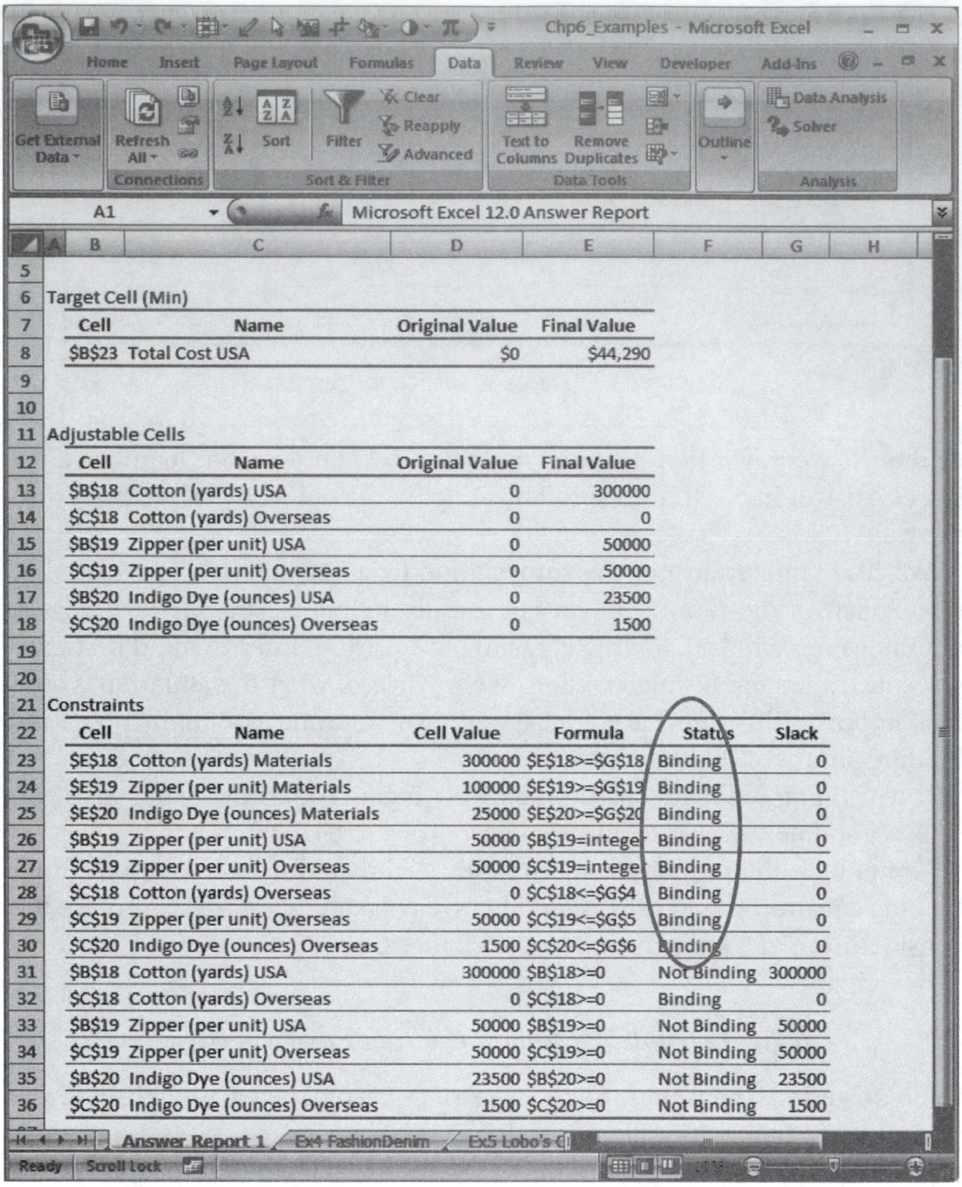

Microsoft Excel 12.0 Answer Report

Target Cell (Min)

Cell	Name	Original Value	Final Value
$B$23	Total Cost USA	$0	$44,290

Adjustable Cells

Cell	Name	Original Value	Final Value
$B$18	Cotton (yards) USA	0	300000
$C$18	Cotton (yards) Overseas	0	0
$B$19	Zipper (per unit) USA	0	50000
$C$19	Zipper (per unit) Overseas	0	50000
$B$20	Indigo Dye (ounces) USA	0	23500
$C$20	Indigo Dye (ounces) Overseas	0	1500

Constraints

Cell	Name	Cell Value	Formula	Status	Slack
$E$18	Cotton (yards) Materials	300000	$E$18>=$G$18	Binding	0
$E$19	Zipper (per unit) Materials	100000	$E$19>=$G$19	Binding	0
$E$20	Indigo Dye (ounces) Materials	25000	$E$20>=$G$2	Binding	0
$B$19	Zipper (per unit) USA	50000	$B$19=intege	Binding	0
$C$19	Zipper (per unit) Overseas	50000	$C$19=intege	Binding	0
$C$18	Cotton (yards) Overseas	0	$C$18<=$G$4	Binding	0
$C$19	Zipper (per unit) Overseas	50000	$C$19<=$G$5	Binding	0
$C$20	Indigo Dye (ounces) Overseas	1500	$C$20<=$G$6	Binding	0
$B$18	Cotton (yards) USA	300000	$B$18>=0	Not Binding	300000
$C$18	Cotton (yards) Overseas	0	$C$18>=0	Binding	0
$B$19	Zipper (per unit) USA	50000	$B$19>=0	Not Binding	50000
$C$19	Zipper (per unit) Overseas	50000	$C$19>=0	Not Binding	50000
$B$20	Indigo Dye (ounces) USA	23500	$B$20>=0	Not Binding	23500
$C$20	Indigo Dye (ounces) Overseas	1500	$C$20>=0	Not Binding	1500

Figure 6.18. Sample output of the Answer Report.

of a population seated in that area. Demands for kitchen work (and thus requirements for kitchen space) will decrease as the size of the bar increases. Implied storage requirements (and storage space) will change depending on how much the restaurant is focused on bar service, as will restroom designs and the need for host stations.

The following is a breakdown of the assumed restrictions with which the restaurant owner is dealing.

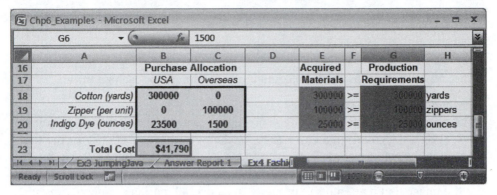

Figure 6.19. Alternate solution after eliminating a binding constraint.

Fundamental Seating Dimensions:
Tables designed to seat four take up 24 square feet of space.
Tables designed to seat two take up 8 square feet of space.
Any seat at the bar (+ bar counter space) takes up 5 square feet.

Additional Requirements:
There must be at least one greeting station that takes up a minimum of 20 square feet. Each host station is expected to provide enough capacity for handling 24 individual tables at most. Each additional host accommodation requires an additional 20 square feet of space.

There must be at least one rear cashier station (taking up 10 square feet of space). Because bar customers pay at the bar, there is no need for rear cashier service. In other words, the need for additional rear cashiers depends only on the amount of dining volume anticipated. Each rear cashier is thought to be able to handle work for up to 20 tables in use.

Minimum kitchen amenities begin with a required 40 square feet of space. Every additional 20 chairs in dining translates into approximately another 5 square feet in the kitchen. However, the current building and sewage code does not allow for a total kitchen capacity beyond 400 square feet.

Minimum cleaning amenities require a minimum of 20 square feet of space. Another 5 square feet of kitchen space is needed for every additional 40 chairs in the dining area or the bar,. Building and sewage codes limit this total space to 200 square feet.

The storage room must be at least 30 feet square. Because of inventory management policies, the restaurant tends to buy alcohol less frequently than food, which it obtains throughout the day from neighboring markets; therefore, each additional seat at the bar increases the storage needs by 1 square foot, while every four seats in the dining area does the same.

Lastly, there must be one male and one female restroom. Each must have a total of 40 square feet to provide the minimal functionality (one sink and "chamber" per restroom). Each additional chamber adds another 15 square feet. The total number of chambers needed in each restroom should be based on expected average need at any given point in time. The forecast the restaurant will use to derive this total is: number of chambers per restroom must be at least equal to:

$$(\text{# bar seats})/30 + (\text{# dining seats})/60$$

The sewage code allows for a maximum of 5 chambers for each restroom.

Profitability and Market Issues:

The owner believes that the average profit his restaurant can generate per dining seat over the course of a day is $340 for the two-seat tables ($400 for the four-seat tables, which are more likely to spend on appetizers), but $560 per average bar seat. However, he is concerned that an excessive bar space might damage the image that it attempts to promote to its overall market segment (consisting of customers who might be attracted to either the bar or seated dining on any given day). With that in mind, he wants to make sure that the bar area never takes up more than half the area specific to dining. If we want Solver to help us, we'll have to translate those specifications into something more formulaic.

Constraints in brief:

The number of greeting stations must be at least ((# of two- and four-seat tables combined)/24); total greeting station space will equal (# of greeting stations × 20).

The number of cashier stations must be at least ((# of two-and four-seat tables combined)/20); total cashier space will be equal to (# of cashier stations × 10).

The kitchen space should be at least (40 + (5 × ((two- seat tables × 2) + (four-seat tables × 4))/20)); total cannot exceed 400.

The kitchen space should be at least (20 + (5 × ((two-seat tables × 2) + (four-seat tables × 4)) + bar seats)/40)); total cannot exceed 300.

The storage space should be at least equal to (1 × ((two-seat tables × 2) + (four-seat tables × 4)) + (5 × bar seats)); the minimum size of this space is 30 square feet.

Total number of "chambers" should be at least ((2 × (bar seats/30) + ((two-seat tables × 2)/60) + ((four-seat tables × 4)/60))); total restroom space should be equal to ((25+25) + (15 × (number of chambers))).

Total area taken up by bar can't be more than half the area taken up by dining.

Figure 6.20 shows an example of how we might structure the various decisions and their relationships to profitability and the functional requirements spelled out in this problem in spreadsheet form. (All constraints and relationships are built in here as in earlier examples.)

Again, if we're using Solver, we'll need to spell out what cells represent decisions and what cell relationships represent constraints. With the appropriate, meaningful cell labeling, we might have the results shown in Figure 6.21 in Solver (lots of constraints here; only a subset is shown in the figure). And if we use this set of constraints, Figure 6.22 show the results from Solver.

Let's do this once again, omitting integer restrictions that can provide for dubious solutions. (I doubt anyone would feel comfortable using a quarter

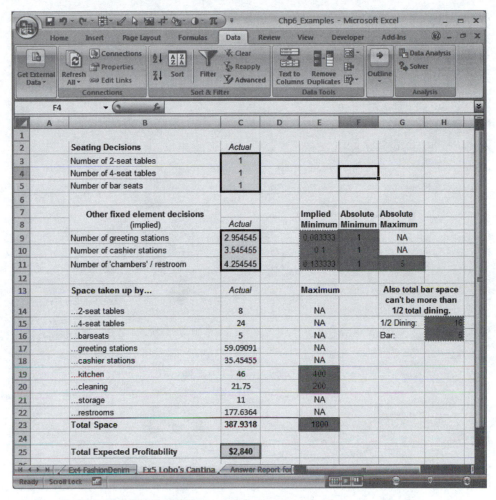

Figure 6.20. Possible spreadsheet set up for layout example.

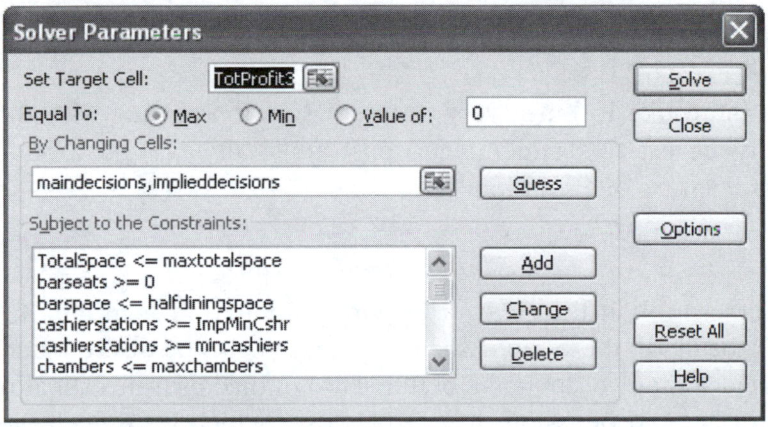

Figure 6.21. Example Solver specification for layout example.

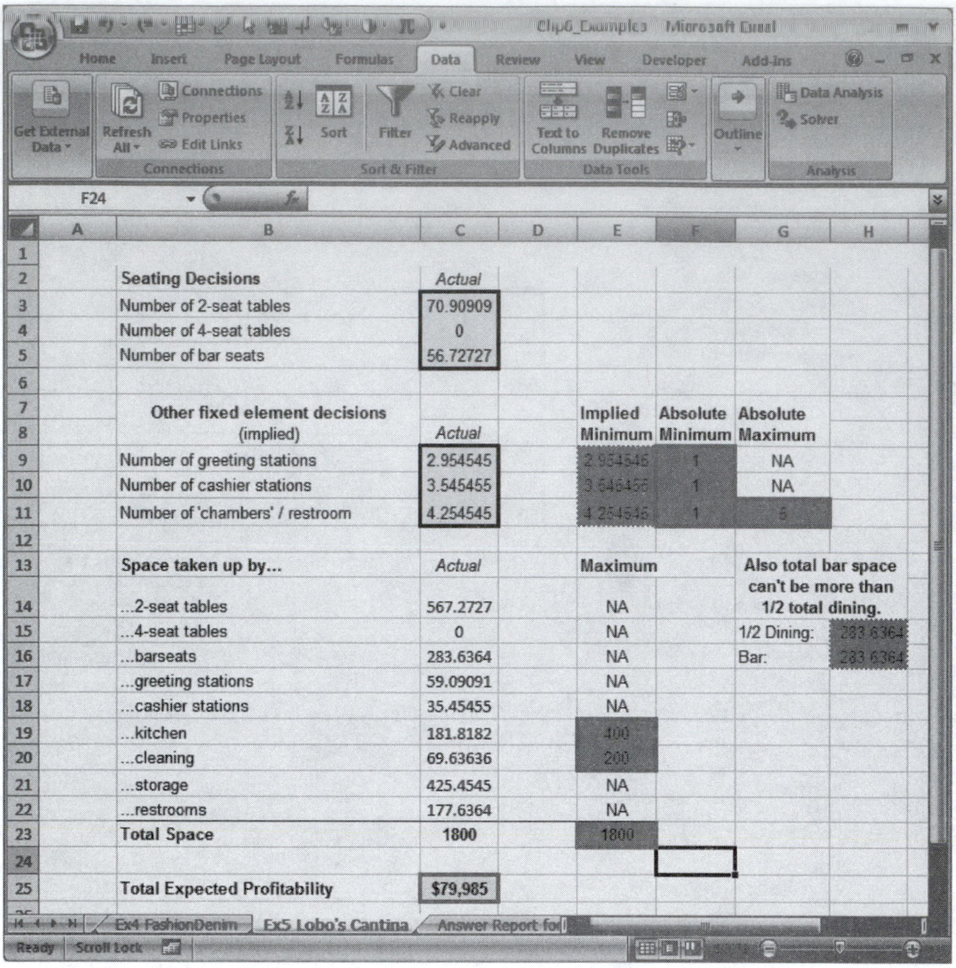

Figure 6.22. Initial solution to layout example.

side of a toilet). So we add appropriate integer specifications and get what's shown in Figure 6.23.

That's more like it, but a very different solution seating-wise than that previously suggested. Again, integer constraints can have a major impact on the general nature of a solution.

6.2.2.1 Interpreting Results

Take another look at the Answer Report generated in Figure 6.24. Again, Solver's labeling in these reports leaves something to be desired, but we get a general idea that we can make better sense of on closer investigation.

Re-phrasing and omission of variables over which we don't have much control (e.g., integer constraints) provides us with the results in Figure 6.25 in which the relative slackness of constraints are ranked from least to greatest.

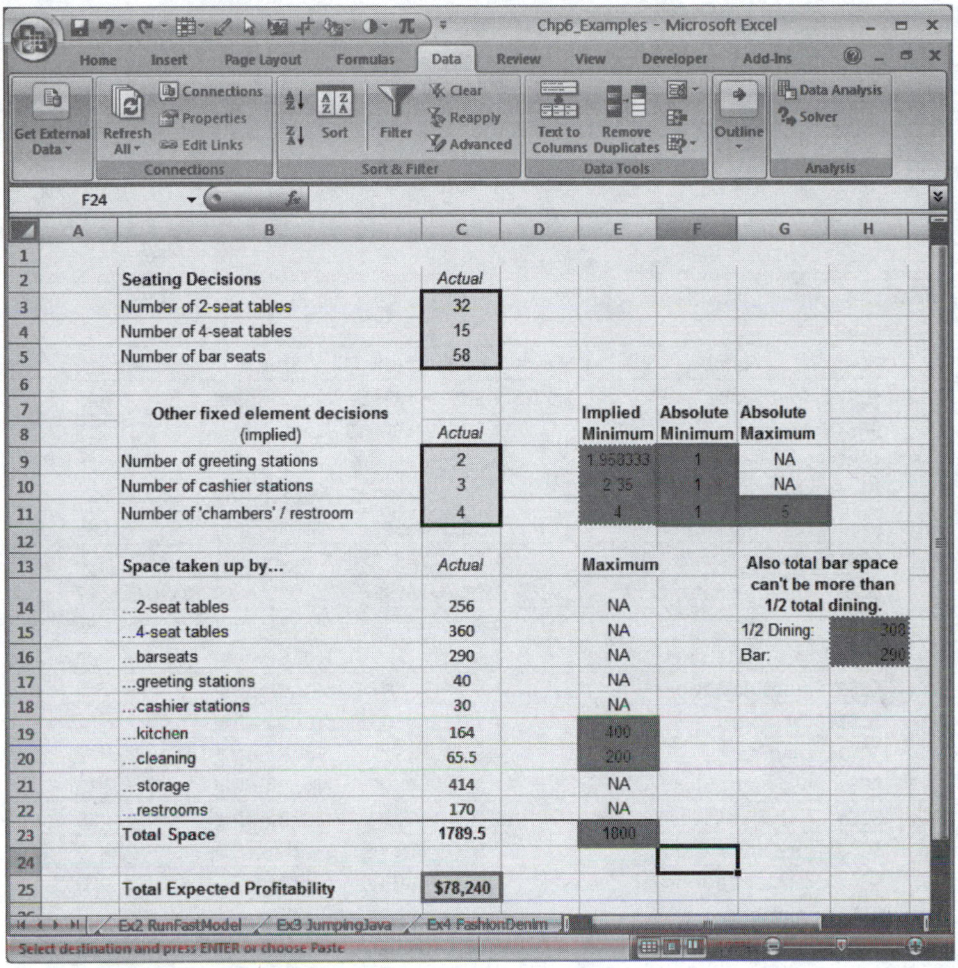

Figure 6.23. Solution integrating meaningful integer constraints.

Now we have a better impression of what's holding us back from doing better, where our next greatest challenges may lay, and where excessive slack might provide other implications on how we use resources.

Interestingly, while we come close to the limits of several of the rules, the only one that is truly binding, aside from the integer limits, is the minimum chamber requirements. (We actually have a little slack on the use of cashier stations, too.) In reality this constraint works in tandem with the total area requirement. We have additional space, but adding even one more seat would increase the restroom size requirements beyond the space available. Oddly enough, coming up with some way of reducing the per-chamber size can impact our solution; reducing it to 14 square feet allows full use of our total space (now a binding constraint) with greater profit (about $500 more) without major changes in our overall solution. A change to a chamber size

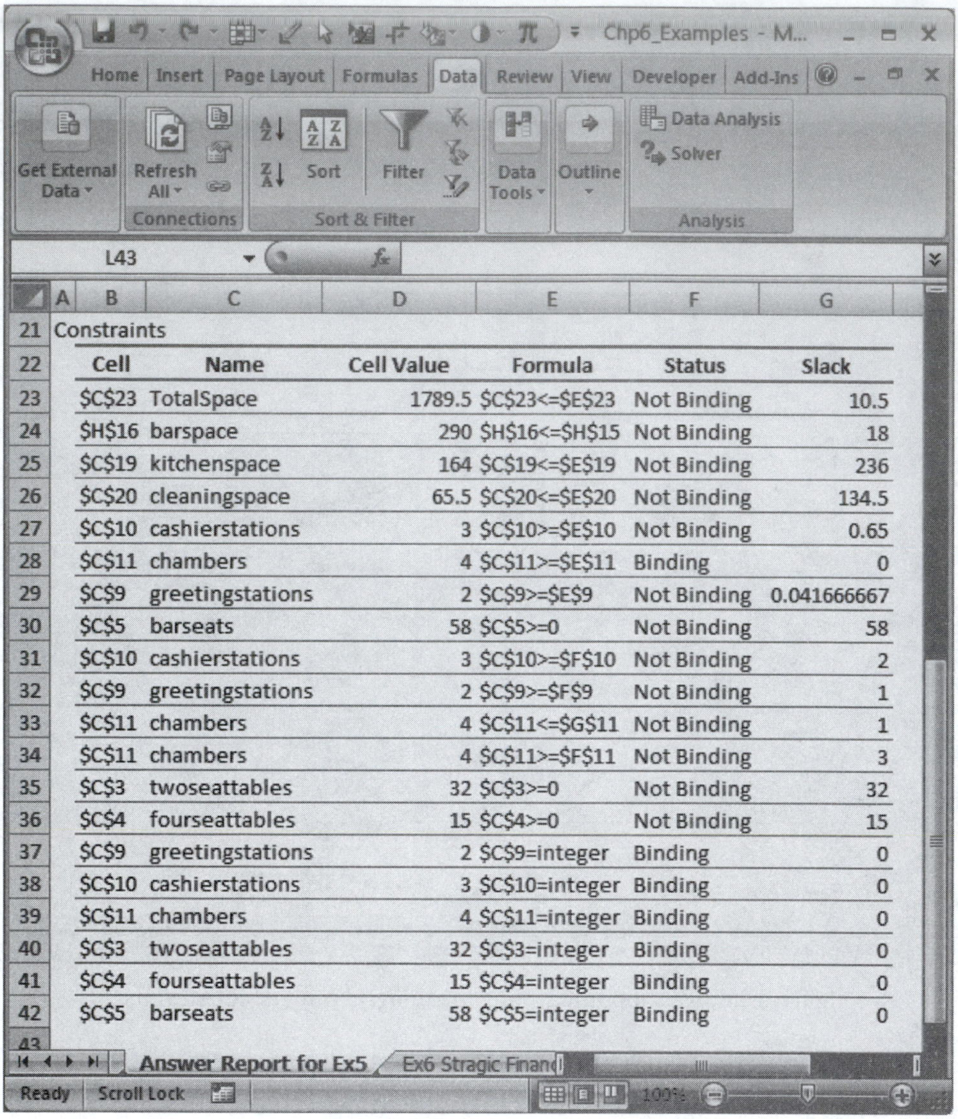

Constraints

Cell	Name	Cell Value	Formula	Status	Slack
$C$23	TotalSpace	1789.5	$C$23<=$E$23	Not Binding	10.5
$H$16	barspace	290	$H$16<=$H$15	Not Binding	18
$C$19	kitchenspace	164	$C$19<=$E$19	Not Binding	236
$C$20	cleaningspace	65.5	$C$20<=$E$20	Not Binding	134.5
$C$10	cashierstations	3	$C$10>=$E$10	Not Binding	0.65
$C$11	chambers	4	$C$11>=$E$11	Binding	0
$C$9	greetingstations	2	$C$9>=$E$9	Not Binding	0.041666667
$C$5	barseats	58	$C$5>=0	Not Binding	58
$C$10	cashierstations	3	$C$10>=$F$10	Not Binding	2
$C$9	greetingstations	2	$C$9>=$F$9	Not Binding	1
$C$11	chambers	4	$C$11<=$G$11	Not Binding	1
$C$11	chambers	4	$C$11>=$F$11	Not Binding	3
$C$3	twoseattables	32	$C$3>=0	Not Binding	32
$C$4	fourseattables	15	$C$4>=0	Not Binding	15
$C$9	greetingstations	2	$C$9=integer	Binding	0
$C$10	cashierstations	3	$C$10=integer	Binding	0
$C$11	chambers	4	$C$11=integer	Binding	0
$C$3	twoseattables	32	$C$3=integer	Binding	0
$C$4	fourseattables	15	$C$4=integer	Binding	0
$C$5	barseats	58	$C$5=integer	Binding	0

Figure 6.24. Answer Report for layout problem.

of 12 square feet has a huge impact on our design (no more four-seat tables, but another $1,000 or so profit; and now the binding constraint is the sewage ordinance).

Another feature that the Answer Report provides is a summary of which constraints seem to be the least binding in a given scenario. The two most slack constraints in the original integer solution are those relating to the building code limits on the kitchen and cleaning spaces. A manager might ask, "If we're so far below our maximum allocations, could we sell the rights to such allocations to another neighboring firm?" (Perhaps one that finds such limits

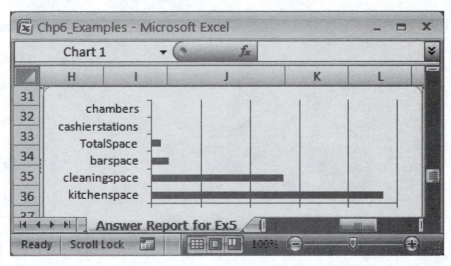

Figure 6.25. Pareto examination of constraints (binding and non-binding).

to be currently restrictive). Furthermore the implied requirements of the cashier station are more than fulfilled by the number of stations we have in the original integer solution. One implication might be that of underutilization. A manager might then ask, "Could these stations be used for other activities as well?" (This makes sense, particularly if they are multipurpose computers and not just mechanical cash registers.)

The use of a Pareto chart in the last example shows how we can link the analysis provided by an automated decision generation engine (Solver) to a graphically meaningful depiction that a variety of managers might use in long-term planning. But there are still more striking examples of how one might present the findings drawn from the sensitivity analysis of optimized solutions.

6.2.3 Example #6: Strategic Focus for Investment Firms

A financial services firm currently provides six kinds of investment packages for its clientele: Debt Payment, College Fund, Small Business, Retirement, Second Home, and Rapid Growth. The development of any one of these investment packages involves some level of the following activities:

needs assessment
asset specification
analysis
option construction
consultation

Based on the specializations of its workforces, number of hours needed to complete each of these activities differs for each package offered, as shown

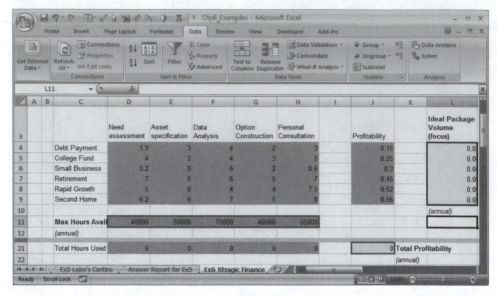

Figure 6.26. Spreadsheet set up for financial strategy example.

in Figure 6.26. Again, based on its workforce, the firm recognizes that realistically (at least in the mid-term) it probably only has a limited level of available hours for work in these various activities over the course of a year. These limits are also provided in Figure 6.26.

At the same time, forecasts suggest that the profitability of each package could remain at the steady estimates shown during such a term. Due to changes in the market for these packages, the firm has decided to consolidate and focus only on a subset of these offerings. Given the numbers, how should the firm refocus its labor hours to maximize its total profit-generation capability? If it were to seek out additional labor-hour availability, what kind of skill sets should it focus on?

Let's start with Solver's initial solution to this problem, shown in Figure 6.27 (assuming at this point we can set it up appropriately in a spreadsheet).

Looking at the total hours used, we can already get an impression of what labor constraints are truly binding here. But we can also ask for that info in Answer Report form (Figure 6.28).

I've shaded those constraints that we really have little hope of changing (i.e., those that ensure we don't pursue "negative" volumes of certain service packages). The three labor-hour constraints that seem to restrict our profitability therefore relate to Needs Assessment, Asset Specification, and Personal Consultation activities.

Because the three packages that Solver suggests focusing on are Small Business, Rapid Growth, and Second Home, the firm might want to consider how sensitive its profitability is to various changes in volume (perhaps

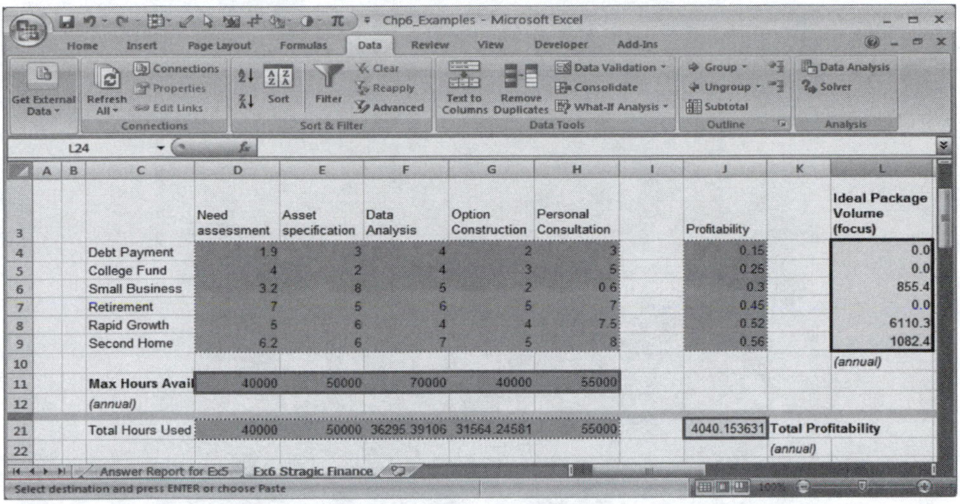

Figure 6.27. Solver's solution for financial strategy example.

market driven), if it decides to focus on these three offerings, and what role the constraints play in this sensitivity. I've used an alternative approach to graphically depicting the critical impacts of constraints. Rather than demonstrating the areas of slack/underutilization as in the Pareto chart of the restaurant example, Figure 6.29 shows how profitability changes with different levels of labor devoted to two of the three suggested packages (keeping the volume of Second Home package work constant).

Ultimately it's just a 3-D surface plot viewed from top down with lighter shades of gray depicting greater profitability. Obviously, higher levels of work on both types of packages would generate greater total profit, but we are

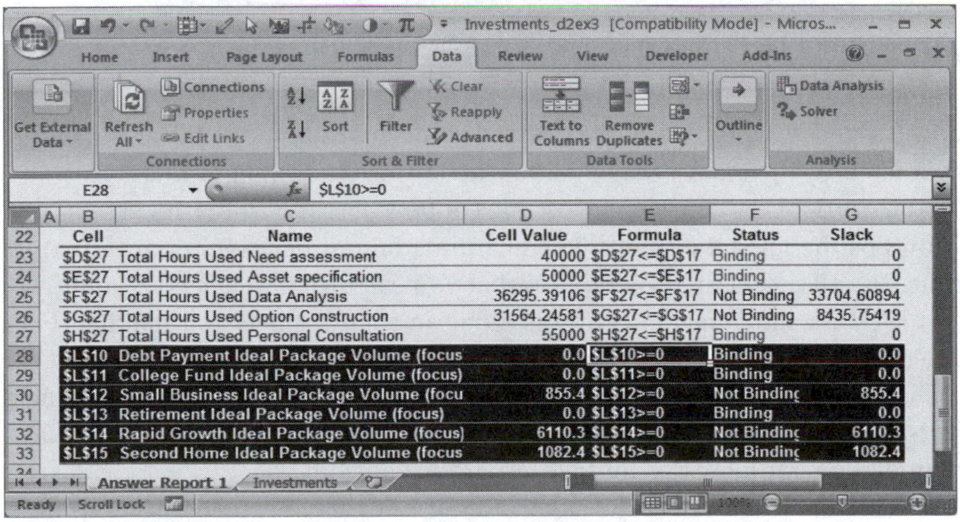

Figure 6.28. Answer Report for financial strategy example.

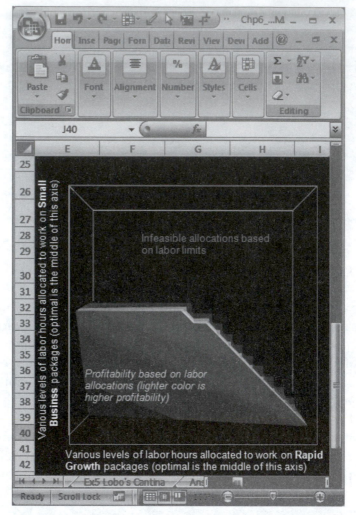

Figure 6.29. Performance landscape as a function of two key decisions.

constrained by labor. We can't consider total workloads beyond certain limits (depicted by the black area in all but the lower left of the graph).

The border between what's possible (or feasible) and what isn't essentially shows us the impact of multiple constraints on our decision all at the same time. Because I set up this graph so that you can turn off each constraint, we can see how individual constraints alone impact our decision making. Figure 6.30 shows the impact of only the Needs Assessment labor constraint.

Figure 6.31 shows similar plots for the other two binding constraints, each in isolation. It is obvious that the presence of only one of the constraints would allow for higher profit levels (perhaps much higher).

One of the more important things that we might learn from this graphical depiction is that although the Needs Assessment labor constraint is officially

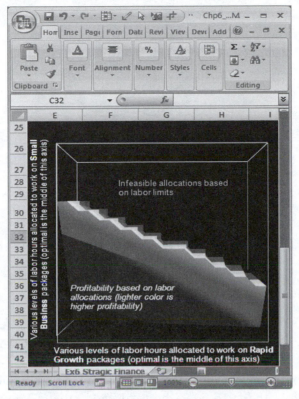

Figure 6.30. Impact of the Needs Assessment labor constraint.

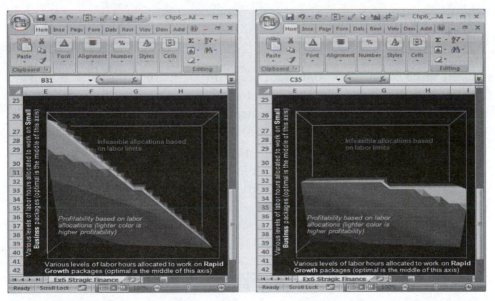

Figure 6.31. Impact of Asset Specification and Personal Consultation labor constraints.

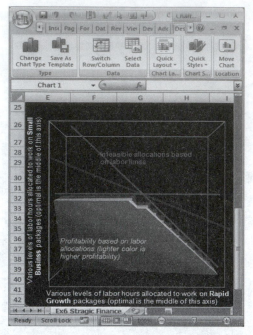

Figure 6.32. Compound impact of three constraints (feasibility frontiers).

binding at the optimal solution level, it doesn't have that much of an impact beyond what the other two constraints already create. Figure 6.32 shows three constraint borders superimposed on the general constraints shown in Figure 6.29.

In this particular case, each of these frontiers intersects at the same point, which happens to be the point of profit maximization. As suggested by the prior plots, there are probably areas of higher profitability beyond this point, and all three constraints could independently limit such pursuits; however, the kinds of limitations imposed by the Needs Assessment constraint are already defined if the other two constraints are active. Efforts to eliminate the Needs Assessment constraint after the suggested service consolidation (perhaps through additional training programs that allowed the firm's staff to conduct such activities in a more time-efficient manner), probably wouldn't have much of an impact on profitability. On the other hand, eliminating one of the other constraints might have a sizeable impact. This is exactly the kind of conclusion that's not easy to get at by simply viewing the nature of managerial prospects by initial reports alone.

PRACTICE PROBLEMS

Practice 6.1

A Fortune 500 company needs to hire a group of consultants from Just Right Consulting to assist with a large technology rollout that will require 24-hour, 7-days-per-week

Table 6.4. *Details Associated with Consultant Staffing Example*

	Sunday	Monday	Tuesday	Wednesday	Thursday	Friday	Saturday
Consultants needed	9	18	15	18	15	15	15

support. The day is divided into eight-hour shifts. The total number of consultants required during the day shift is shown in Table 6.4.

The client would like to minimize the labor costs associated with staffing the project. Consultants from Just Right work five days a week, and are entitled to two consecutive days off each week. We know there are only seven ways that each consultant can have two consecutive days off, with each break starting on a different day of the week (staggered approach). One straightforward way to structure the problem is to determine how many consultants of each break type to have staffed each day.

One twist in the problem is that any consultant required to work on Saturday receives an additional 5 percent of overtime pay (think of their current pay level as 100%), while those that require work on Sunday require an additional 7 percent of overtime pay. This will undoubtedly result in a tendency to avoid excess weekend scheduling whenever possible.

Determine how many consultants of each break type (i.e., beginning their two-day break on a specific day) would be needed to at least cover the demand, while trying the keep the total cost (again accounting for weekend premiums) as low as possible.

Practice 6.2

Fun Viewing Inc. is a new television network that has become extremely popular in recent months. Fun Viewing is trying to decide which TV shows to air during the Fall lineup. The creative staff has worked tirelessly reviewing market research reports to give Fun Viewing an idea of how profitable each show will be (based on the number of viewers, ad sales, competing shows, and so on). Fun Viewing has allocated $28,000 for new TV shows. The objective is to generate the highest possible return on investment.

Eight scripts have been reviewed and deemed worthy to air on the network. Table 6.5 specifies the estimated ROI (return on investment) for each of these shows.

If a script is chosen, at least $700 must be allocated to developing the show. To maintain a variety of shows, the board of directors has stipulated that at most $7,000 can be invested in any project. A show's total return is the product of its ROI and the amount invested in the show.

Table 6.5. *Details Associated with TV Script Selection Example*

Show#	1	2	3	4	5	6	7	8
ROI	7%	9%	4%	25%	21%	14%	8%	16%

The decision to finance some shows cannot be made independently of other funding decisions. The following constraints must be met:

Show 2 can't be pursued unless Show 1 is	Show 4 can't be pursued unless Show 3 is
Show 3 can't be pursued unless Show 1 is	If Show 6 is funded, so MUST Show 7 (and vice-versa)
Show 4 can't be pursued unless Show 2 is	Shows 5 and 6 cannot be funded at the same time

Determine which shows to invest in (1=yes, 0=no), and how much to invest in each so as to maximize the total ROI of the resulting portfolio of TV shows (subject to the rules outlined in the previous chart).

Practice 6.3

Art Share is a shipping company that specializes solely in the transportation of fine art to and from museums around the world. The majority of the art is part of a French Impressionist traveling exhibit (from the Louvre in Paris) that is transported from one city to the next. Due to space issues, different museums have different requirements for the number of paintings to be displayed in each exhibit. Unfortunately, this means that most of the paintings in the exhibit travel in pieces and are not always at the desired location when needed. In fact, each month, there are usually seven too many paintings in Paris, eight in London, and four in New York. In addition, there are three too few paintings in Prague, and six in Stockholm. Art Share wants to determine how to redistribute paintings from those locations with an excess number to those locations with shortages, and it wants to do this at the lowest cost possible.

Table 6.6 shows the costs to transport one painting directly from one city (in the left column) to another (in the top row). In this table, the significantly higher cost figures of 999 are there to reference routes that the company does not want to consider (liability issues). The possibility of indirectly redistributing a painting should also be considered (e.g., moving from one city to another and then on to a final destination). In some cases (Paris to London to New York vs. Paris to New York, for example), indirect

Table 6.6. *Details Associated with Transportation Example*

	Redistribution Costs	To:				New York	Demand ("Supply" if "-")
		Paris	Prague	London	Stockholm		
From:	Paris	999	13	17	999	16	−7
	Prague	14	999	999	19	12	3
	London	18	999	999	16	999	−8
	Stockholm	999	999	17	999	19	6
	New York	999	13	999	18	999	−4

Table 6.7. *Details Associated with Football Fanatics Example*

		Labor (hours/football)		Material Requirements (gram/football)		
	Revenue	Cut	Assemble	Rubber	Leather	Stitching
Pro Player	55	0.3	0.5	250	200	60
College Canon	48	0.2	0.4	225	180	50
Pee Wee	30	0.1	0.3	150	100	40
	Max Available	40	100	35,000	28,000	5,000
	Cost issues	15	20	0.02	0.05	0.03
			[$ /hour]		[$ /gram]	

routing may actually make indirect transfers more cost effective (taxes, insurance, and so on).

How many paintings should it move from one city to another to fill current deficits and eliminate existing surpluses in the various cities, all at least cost?

Practice 6.4

Football Fanatics, Inc. makes three types of footballs – the Pee Wee, the College Canon, and the Pro Player. The labor and materials requirements for each football are shown in Table 6.7 with information regarding the maximum amount of labor hours available (for a given activity) and the maximum amount of each material available.

The firm purchases only as much of the three materials (rubber, leather, and stitching) as it uses at the prices shown in the table. It wants the Pro Player to comprise at least 10 percent of all the footballs it produces and sells. In addition, the number of Pro Player and College Canon footballs (in total) must not be more than 50 percent of the total number of footballs produced and sold.

How many of each type of football should be produced to maximize its profits, subject to the availability and sales-planning constraints given? Which input constraint appears to be most limiting? How does this result differ when integer decisions (i.e., whole numbers of footballs) are no longer assumed necessary for planning estimates?

7

Complex Optimization

As an extension to the discussion of Chapter 6, it's relevant at this point to reconsider how a feature such as Solver comes up with a solution. Although it's not necessarily critical for developers to understand the detailed technicalities of these packaged programs, any developer worth his or her salt should at least understand the limitations of these algorithms.

7.1 How Solver "Solves"

Many people use Solver with the expectation that it can find the optimal solution for any kind of problem (of reasonable size). But even small problems can have their nuances that make the job of the standard Solver add-in extremely difficult, and the resulting solutions prone to poor performance (substantially less-than-optimal managerial recommendations). One of the mechanisms that engines such as Solver commonly use to search for optimal solutions is a hill-climbing algorithm. In reality, this is just another heuristic (as discussed in Chapter 5). It starts with a guess for what the solution might be and then sees if small changes to any of the decision variables of that solution can result in better value for the objective function, subject to constraints.

Hill-climbing algorithms typically look into only one solution at a time. For example, consider the following hypothetical performance surface (where performance along the z-axis is some function of the two decision variables X and Y). In Figure 7.1, a shaded dot represents a possible solution, one that at this point appears to be less than ideal. From a local perspective, it certainly doesn't represent the apparent peak value of Z attainable (shown by an ellipse).

7.1.1 Problems with Multimodality

From Figure 7.1, we get a visual impression of the objective landscape or terrain over which possible decision options may reside. Based on our limited view of this landscape, we might immediately conclude that the best decision

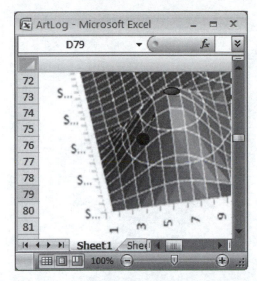

Figure 7.1. Hill-climbing active in a nonlinear frontier.

exists at the top of the hill. This immediacy is the result of the availability of the graphic visualization of this terrain as well as our ability to interpret it. This does not typically represent the starting condition of a computer algorithm such as Solver, charged with delivering an optimal solution. Instead, such algorithms are more or less restricted to information on the most recent solution considered (starting with the solution it was initially provided) and the nature of the terrain only incrementally around it. It will pursue changes in the solution that improve upon the current objective (i.e., climb a hill) and then stop when it gets to a point where it can't make any more improvements (i.e., at the peak) but it doesn't recognize that as the best solution until it is actually there.

This seems simple enough; however, we can get into some pretty serious problems with this approach when performance landscapes are more complex. Depending on where our first guess is, we might essentially climb the wrong hill (one that's not the highest overall). Even we, as visual observers and integrators, might make such a mistake if we were limited in our overall view of the landscape shown in Figure 7.1 as opposed to a more global view shown in Figure 7.2.

In such cases, the algorithm provides us with what we call a local optimum, whereas the global optimum (best solution, represented by the shaded dot above the ellipse) eludes it. Because the standard Solver uses such an approach to handle non-linear objective functions in optimization, problems with more than one peak may be impossible for Solver to solve well – or at least impossible for Solver to guarantee us that it has provided us with the best option available.

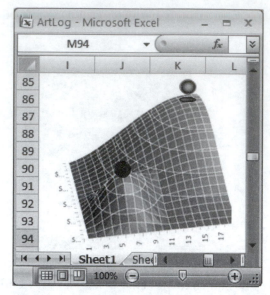

Figure 7.2. Hill-climbing stopped at a local peak, missing global optimum.

Is this something to be concerned with? Do difficult objectives and decision terrains really exist in practice that would make a reliance on hill-climbing algorithms alone problematic?

Marketing example: Demand is often dependent on price. If revenue is a multiplicative function of both demand and price, it's going to be nonlinearly related to the price decision. Beyond this, demand for one good often impacts demand for others that are either complements or alternatives. Therefore, when faced with multigood pricing decisions, the objective landscape for expected revenue may have many distinct peaks.

Finance example: Think about all of the complex calculations financial planners have to deal with on a regular basis, beginning with even some of the simplest like NPV. Nonlinearity typically pervades their work. In cases where complex portfolio management decisions need to be made, particularly when the performances of options are thought to be interrelated, it is difficult to simply assume single peak dynamics automatically apply. More to the point, making such an assumption and relying on a hill-climbing approach cannot only result in suboptimal decision, but will reduce the overall value provided by such analysts.

7.1.2 Problems with Discontinuity

Complex nonlinearities in themselves aren't the only bane of simple optimization mechanisms. Solver's approach also expects that the objective function for which you are trying to develop a set of decisions is a continuous one, not choppy, subdivided, or staggered (Figure 7.3). If your objective model includes elements such as IF statements or LOOKUP values, or relies on

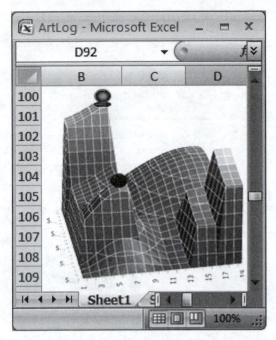

Figure 7.3. Hill-climbing efforts further complicated by discontinuity.

noisy, real-time data, Solver really has its work cut out for it; however, *don't bet on getting a great solution in such cases!*

As a simple thought experiment, consider a firm that makes and ships a bunch of items over the course of a week (e.g., 12,500 low-end wrist watches). Say that the total cost to run that operation is $28,125. Let's say we want to reduce how many watches we produce. If we produce only one watch, would we assume it would cost us just $2.25 ($28,125/12,500) to run that kind of operation? Of course not. We assume that there are fixed costs that don't diminish as a function of scale in most organizations. Furthermore, in many cases organizations gain from nonlinear economies of scale due in part to efficiencies gained by processing (buying, assembling, shipping, etc.) in bulk. Whenever decision variables (e.g., how much to produce in this case) have a nonlinear impact on objectives (e.g., maximization of profit), the task of coming up with good solutions becomes more complex.

With multiple and distinct nonlinearities, as well as conditional dependencies (e.g., often bulk purchase rates are adjusted not on a continuous scale but on a tiered scale such as $0.5/unit for 0–99 units of raw materials, $0.35/unit for 100–499), problems are even more complex and harder to solve.

7.2 The Benefit of Alternate Optimization Options

As a buildup to more effective approaches to complex optimization, let's further scrutinize the capabilities of the hill-climbing algorithm through a full-blown numerical example.

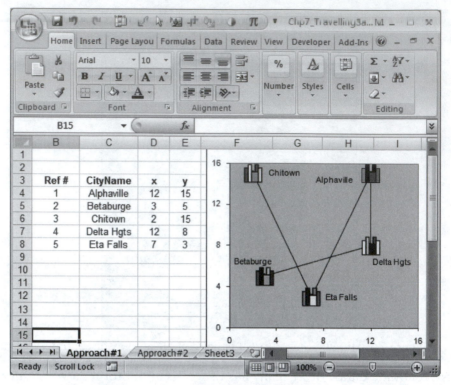

Figure 7.4. Five-city traveling salesman scenario.

7.2.1 Problems with Vehicle Routing

The classic Traveling Salesman/Vehicle Routing problem is the same one we introduced when talking about heuristics in Chapter 5. It's a tough one to solve, especially when there are a large number of sites to visit. It's worth noting that this is essentially a "sequencing" problem, and although it is often applied to routing, it has similar applications in work scheduling (what to work on first), investment planning (where to transfer cash to next), training (what sequence of skills should be taught and in what order), marketing (what sequence of marketing activities will yield the best results), and so on. Because we're already familiar with this setting, we'll stick to the routing case. Figure 7.4 shows five cities.

As with many problems, there are multiple ways to structure the decision-making framework. I have two approaches provided in the document TravelingSalesman.xls. Figure 7.5 shows an image of the first approach.

I'm using both city names and reference numbers (Ref #s) to refer to the sites along the route. I have a matrix that approximates travel distance based on straight-line distances (I could change that, but there's no reason to for this example). Although appearing in gray scale in this text the available workbook in which this is developed contains color demarcations for clarity.

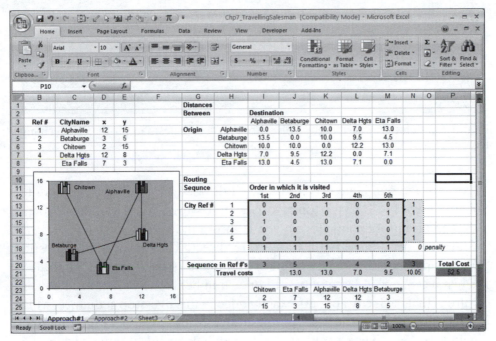

Figure 7.5. One approach to traveling salesman problem setup.

For example, in the worksheet in blue (gray in text) I show the decision variables; in this case, they answer the following questions: "For a specific city will it appear in the route first? Second? Third? Fourth? Fifth?"

Those 1s and 0s basically represent true or false. The row below those decisions provides the sum of the (0,1) decisions above it. Because exactly one of the cities should be visited first, and only one should be visited second, that lower blue row should be all 1s. Similarly, the column to the right of that table is the sum of all (0,1) decisions to the left of it. Because each city must be visited exactly once, those sums should also be all 1s. Rather than create a formal constraint in this case, I'm going to create a heavy penalty for any attempted solution that breaks these rules (one that the computer will try to avoid in minimizing total travel cost).

The numbers in shaded gray depict the actual routing sequence based on all those (0,1) decisions. I could try to use Solver to come up with an optimal solution, trying to minimize total travel cost (which includes that penalty function) by changing the decisions in the blue box. The necessary constraint is that those decisions must be (0,1) or binary in nature. Unfortunately, the relationship between the objective and the decision variables is far from a simple linear solution. If I try to use Solver (with target cell of $P$21, changing cells $I$13:$M$17, and subject to $I$13:$M$17=binary), Figure 7.6 shows what I get. In other words, Solver doesn't suggest a change in the solution, although we know visually that better solutions exist.

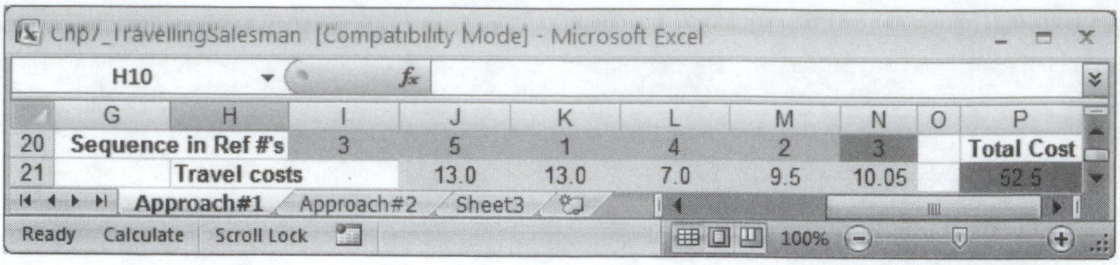

Complex Optimization

Figure 7.6. Solution provided by Solver for traveling salesman problem (no change from original).

Perhaps the real issue was in the way I decided to set up the problem for Solver. Maybe I made it too tough for Solver to work with. Another approach, although also problematic for Solver, is shown in Figure 7.7.

Here the decision variables are more direct. They answer the question "What is the sequence of city reference numbers associated with the route?" It's just a sequenced list of city reference numbers. The only thing I have to ensure is that each city appears exactly once in this five-stop sequence, which is what I'm doing in the last column above using a COUNTIF statement. Again I'm going to use a penalty function to help avoid situations where any one city appears in the sequence more than once.

What do I get from Solver using this approach? Same thing as before. Solver can't devise how to improve the current solution.

With just five sites this really is not an extremely complex problem. Using a heuristic (e.g., Nearest-Next), or just by visual inspection, we'd probably be able to come up with good alternatives to the current solution. But Solver doesn't know how to think that way. When problems become much more complex – for instance, 15 cities, or 30 cities, or more – we're not going to want to figure things out by visual inspection. And we may like to have an

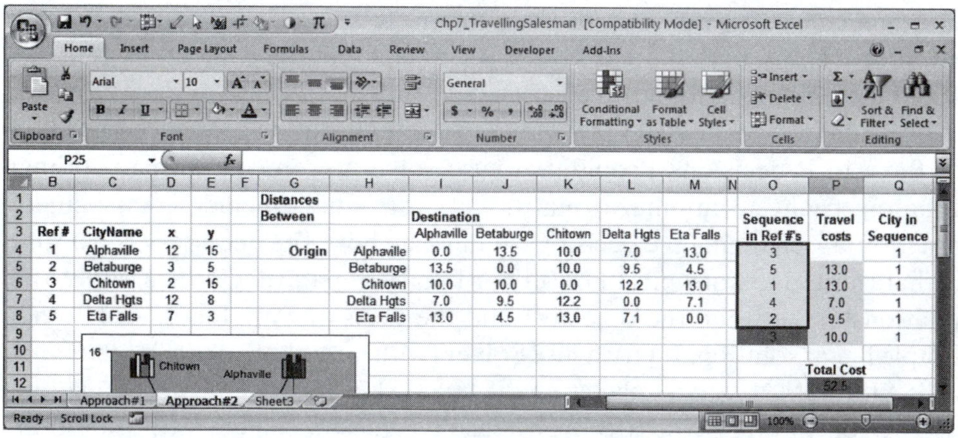

Figure 7.7. Alternative approach to traveling salesman problem setup.

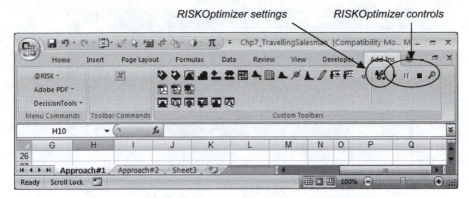

Figure 7.8. RISKOptimizer interface access.

alternative mechanism that is more sophisticated, possibly more effective than a heuristic to try to get to a good solution.

7.2.2 *RISKOptimizer on Vehicle Routing*

To get the job done we'll be demonstrating the use of Palisades' RISKOptimizer package. As with XLStat, RISKOptimizer is a package that can function similarly to other standard add-ins in Excel. Its power in this case stems from its capability to tackle complex optimization problems and come up with good solutions by making use of what is referred to as a genetic algorithm (discussed in greater depth in the chapter supplement). Basically, a genetic algorithm starts by forming and considering a range of solutions to an optimization problem, and then step by step (i.e., iteratively) expands and discards sets of these solutions in an attempt to capitalize on the information they each provide. New solutions for consideration are based in part on the structure of good existing solutions (attempting to modify these towards improvement of the objective function) and in part on some random number pulls (to help investigate areas of the solution terrain that may not have been represented by earlier solutions). In this way, the best solution evolves from often less prospective beginnings that would otherwise render a simple hill-climbing algorithm useless.

Ensure first that the application is installed. To make the most out of this application, open the program called @Risk followed by the associated program RISKOptimizer. (These are both Palisades products that come with an installation of the Palisades suite and should be found in the Palisades folder.) If asked about running macros, say yes in this case. When the program opens it should look similar to what you typically see in Excel, except for a variety of new tool icons under the Add-ins tab (see Figure 7.8). Many of these tools provide statistical analysis similar to the capabilities of XLStat.

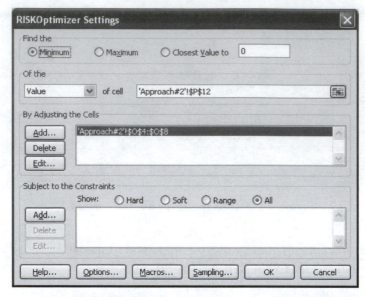

Figure 7.9. Specifying objectives, decision variables, and constraints in RISKOpti-mizer.

For now, however, we are interested only in approaches to solving complex nonlinear optimization problems, and there are only a few specific tools in which we're particularly interested.

To demonstrate the use of RISKOptimizer's genetic algorithm in optimization, we'll use the second traveling salesman/routing setup for illustration. Make sure this file is open and then select the RISKOptimizer settings icon (a double helix with a red distribution curve to its upper left).

A dialog box should appear. As with Solver, we need to first say what we want to do. In this case, we want to minimize the total cost; located in $P$12). And, as with Solver, we also need to specify where the decision variables are (See Figure 7.9).

With RISKOptimizer, however, we're given a more sophisticated interface that allows us to actually help the computer approach the task we're giving it. In this interface we can essentially describe the nature of the sets of decisions we want it to consider. And in this case we want it simply consider alternative sequences or orderings (see Figure 7.10). That's actually an option here, and specifying this will help.

Other available solution mechanisms are better suited to other kinds of problems. A summary of these methods are provide in Table 7.1.

With the appropriate solution mechanism selected, we can now specify the decision variables – in this case, the cells in $O$4:$O$8.

RISKOptimizer actually takes into account the possibility that our problem might have some uncertain (e.g., random) numbers built into it. Unless we tell it otherwise, it'll try to evaluate each solution it comes up with numerous times

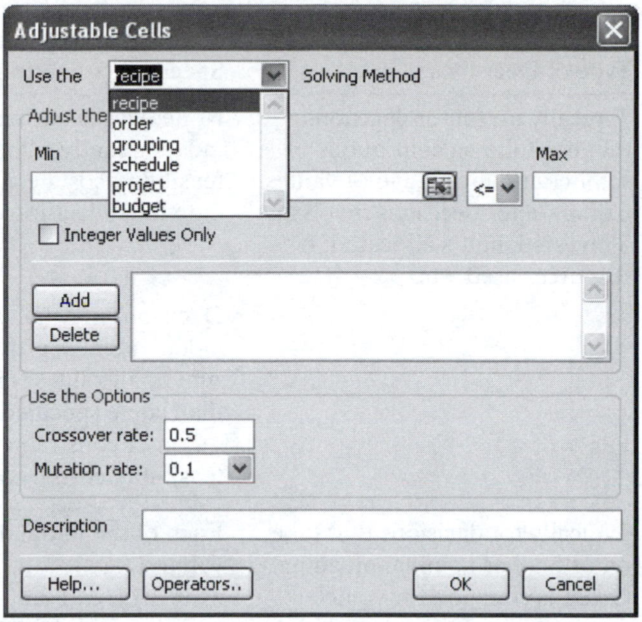

Figure 7.10. Selection of solving method when specifying decision variables.

to create some typical performance level. We don't have random numbers in this case, so specify 1 iteration per evaluation (under RISKOptimizer Options shown in Figure 7.11). We'll get back to playing with this option more in Chapter 9.

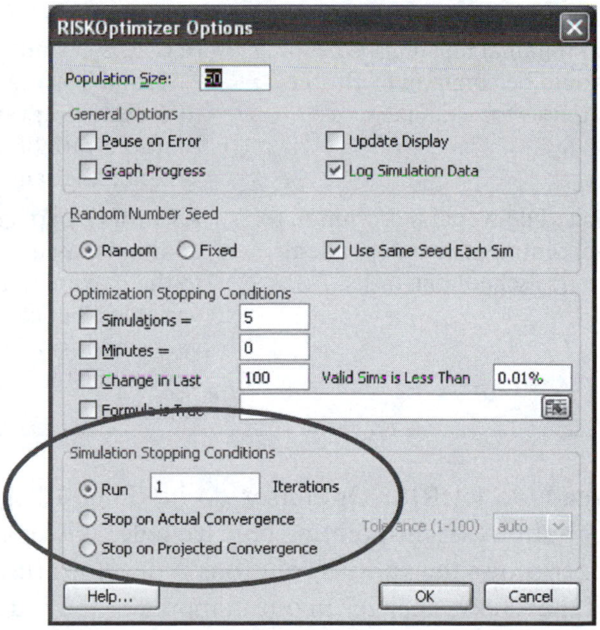

Figure 7.11. Specification of single iteration conditions on search.

Table 7.1 *Types of Solutions Approaches Available through RISKOptimizer*

Method	Type of Decisions	Special Assumptions
Recipe	Typically useful for decisions that can take on continuous or semi-continuous range of values. Common for decisions involving $ invested, hours allocated, # resources used, etc.	None. Decisions may be varied independently (s.t. constraint feasibility/costs, e.g., bounds on individual decisions)
Budget		Decisions may be varied independently, provided the sum of all values is no greater than some specified value (and s.t. other constraint feasibility/costs).
Order	Typically for decisions that take on ordinal or nominal meaning. Order is common for vehicle routing tasks; Project would be common for project scheduling tasks.	Each of the initial decision values (e.g., 1, 2, 3, and 4; or even 3.14, 2.31, and 2.41) used exactly once in final solution (only order is manipulated)
Project		As with Order, with the additional assumption that some decisions must take on smaller values than (i.e., come before) others.
Grouping	Typically for decisions that take on nominal meaning. Grouping would be common to cluster analysis for example.	Only the initial decision values (e.g., 1, 2, 3, and 4; or even 3.14, 2.31. and 2.41) can be assigned to the decision variables. Multiple variables will be assigned the same value.
Schedule	Schedule would be common to appointment or independent course scheduling tasks.	As with Grouping with additional assumptions relating to the maximum number variables that can take on each value, and (similar to Project) any applicable precedent constraints.

We're now ready to let RISKOptimizer do its thing. Click on the Start RISKOptimizer button (a right-pointing blue triangle, akin to a Play button).

RISKOptimizer shows the various solutions it develops (using its genetic algorithm), and that shows changes in our mapping of the route. RISKOptimizer quickly comes up with better solutions, shown in Figure 7.12.

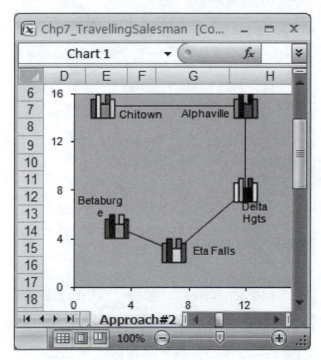

Figure 7.12. Solution derived by RISKOptimizer.

The one limitation is that RISKOptimizer doesn't always know when to stop trying, but that's where that little red Stop button in the RISKOptimizer controls comes in. We could also have chosen an additional option to stop the search after, say, five minutes; we'll talk more about this in Chapter 9.

Another useful feature of RISKOptimizer worth noting at this point – particularly for those interested in getting a feel for how much progress is being made toward better and better solutions as time goes on – is the Graph Progress option. Checking this option (Figure 7.13) provides a graphical mapping of the objective function as it evolves with alternative better solutions encountered. Through such a visual representation, an analyst may be able to assess whether it is worth continuing the search for an appreciably greater length of time, or whether a termination of the search can be made early on.

In a post-hoc sense, a similar capability is provided by the Log Simulation Data option, which triggers a prompt for what kinds of rich summaries of the search an analyst might be interested in after the search has terminated. A demonstration of the nature of those data summaries is provided in the next example.

7.2.3 RISKOptimizer on Cluster/Group Development

As suggested, RISKOptimizer is also capable of finding solutions for clustering and grouping problems. We've already discussed the potential value

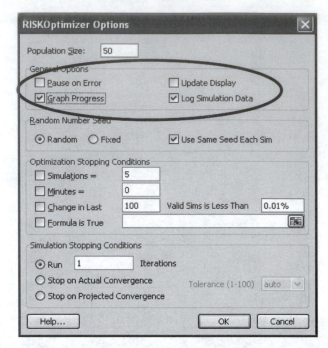

Figure 7.13. Output options in RISKOptimizer.

of cluster analysis in Chapter 5 and the Dodecha solutions case (which we'll get back to in the practice set later in this chapter). However, the ability to develop meaningful clusters often transcends standard assumptions made by statistics programs (e.g., that the best clustering solution minimizes the ratio of within-to between-group variance). In practice, the objective of our clustering may be much more idiosyncratic to our context and the perceived interpretation of managers. Let's consider an example with a very different sort of objective function.

Imagine a scenario where a manager is given the task of breaking a workforce up into four groups, each of which will be responsible for one of four projects. Before assigning workers to project groups, the manager surveys the workers to try to assess the contribution each worker thinks he or she can make to each project group, and the level of satisfaction he or she thinks they will get from working in each project group. Surveys responses range from 0 (low contribution/satisfaction) to 10 (high contribution/satisfaction).

Given an interest in both high levels of contribution and satisfaction, as well as an interest in keeping group sizes relatively equal (making sure all groups are composed of between 18 and 22 people), how should the manager assign the workers? The workbook Chp7_WorkGroupSelection.xls sets up this problem for us.

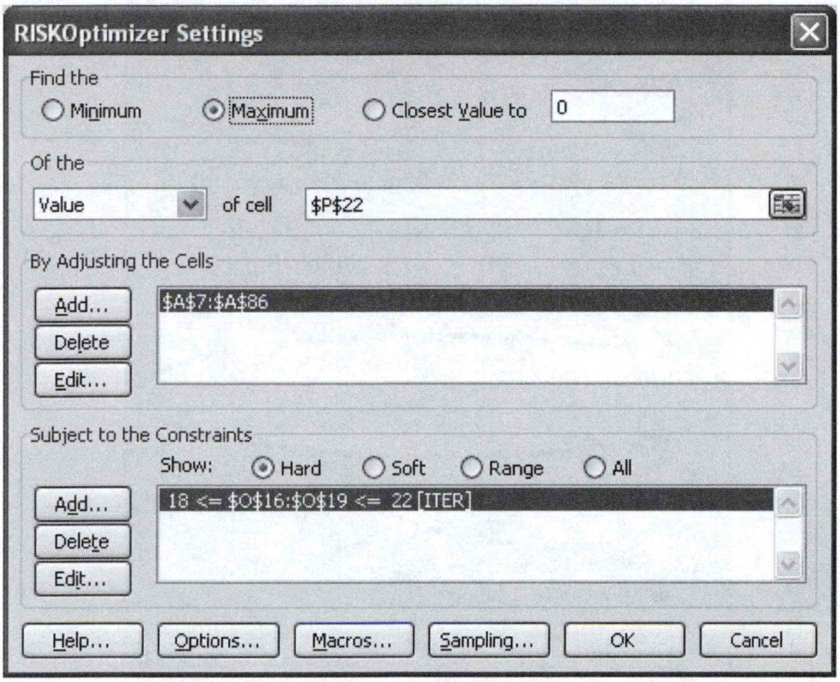

Figure 7.14. Specification of workgroup formation problem in RISKOptimizer.

We'll use RISKOptimizer on this one as before. Unlike the traveling salesman problem, which simply required RISKOptimizer to consider several different sequences of numbers, the problem structure here is less defined. We're trying to maximize the sum of perceived contributions and satisfaction levels, while limiting group sizes to between 18 and 22 people. All RISKOptimizer needs to do is assign workers to group 1, 2, 3, or 4 (so 80 decision variables, each of which is an integer from 1 to 4). Because this is not a sequencing problem, I'm going to ask RISKOptimizer to use the Grouping approach to a genetic search for new solutions (Figure 7.14).

An alternative approach, also set up in the example workbook, is the potential use of a penalty function for group sizes outside the 18 to 22 range. These penalties become part of the objective function (negative contributors). If the penalties are appropriately designed (i.e., large enough to ensure the desired group sizes), there shouldn't be a need to explicitly designate constraints. The approach often makes RISKOptimizer's search a little easier, and is similar to designating constraints as soft in RISKOptimizer.

Allowing RISKOptimizer to run for about one minute, the algorithm is able to develop a grouping solution with an objective value of 1024 (vs. the original 795). After two and a half minutes we're at 1070. After 10 minutes, we're at 1087. Things don't change much after that point. We might manually

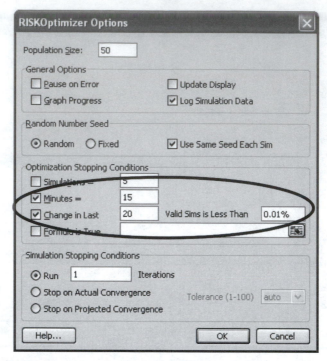

Figure 7.15. Specification of search stopping conditions in RISKOptimizer.

stop the routine, or perhaps we could have been savvy enough to preset stopping conditions as an option of the run. For example, Figure 7.15 shows designating the amount of maximum search time in minutes or the degree to which the objective solution appears stable (here the run is set to stop if either the 15-minute mark is met, or very little change is observed in the objective function of the last 20 valid solutions).

After any run is stopped, RISKOptimizer provides the option of giving you a summary and log of all solutions it has considered up until the point at which the search stops. This could be useful for you if you wanted to do further analysis on other nearly as good solutions. My recommendation to you: Ask only for reports on best solutions (Figure 7.16) unless you have a very strong reason otherwise. The number of solutions considered by RISKOptimizer over the course of 10 minutes is enormous, and simply the reporting of all of these solutions (both great ones and very poor ones) is going to take up a lot of time and space, often with little added value in analysis.

This is quite a bit of summary data. How could we use it to interpret the effectiveness of our investigation? At the bare minimum, we could use the log file to get a visual impression of how progress on getting better solutions was being made, and perhaps to project how long it would take to get a solution that yielded a specific target objective (performance) level. For example,

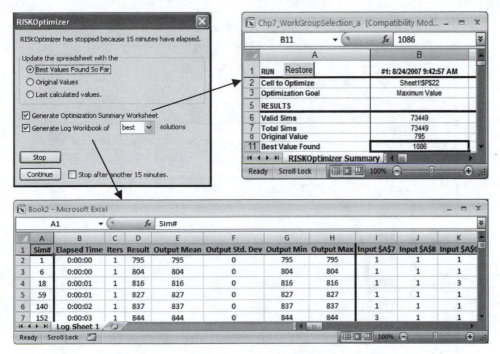

Figure 7.16. Sample output reports available from RISKOptimizer.

simply selecting the Elapsed time and Result columns, I could generate a connected scatter plot to show how much of an improvement we were getting the last 10 of the total 15 minutes that elapsed (Figure 7.17), which isn't much.

Not to say that there isn't some fantastic solution we could have arrived at by waiting another hour, but such an improvement definitely doesn't appear promising at the 15-minute mark. Don't give up too early on a search process. Extending the length of the examination is ultimately the analyst's call, but there is virtue in knowing how best to use one's time.

7.2.4 RISKOptimizer on Schedule Development

As a last example of the kind of complex problem for which RISKOptimizer might provide analysis strength, consider the task of developing a schedule that outlines the sequence and potential simultaneity of the work required for a large-scale project. Such projects typically consist of a series of discernable steps, many of which cannot be started before work on other steps is completed. The availability of individual project workers is an added complexity. In many cases, some workers cannot easily handle more than one step of a project at a time. Because of the costs of transferring in-project experience from one worker to another, however, it is often beneficial

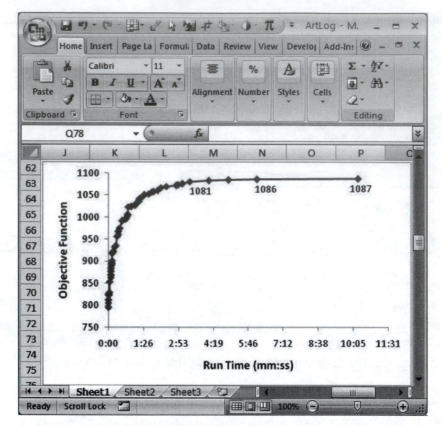

Figure 7.17. Improvements in search over time.

(if not necessary) to make sure that certain sets of steps are handled by the same individual. Aside from the implied human resource and organizational issues, such complex constraints on the decision-making process, coupled with potential nonlinearities in the value of getting a project done both quickly and at a high level of quality make project management a complicated duty (see Figure 7.18).

The spreadsheet within which these facts are applied in developing relationships between the decision variables to whom to assign project steps, and when to start them) and the objective (how much time total should be expected for project completion) should also contain the mathematically codified forms of all relevant constraints (i.e., both precedent and no-double-working rules). An example workbook that captures this is provided in Chp7_ProjectScheduling. The main decision interface with a sample start solution is shown in Figure 7.18.

Keep in mind that even RISKOptimizer may be sensitive to the nature of starting solutions, especially as in this case when so many possible solutions and discontinuities exist. The more thought you put in your initial solution

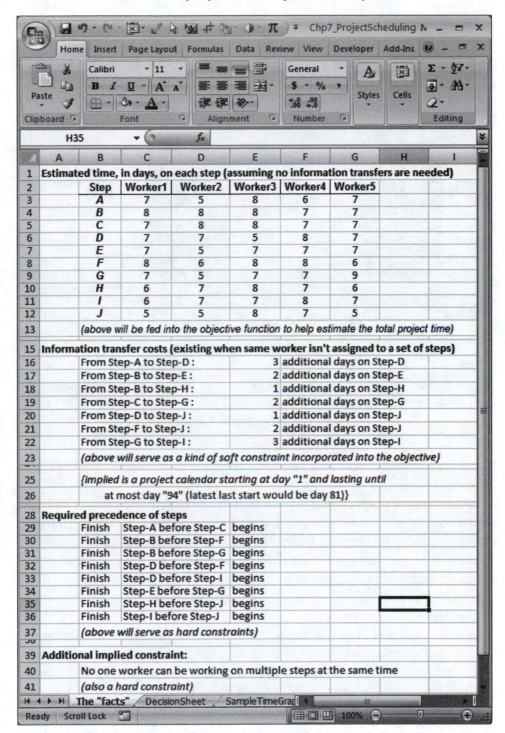

Figure 7.18. Facts and rules critical to the project scheduling problem.

	A	B	C	D	E	F	G	H	I	J	K
5		Worker#	Planned Start Day		Baseline Estimated time to complete	Additional transfer cost	Estimated Completion	Earliest Start Time			
6	Step-A	1	1		7	0	8	1		Any start before	
7	Step-B	2	1		5	0	6	1		earliest start time?	
8	Step-C	3	9		8	0	17	9		0	
9	Step-D	4	1		6	3	10	1			
10	Step-E	5	1		7	2	10	1			
11	Step-F	1	17		7	0	24	11			
12	Step-G	2	17		5	2	24	11			
13	Step-H	3	18		8	1	27	1			
14	Step-I	4	17		6	3	26	11			
15	Step-J	5	28		7	5	40	28			
16						MAX :	40				
17											
18	Number of times a worker has more thank one Step to handle (from below estimated calendar)										
19	0										
20		Worker									
21	Day	1	2	3	4	5					
22	1	1	1	0	1	1					
23	2	1	1	0	1	1					
24	3	1	1	0	1	1					
25	4	1	1	0	1	1					

Figure 7.19. Setup for project scheduling optimization.

based on what you know as a planner, the more algorithms like RISKOptimizer will serve you.

In this case we're specifying two kinds of decision-variable search methods:
recipe for the worker assignment, and schedule for the start dates. In truth,
this isn't the best example of how the schedule was designed to work – it
actually is more useful when all project steps take both a fixed and equal
amount of time. However, because that it often not a luxury in the real world,
it is probably more helpful for you to be able to see a more realistic problem
getting solved.

In any event, and even starting with a reasonably intelligent starting solution, RISKOptimizer is still able to provide an improvement – from a starting
solution's project completion time of 40 days to a project completion time of
34 days after about 6.5 minutes of search time. To help visualize any meaningful changes in the solution, I've also included in this workbook a couple
of bar charts that have been customized to depict resulting solutions (i.e.,
as would Gantt charts common to project management). For contrast, Figure 7.20 shows what the initial solution in Figure 7.19 looks like in graphical
form.

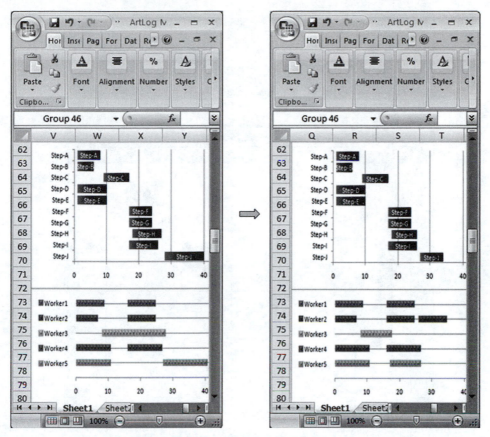

Figure 7.20. Before RISKOptimizer vs. after 6.5 minutes of search.

Visually, the modifications to the initial schedule suggested by RISKOptimizer are clear and the benefit provided rather striking (a 10 percent reduction in project completion time can provide a significant cost saving while potentially freeing resources up for other work).

As a final reminder, as valuable as graphical depictions of solutions can be, they can appreciably slow down processing time. If you want RISKOptimizer (or any other routine) to quickly run through a large number of solutions/calculations, you might consider postponing graphing only until after each search.

Chapter 7 Supplement: A Primer on Genetic Algorithms

Genetic Algorithms in General

As mentioned, genetic algorithms represent an alternative to search tactics such as simple hill-climbing. They are based on at least two principles fundamental to biological science:

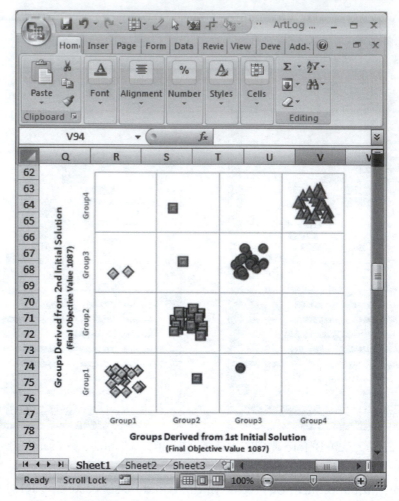

Figure 7.21. Reconsideration of complex objective terrains.

- Entities, scenarios, and solutions that do well in nature also tend to be replicated in nature (i.e., "survival and progenation of the fittest").
- For improvements in nature to develop, there must be opportunities present for diversity. Such diversity is typically the result of either the intermingling of sufficiently large populations, or the result of perturbations (mutations) that introduce novel changes.

These same principles can be used to help analysts develop high-performing solutions in the professional world.

Consider one of the more complex decision landscapes depicted in Figure 7.3 (here, as before, the global optimum is designated by a gray oval) (see Figure 7.21). This is certainly a difficult problem for a simple hill-climbing algorithm alone to solve. On the other hand, genetic approaches to solution searches, driven by the principles stated in the above two points, operate

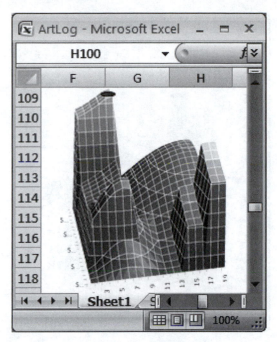

Figure 7.22. Possible initial solution set used by a GA.

very differently and are generally not impeded by false signals relating to local optima and complex nonlinearities (or certainly less prone to failure than hill-climbing in such cases).

For a genetic algorithm (GA) to start its work, it needs to begin with an initial pool of solution possibilities, an initial population in which traits are often simply random. Some of these solutions will certainly be better than others vis-à-vis the performance landscape. A starting population of eight example solutions (gray scale dots) is depicted in Figure 7.22.

The next step allows the survival-of-the-fittest concept to kick in by eliminating many of the poorer solutions (perhaps half). If our initial set consisted of eight solutions, this first cut would bring our solution set down to four. To reinforce the potential for future diversity and development, the algorithm would then temporarily duplicate each of the four remaining solutions, bringing the number of solutions back up to eight. We say temporarily because the nature of these solutions are about to change considerably.

Again, drawing on the first natural principle, a random pairing of each solution with another in that set of eight (four pairs of two) provides for the foundation of a mechanism by which new solutions can be generated for consideration. The generation mechanism itself requires that some of the decision-variable values get swapped with those of the other partner. In the case illustrated in Figure 7.22, this might involve the X values only, with the Y values retained. This swapping activity is referred to as cross-over and

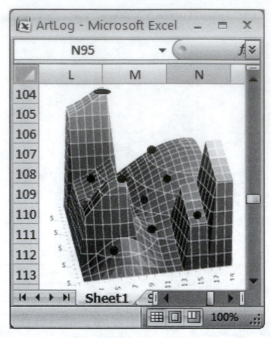

Figure 7.23. Possible first evolutionary iteration by a GA.

is akin to the passing along of a mix of genetic traits to offspring in nature. The result is not only new solutions with mixed traits (i.e., X and Y values in the graph), but also potentially novel performance characteristics (i.e., Z values) based on those traits (see Figure 7.23).

Overall, this process will give us a new population of possible solutions that *may* be very different from the initial set. Some of the new solutions may be much worse than their parents, some equivalent; however, some may be better – and that's the important point because we're going to repeat this procedure, cutting out worse performers and basing the next generation off of the best. If we allow the population to evolve (eliminating the worst and then reproducing and swapping from the best) for yet another generation, we might find further improvements in our solution set, some of which may be very close to a globally optimal solution.

With only a fixed initial population and the cross-over mechanism, however, we're going to hit some limits in the extent to which we can find better solutions (i.e., at this point our gene pool is fairly limited). However, even small gene pools are capable of seeking out and attaining globally optimal solutions if we throw in the element of mutation. Along with the cross-over mechanism, we could also pick a specific attribute (X or Y) in a solution and randomly alter it in a way that creates something that cross-over would never achieve by itself. The subsequent solution may put us in a position much closer to the global optimum, or further away, but in any case it's different

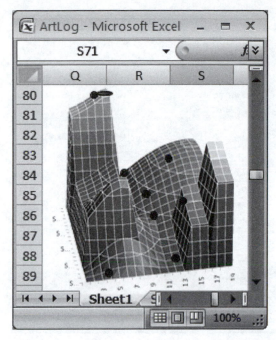

Figure 7.24. Specifying solution population size in RISKOptimizer.

and its strengths and weaknesses as an alternate line of investigation will become apparent to use in future generations.

GA Options in RISKOptimizer

RISKOptimizer uses both cross-over and mutation in its search for globally optimal solutions to complex business problems. To make use of these mechanisms, and in accordance with the conceptual nature of genetic algorithms just described, it will need to have available a set of alternative solutions from which to draw (i.e., to develop next generation solutions). Analysts can specify the size of this pool in the RISKOptimizer Options dialog box, as shown in Figure 7.24.

The specification of the size of the retained population (i.e., the gene pool) can have a significant impact on the effectiveness and efficiency of the search. Too small a pool can impair the development of novel superior solutions because only a limited set of existing ideas are available upon which to draw. Too large a pool can relate to the retention of too many inferior solutions that can similarly distract from effective searchers. So, what's a good population size? This is likely to differ for each and every problem type. The problem is that early on, most analysts won't know what that size is, and only learn through experience running similar optimizations again and again. The makers of RISKOptimizer do, however, suggest a population size of 30 to

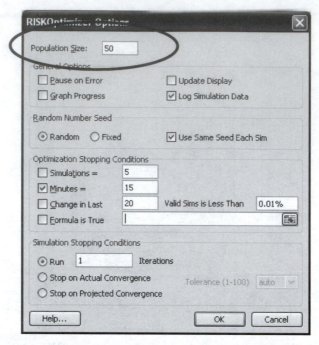

Figure 7.25. Specifying evolutionary dynamics in RISKOptimizer.

100 for most problems, with bigger populations relevant for bigger problems (i.e., those with large numbers of variables and more complex relationships between those variables, constraints and the objective function).

As for the nature by which the solutions in this population are used toward the search for still better solutions, RISKOptimizer also provides the means by which to specify how certain decision variables are mixed and matched by the GA and potentially subjected to mutation during the search. For any set of decision variables (the settings can differ for different decision variables), these options are available when the variables are initially specified or when users elect to edit them in the RISKOptimizer interface (see Figure 7.25).

The cross-over rate specified in RISKOptimizer can be anything between 0.01 and 1.0. For any two solutions being used in cross-over to generate new offspring solutions, a cross-over rate of 0.85 would mandate that 15 percent of all decisions variables involved in a composite solution will be substituted for during cross-over using other existing decision variable values (from the partnering parent solution). In contrast, a cross-over rate of 0.5 suggests that only half of existing decision variable values will be retained. A cross-over rate of 1 essentially equates to zero cross-over (supposedly the generation of new solutions are handled predominantly through mutation instead).

Of course the mutation rate is also modifiable and can be specified as anything between 0.0 and 1.0. A mutation rate of 1.0 specifies that any individual decision variable value in a composite solution involving multiple decisions to be made is subject to random modification for the generation of new solutions. A mutation rate of 0.5 suggests that half of all decisions are subject to random mutation, while 0.0 relates to zero mutation in new solution development. The abundant use of a mutation rate also relates back to the specific selection of population size. If new solutions are being generated largely by mutation rather than cross-over, the need for large populations is reduced. (Random mutations allow even relatively small genetic pools to evolve.)

PRACTICE PROBLEMS

Practice 7.1

Recall the application of cluster analysis to the Dodecha Solutions, Ltd. case. The clustering algorithm used was a tool made available by XLStat. One of the implied goals of the clustering algorithm was to minimize the ratio of within- to between-group variation, subject to the constraint that we were interested in distinguishing a total of four groups. The criteria for grouping (and the source of variation) were eight higher-level factors that were derived through Principle Components Analysis (PCA) conducted on an original set of 32 items.

Recognizing the semi-random nature of the grouping process (both in XLStat and through RiskOptimizer's genetic algorithm), attempt to replicate the groups derived in the XLStat example. Using the data set from the Chp5_DodechaSolutions workbook, compare how the resulting groups compare across the performance measures. Can a similar story be told? Given our previous discussion in this chapter regarding the implications of random features to the grouping process, what might any significant differences imply for an analyst attempting to discriminate among project types?

Practice 7.2

Recall the issues of randomness brought up in the clustering discussions of Chapter 5; the same kind of randomness inherent to XLStat's search for groups applies here. RISKOptimizer isn't providing a complete search over $4^{80} = 1.46 \times 10^{48}$ solutions, just an evolving series of smart guesses.

Try to make a major manual modification to the initial solution, making sure that group sizes are still between 18 and 22. Look at the best solutions log and then compare it to that derived in the example solution presented in this chapter. Are similar objective function values obtained? Does convergence seem to occur much earlier for one start solutions?

Try to develop a plot of best solutions at each of 10 second intervals with your solutions on the Y and the example solutions on the X axis (i.e., organize the data so that best solutions at each 10 second interval are outlined for comparison purposes, then line up and plot the solutions corresponding to each interval). How could this depiction help to describe the relevance of starting solutions?

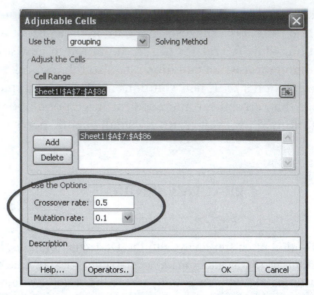

Figure 7.26. Example summarization of clustering result distinctions.

Regardless of group number, how similar are the group constituencies derived at the end of the two initial solution approaches? An example of how to depict this might involve the use of a scatter plot for four separate series of data (designated by the groups derived from the first best solution). Group membership from the first approach might be graphed against that from the second set of runs, with a little jitter added in. Perhaps something along the lines of that shown in Figure 7.26.

Section 3

Leveraging Dynamic Analysis

8

Controlled Simulation Analysis

We've talked about how difficult it can be to find or construct an optimal solution to real-world management problems – where we're faced with nonlinear relationships and constraints that make it difficult to predict how specific decisions work together to impact performance. But in a certain way we've continued to simplify these real-world problems. There may be some shortcomings in the approaches we take to finding solutions, but what about the approaches we use to come up with the problems that we're trying to solve?

When we create a mathematical form to represent reality so that we can ultimately use analytics to provide a solution that might apply to reality, are we missing something? And how much does that impact the real-world applicability and effectiveness of the solution we develop?

These are critical questions for managers who want additional support in their decision making. Project managers don't want suggestions that come out of inappropriate assumptions.

What steps can we take to help ensure that we are, in fact, providing appropriate characterizations of reality when we structure problems and make sense of solutions? Although there are a lot of good places to start, one obvious place is an attempt to take into account the uncertainty associated with just about everything that takes place in the real world. In the problems we've examined in the last few chapters, we really haven't dealt much with this issue; instead we've assumed that certain elements of our decision context are relatively fixed or constant, such as:

- the amount of demand we need to cover in the next few days
- the amount of time it takes a worker to serve a customer
- the nature of the transportation infrastructure (e.g., traffic) on which we base cost and time estimates in routing
- the rate of return on stocks and other options in portfolio selection
- the actual cost to complete a project or new venture we may be considering (among a set of other options)

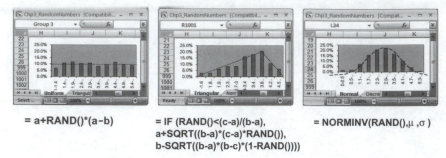

= a+RAND()*(a−b)   = IF (RAND()<(c-a)/(b-a),   = NORMINV(RAND(),μ ,σ)
                          a+SQRT((b-a)*(c-a)*RAND()),
                          b-SQRT((b-a)*(b-c)*(1-RAND()))))

Figure 8.1. Pervasive role of the random number generation in simulation.

But in the back of our minds, do we really believe any of these are constant? If the answer is no, we should probably look into the potential impact that variation in these assumptions may have on the effectiveness of any given solution relative to other solutions from which we might be able to pick.

If we want to incorporate variation into our models, how do we do it? We can start with the notion that most real-world data can be described not only by a characteristic value (e.g., a mean) but also by a measure of uncertainty (e.g., standard deviation). The ability to simply generate random numbers based on those two kinds of information is a first critical step towards formally incorporating variation in our decision-making process.

Remember that in Excel, we have a building block for generating just about any kind of random number that you can dream up – the RAND() function, shown in Figure 8.1. All random numbers created within cells of a spreadsheet make use of this function.

8.1 Approaches to the Use of Simulation in Analysis

Simulation-based models can take on many forms, depending on how random numbers are used to construct various scenarios for evaluation. Two general categories that are worth distinguishing can be referred to as simulated variants and system simulations.

8.1.1 Simulated Variants

Simulated variants generally refer to a set of structured management problems or decision-making scenarios that are equivalent in structure but differ in the actual values of the parameters (e.g., work rates, interest rates, levels of demand) used to describe them. Simulated variants are useful in what managers call what-if analysis. For example, a manager might need to know how different the optimal solution to a problem would be if only slightly different numbers (again e.g., work rates, interest rates, levels of demand) are applied;

that is, would Solver or RISKOptimizer come up with a different solution if the numbers were slightly off. We might call this a pre-construction approach to considering variation. Alternatively, a manager might like to take a derived optimal solution (based only on best estimates; i.e., mean values of demand) and test how well the resulting solution set of decisions would do if the numbers describing the problem changed; would it always ensure profitability? Would it always be technically feasible? We might call this a post-construction approach to considering variation.

Still more sophisticated use of simulated variants would involve considering both issues in tandem. For example, a manager might need to come up with a set of potential of solutions based on slightly different initial problem parameters, and then see how each does under a range of alternative parameters. The manager might find that one of the solutions (that might not appear to be the best based simply on the average values of the problem parameters) might be much less sensitive to variation. As a result, that option might be much less likely to incur unacceptable costs or difficulties in applying it in an uncertain world. That might carry a great deal more appeal than otherwise suggested based on a simple average-driven assessment.

8.1.2 System Simulations

Many management problems require the consideration of decisions that impact not only one point in time, but actually have repercussions across time where later phenomena remain highly dependent on choices made early on. For example, the decision to put in place a specific inventory ordering policy will impact the level of inventory available to a firm for the length of time during which the policy is in place. In fact, even the amount of inventory bought at a single point in time can have implications for performance in many subsequent periods. A decision to hire additional full-time staff or restructure the layout of a facility has similar long-term implications. In such cases, the impact of managerial decisions are still more difficult to assess because they involve numerous events that will take place in the future and about which we may know very little at any level of certainty. Impact can also be affected because these decisions may set into motion a series of events whose repercussions may be difficult to assess in a single closed-form calculation.

A system simulation is often used in such cases to provide a description of how a particular system operates, and how management decisions impact that operation. Variation is built into the activities of that system at each step through time. After the system (the set of codependent and interactive resources, activities, and outcome measures) is allows to run in this manner, subject to a pre-specified set of management rules for a particular length of time, it's overall performance is typically recorded. Additional runs of that

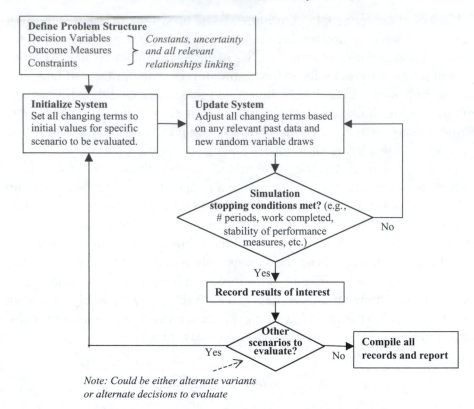

Note: Could be either alternate variants
or alternate decisions to evaluate

Figure 8.2. General design structure for simulations.

system (i.e., with different random numbers in play) are then performed, and some general picture of average and variation in system performance is derived. Those summaries are typically compared to other summaries generated for systems subject to alternative management policies to try and determine which management decisions are in fact preferable. as in the simulated-variant cases.

Because the result of a system simulation is, by its very nature, bound to be characterized in part by the kinds of random variables drawn upon as the system evolves, one full iteration of a system may be different than another full iteration. System simulations are often used to generate complex versions of the simulated variants previously discussed in this chapter, and can be used in both pre- and post-constructive approaches to analysis.

8.1.3 Basics of Simulation Design

Regardless of the kind of simulation approach, the development and use of any simulation model fundamentally involves a set of common steps, shown in Figure 8.2. With this outline in place, we're now ready to consider a codified structure for all varieties of spreadsheet-based simulation models.

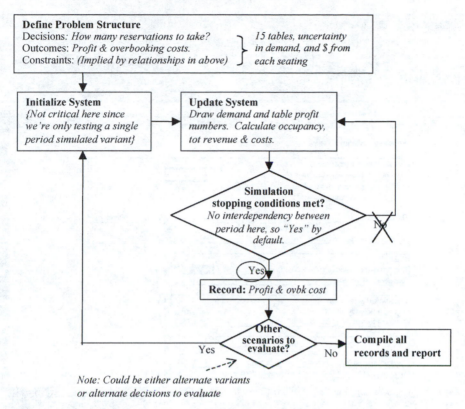

Figure 8.3. Design structure of the reservations simulation variants.

8.2 Assessing Simulated Variants

Consider the case of Lobo's Cantina introduced in Chapter 6. One of the many policy decisions currently under re-evaluation is that of its reservation policy for four-seat tables. Specifically, a standard policy for service firms wishing to capitalize on fixed investments and facing uncertain demand is to overbook their seating capacity. The big question is by how much.

To limit the scope of our example, let's assume that they've decided to have 15 four-seat tables. Performance will be based on two factors: expected total profit (across all groups seated) for a particular reservation policy, and expected implied additional costs associated with not being able to seat customers that arrive with reservations because of overbooking (i.e., loss of good will, future business). The decision, along with variable demand, implicitly constitute the constraints to performance (i.e., limits in actual demand and in reservation policies limit both revenue and costs). Also impacting profit is uncertainty regarding the amount of money spent by each group seated (i.e., profit is impacted both by number of people seated as well as dollars spent per group seated). Having said this, and drawing on the previously presented generalized flow chart (Figure 8.2), we might outline an approach to generating simulated variants as shown in Figure 8.3.

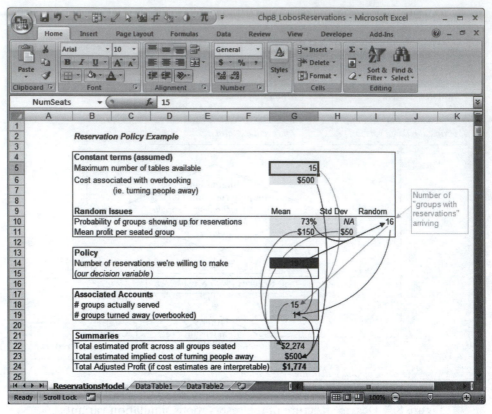

Figure 8.4. Example of the implemented simulation variant template.

With a well-designed view of what needs to be done (Figure 8.3), the structure of a spreadsheet designed to execute the simulations should be fairly straightforward. Some additional assumptions regarding the nature of the random variables to be drawn (e.g., what kind of distributions they follow, means and standard deviations) will be needed, but in this case not much more in terms of complexity of design is required. Workbook Chp8_LobosReservations and Figure 8.4 provide an example of how this might be set up.

Although this spreadsheet structure is sufficient in providing an estimate of how well a specific policy might do given one set of random variable draws, a single variable draw can be misleading. It shouldn't form the basis for final consideration by decision makers. We'd like to be able to have stable estimates of policy performance representative of a full range of random draws, and we will want to be able to compare these results of various policies assessed the same way. A Data Table is a convenient tool that can be leveraged to this end. The Data Table tool is found by selecting Data>What-If Analysis>Data Table (Figure 8.5).

A Data Table is used to provide a series of permutations of a simulated variant structure (i.e,. a series of variants of outcomes based on the simulation

Figure 8.5. Accessing Data Table functionality in Excel.

design, each independent of one another). This tool is fairly straightforward after a spreadsheet structure such as the one demonstrated in this case is set up. To make clear a couple of approaches to the leveraging of Data Tables, we'll start our work on a new worksheet.

Let's store our Number of Reservations decision variable in cell A1 of worksheet DataTable1 in Chp8_LobosReservationsBook. In cell A2 we can store the assumed cost associated with overbooking. To control the simulation outcomes from this sheet, go back to the ReservationsModel worksheet and replace the content of these respective cells (located in G14 and G6 of that first worksheet) with references to =DataTable1!A1 and =DataTable1!A2, respectively. Now we need to outline the structure of the Data Table to be filled in. If we want a table of 100 runs, we might enter the numbers 1 to 100 in the cells DataTable1!B6:B105 (mostly this is just for our own reference). To designate the kinds of scenarios we want the Data Table to collect data, we enter a variety of alternative reservation policies; 15 to 25 reservation bookings in cells C5:M5 in this worksheet. Finally we need to designate what kind of outcome measure we want summarize in the table. For now, let's go with the Total Adjusted Profit figure (a merger of estimated profit across seated groups minus assumed costs due to overbooking). In the upper-left corner of our table outline, cell B5 in this case, we want a direct reference to that outcome measure (ReservationsModel!G24).

Now we're ready to let the Data Table tool do its work. Select the entire area of the table that contains the row labels (1–100), the calculation reference (here in cell B5), and the various scenario inputs (cells C5:M5). Select the Data Table tool to generate the Data Table dialog box, shown in Figure 8.6.

In the field labeled Row input cell, select A1, which is the cell we are using to store our decision variable and using now to control the nature of the simulation. This tells the table generator that you will effectively want to be substituting in the various alternative policies you've designated at the top of the table into this input field for generating your results. In the Column input cell field, select any blank cell to the left or above of the table area (a blank cell must be designated here for the syntax to work). The result should be a

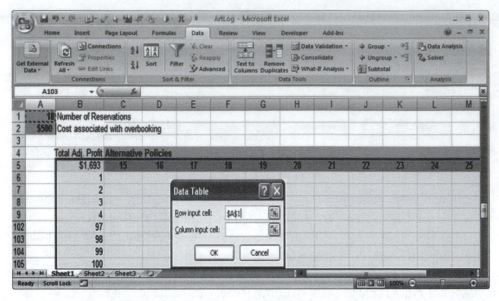

Figure 8.6. Developing a Data Table in Excel.

table of data populated with outcome data for 100 variants of the simulation for each of the scenarios represented in the top row of the table, shown in Figure 8.7.

The nice thing about this table is that you can change just about any of the features of the simulation, including both constants such as cost figures and the nature of relationships (i.e., formulae), and the Data Table should provide updated information more or less instantly in response to these changes. For example, try changing the cost figure in cell A2 or replacing

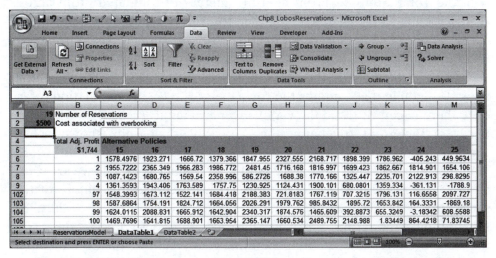

Figure 8.7. Data Table content for multiscenario runs on a single outcome.

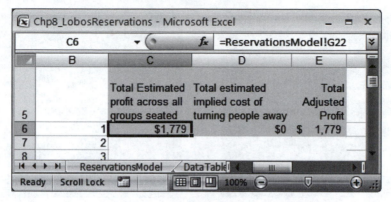

Figure 8.8. Setting up a Data Table for multiple outcome use.

the reference in cell B5 (currently pointing to Total Adj. Profit) with a reference to ReservationsModel!G23 (implied cost of turning people away).

Somewhat less convenient is the Data Table's general dedication to a single outcome measure (i.e., here we can select any one outcome measure to generate variants on, but only one at a time). We could create any entirely separate table for another outcome, but those measures would be in no way linked to the values in this table (i.e., the outcome in the first data cell of this table would be based on entirely different random number pulls).

Similarly we could try to generate a single Data Table that generates variant outcomes for a set of different measures under a specific decision (policy) scenario. The worksheet DataTable2 actually does this. The table was developed by starting with a structure similar to Figure 8.8 in which the top row references each of the three outcomes stored in the cells on the main simulation worksheet.

Selecting the table area that includes the left-most column and all three subsequent columns for which calculations are provided, and again calling on the Data Table tool, again the Data Table dialog box will ask for information. This time the only information we want to provide is a reference in the Column input field to a blank cell outside of the table, e.g., cell A4. This indicates to Excel that we want to use the default calculations in the top row to build the rest of the table, and we don't want to use any information for separate calculations. The result is shown in Figure 8.9.

The values in each individual row of this table are related, as evidenced by the fact that the Total Adjusted Profit values really do represent the difference between the values in the first two columns, even though they are generated by the Data Table as opposed to a post-hoc calculation. In this case, because we're evaluating only a single policy scenario, each row essentially represents a single variant (a single random number pull). This means that complex relationships between any two outcomes (e.g., covariance structures) can

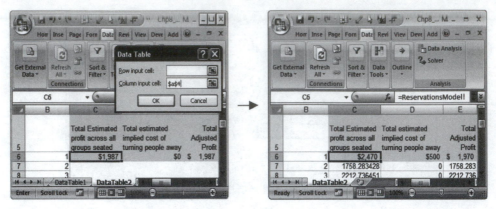

Figure 8.9. Specification of Data Table parameters and subsequent refreshed result.

be assessed and visualized. In some cases the ability to visualize possible interdependencies in this way proves critical in meaningful and intelligent approaches to trade-off analysis.

8.3 Assessing System Simulations

While Data Tables can be extremely useful in providing quick results for a variety of simulated variants, they are less useful in cases where iterations of calculations need to be conducted. In such cases, more sophisticated approaches to assessment must be used. For illustration, consider another decision policy that Lobo's needs to make: inventory re-ordering. Inventory policies critically impact the availability of certain stocked items (e.g., liquor and dry goods, in particular), but are also highly dependent on uncertain issues such as periodic demand and fulfillment lead times. For some complex policies, or those subject to complex forms of uncertainty, the use of system simulations may be the only mechanism for assessing their overall effectiveness.

The flowchart shown in Figure 8.10 presents a fairly simplified inventory system, that nevertheless is sufficiently complex to warrant a demonstration of the shortcomings of Data Tables and the value of alternate approaches to assessment.

The primary decision variable in this case is the re-order point, or the specific level of current inventory that triggers a call to our suppliers for a shipment of new supply. Ostensibly the quantity of the resulting new order is also a policy decision, but one that we'll put aside for now in the interest of simplicity. For now, we'll assume that the size of each re-order is designed to cover average expected demand over average expected lead times, and recoup the deficit between re-order point and most recent supply level

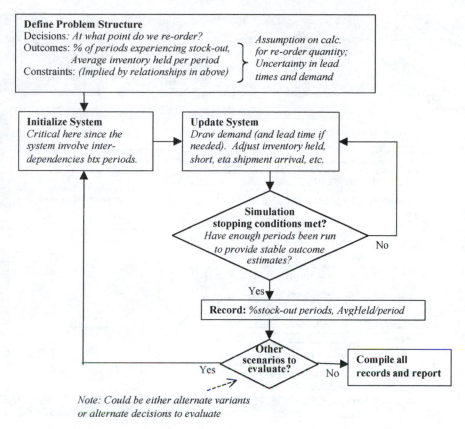

Note: Could be either alternate variants
or alternate decisions to evaluate

Figure 8.10. Design Structure of the Inventory System Simulation.

(i.e., the one which triggered the re-order). This can all be formulaically built into the spreadsheet.

As in the simulated variants example, we could have multiple outcome measures worth noting. One would certainly be the average amount of inventory held per period. This outcome would be implicitly traded off against some measure of stock-out costs, and hence the basis for decision making (policy selection). This other outcome measure might simply be the percentage of periods during which we would anticipate experience stock-out conditions. A related valuable outcome might be the average level of inventory short, either for the timeline as a whole or specific to those stock-out periods. We'll keep things simple here and just focus on the first two of these – % of periods experiencing stock-outs, and average per period inventory holdings. The workbook Chp8_LobosInventory provides an example of how this design might be implemented (see Figure 8.11).

As mentioned in previous chapters, F9 provides a mechanism for iteration, although admittedly F9 only progresses the simulation through a single iteration of the simulation. But realistically, overall summaries of the effectiveness

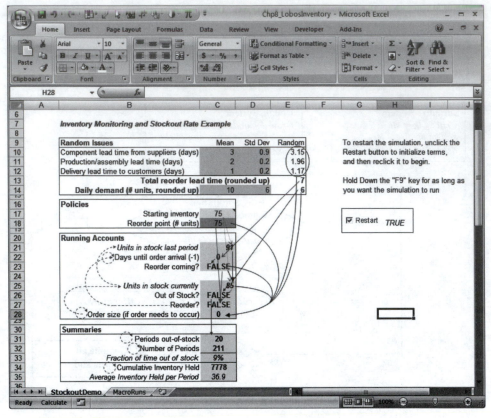

Figure 8.11. Example of the implemented system simulation.

of any policy need a much larger set of iterations for true representation. Furthermore, decision makers are likely to be interested in the comparison of multiple policies. What are the implications of all of this?

Let's think about it. Say we want to slightly change the policy under consideration so that the re-order point is 75 units. To record the summary results for that policy we would have to first change the policy we wanted to evaluate (i.e., typing in 75 for the reorder point value). Then we would have to carry out the following steps at the minimum:

1) Reset the spreadsheet's summaries (i.e., type False and True for Reset).
2) Press F9 as many times as you think is necessary; some logical stopping rule could apply here.
3) Pick a clear spot in the workbook to save those summaries.
4) Copy and paste-special the values of those summaries.

We could do all of these steps manually, but that would add up to a lot of work if we want to generate and store summary measures for many different management policies.

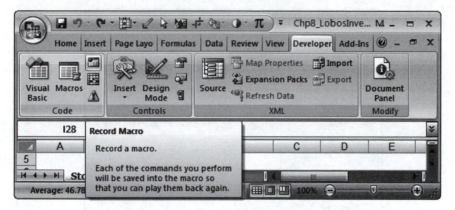

Figure 8.12. Accessing macro capabilities in Excel.

We can use the Macro function to record a set of actions so that we could get Excel to repeat that same set of actions on command (and in one click). Macro functionality is found under the Developer tab, as seen in Figure 8.12.

For now we'll start with a demonstration of one of the simplest forms of macro recording – simulation data recordkeeping. To keep things organized we'll store this data in an additional sheet called MacroRuns. I've set up a duplication of some of the data relevant to our assessment of this system in another area (cells K32:K35) of the main worksheet to make all subsequent copying easier. Selecting the Record Macro option in the Developer tab to open the Record Macro dialog box, shown in Figure 8.13.

In this dialog box, we can name our macro, describe it in depth, and even create a shortcut key for later execution. The default name Macro1 has been selected by the system. If we don't want to specify any information of our own, we can simply click OK and the macro will start recording the actions

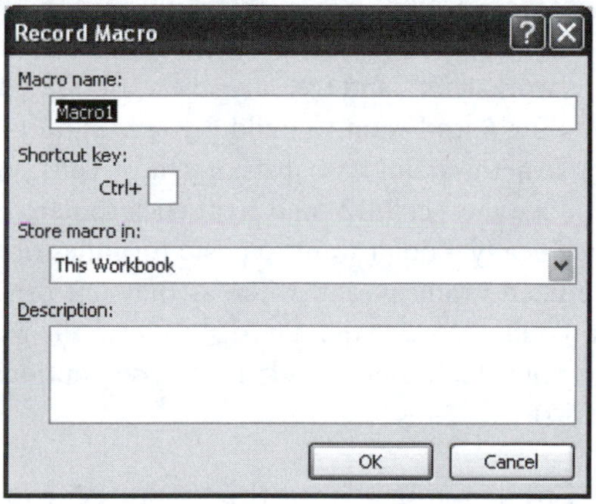

Figure 8.13. Initial specification interface presented for macro recording.

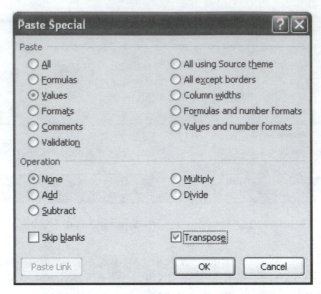

Figure 8.14. Using the Paste Special option during a simple macro recording.

we take in the spreadsheet (within certain limitations that we'll discuss in more depth in Chapter 11).

The following are the actions that the macro will record.

1) Again, as stated, I've got to re-initialize this system simulation to get clean results, so I'm going to reset the spreadsheet's summaries (i.e., type "False" and return, then "True" and return for the Reset value in H18). For now, we'll just type these things in rather than use the check-box shortcut I've included (Excel 2007 circa 6/12/2007 doesn't record actions on an object, a bit of a devolution from the Excel 2003 version).

2) To generate the kind of summary outcomes I want, I'll hold down F9 until I cover 200 periods worth of iterations. Tedious but we'll talk about better ways to get this done later as well.

3&4) I've already picked a clear spot in my workbook to save those summaries (the MacroRuns worksheet), and I've already consolidated the critical system parameters and outcomes I want to build my record off of (cells K32:K35 on the main sheet), so at this point I can just copy those cells, go to the MacroRuns spreadsheet (for instance, cell B2) and right click to perform a "paste-special operation." Specifically, I don't want to paste formulas or references. Instead I want to paste fixed "values," and whereas they are organized vertically in the main sheet, I'd like to paste them horizontally in the MacroRuns sheet; so I'll be selecting both the "values" and "transpose" options in my paste (Figures 8.14 and 8.15).

And that's it. Now I'm just going to hit the "stop recording" button (small square at the bottom of the screen). The square icon shown in Figure 8.16

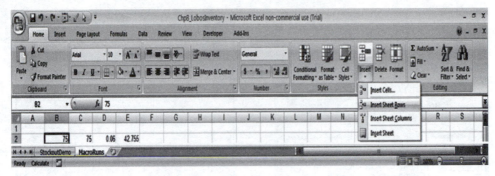

Figure 8.15. Inserting rows during a simple macro recording.

will change at this point to represent the record button. These buttons are usually more convenient than the menu-driven system.

The macro is now saved and available for future use. There are several ways to activate a recorded macro, and the first is menu driven. Select the Macros option on the Developer tab to open the Macro dialog box. Choose the macro you want (in this case Macro1) and then click Run (Figure 8.17). Another way to open and run a macro is through the use of the shortcut key that you specified when you created the macro.

There also an object-based approach available for any developed macro called Make a button. The easiest way to use this is to draw your own button Insert>Shapes to open the Shapes drop-down (see Figure 8.18).

For any object such as a drawn circle (or even an inserted.jpg), right-click on that object to see a number of property options including Assign Macro (shown in Figure 8.19). Selecting that option then allows you to specify what macro will be associated with that object.

After a macro is assigned, place the cursor over the object to change the cursor icon from that of an arrow to that of a pointing finger (indicating that the object can now be clicked to run the assigned macro). The use of text to add immediate clarity regarding the role that new button adds to its usefulness as an intuitive and readily accessed means of executing macros

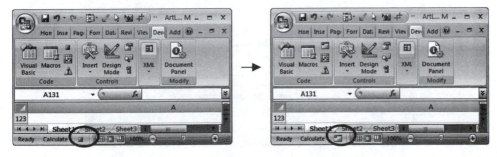

Figure 8.16. Quick stop to a macro recording.

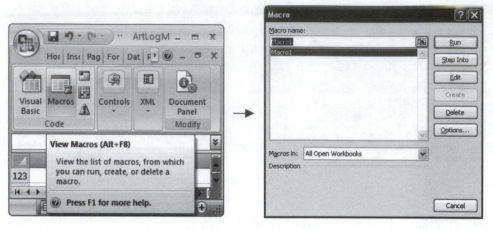

Figure 8.17. Menu-driven activation of a macro.

(for you as well as others using your workbook). And there's no limit to the number of macros and buttons you can place within a workbook.

As we will discover in particular Chapter 13, there is a range of related button approaches to interfacing with macros, although having introduced three different approaches it's worth emphasizing that any one of these should work to replicate the system simulation recording procedure that we set out to perform (provided we recording our actions correctly). The macro currently recorded in the Chp8_LobosInventory workbook works as expected.

We could run this for any number of scenarios to try to assess which one works best for our interests; however, if we wanted to be still more sophisticated in our simulation development, we could (if we knew how) consider making this whole process even more automated by not just recording our actions in a macro, but also editing the recorded actions. That's going to

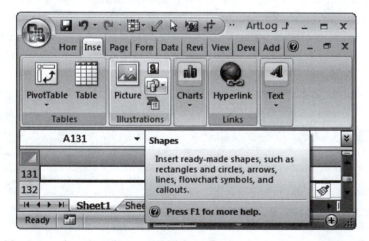

Figure 8.18. Accessing drawing capabilities to generate a macro activation button.

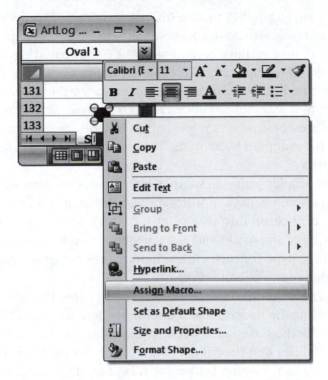

Figure 8.19. Assigning a macro to a drawn button.

require some knowledge of how to access how Excel recorded those actions in the first place (i.e., in VisualBasic code), and that will be the focus of Chapter 11.

8.4 An Introduction to Stochastic System Structures

As valuable as the approaches to simulation presented thus far may seem, it is worth noting that most real-world systems are more complex with uncertainty built into not just the characteristics of events (e.g., how many customers arrive) but also whether or not certain subsequent events take place (e.g., upon arrival do all customers request comparable services, which ones will require payment by credit, which of those will want to split the bill). All of this is, of course, important to those trying to manage the kinds and amounts of resources needed to fill all these different needs at any given point in time.

A key term used to describe the complexity associated with these real-world systems where uncertain events are followed by still other uncertain events is stochastic. Stochastic processes can be thought of as a series of specific steps, stages, or states where the transition from one step to another is characterized by some amount of uncertainty. For example, although loan processing at a bank may involve a pre-established series of steps, and although one might be able to describe the progress through this process by a specific and typical ordering of these steps, mistakes or simply variations in requirements may require certain steps to be repeated before the process is successfully completed. If these alternative sequences through the process cannot be predetermined prior to entry into the processes, but are rather subject to issues that are uncertain or only made apparent in process, a common representation of the probabilistic tendency for such sequence variation is often adopted by analysts. This representation is referred to as a transition matrix.

In a slightly simpler process example, let's consider a three-state process. Specifically, assume we have a prototype development process that can be meaningfully broken up into three steps. At each step, a different worker takes possession of the work; and at each step, a decision is made to either advance the prototype for further development/testing or to send it back to a previous stage of consideration/rework.

The Chp8_TransitionMatrices workbook depicts how the information relevant to capturing the uncertain and interdependent nature of this system is used. Specifically the boxed area of cells labeled Transition Matrix provides a set of probabilities that describe how likely it is for a job currently in one state (1, 2, or 3) to transition (move) next into another state. In this table, the probability of transitioning from State 1 into State 2 is 0.7, or 70 percent. Because any job in State 1 must go somewhere, the sum of transition probabilities in each row should sum up to 1 (as demonstrated in the column labeled Sum shown in Figure 8.20).

In the adjacent table labeled Quasi-Cumulative Transition Matrix, I've used some simple addition to help indicate probability thresholds, useful in getting a random transition between discrete states to actually work. It's a bit sloppier than necessary, but fairly transparent for the purpose of introducing how such random transitions might be generated. Specifically, I've developed this adjacent table with the sole intention of using it with the conveniently provided HLOOKUP function in Excel. As discussed in Chapter 2, HLOOKUP can be used to search for a specific term (e.g., 12, or 3.14, or Mike) in the top row of a table and return information from a lower row of the same column in which the entry was found. However, provided entries in that top row are sorted, VLOOKUP can also conduct a search for the last closest entry that doesn't exceed what's being looked for (e.g., 3 if 3.14 is being looked for in a sorted array of integers, or perhaps Michael in a sorted list of first names). To ensure such a search takes place, simply make sure that the last term in the HLOOKUP is a 1 (e.g., HLOOKUP(RAND(),J8:L13,3,1) to indicate a sorted search).

In this case, where the next state is in part determined by a random decimal ranging from 0 to 1, the use of HLOOKUP with a table that contains both

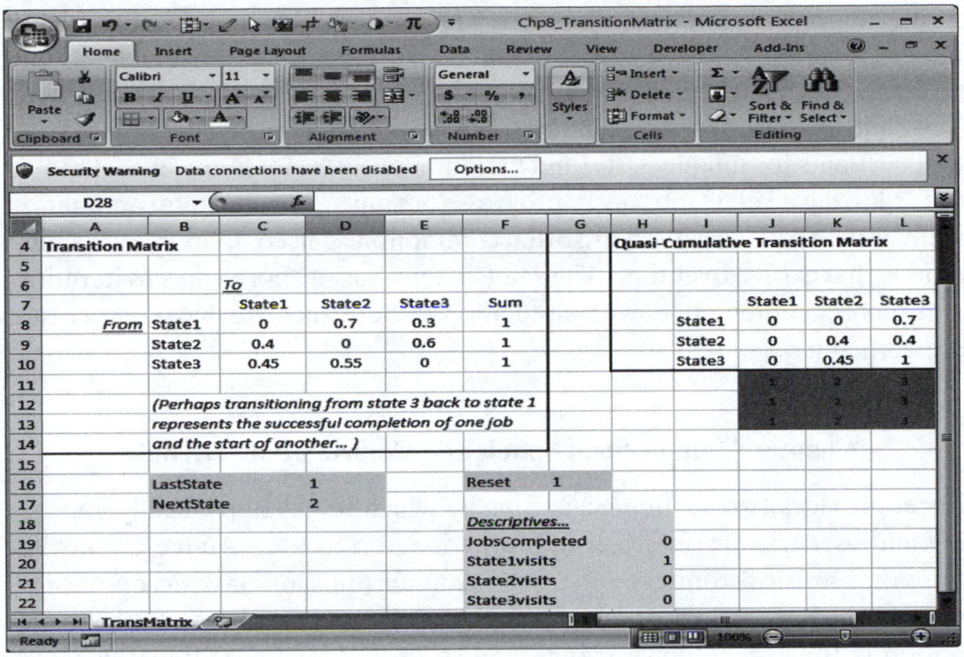

Figure 8.20. Example of transition matrix as a possible component of a system simulation.

these quasi-cumulative probabilities and some indication of the associated next state works well provided we are able to consistently indicate where those next state references are. That consistency is provided by the deliberate indication of state references numbers $(1, 2, 3)$ in the three rows (rows 11–13) below each of the quasi-cumulative probability rows (rows 8–10). Think of rows 8 to 13 as constituting the template from which appropriate sub-tables for lookup will be formed. The use of the OFFSET function allows us to specify which sub-table, and hence which starting row for use in a lookup, should be focused on.

As an example, if a job is currently in State 3, we would use an OFFSET function to shift our focus from the sub-table J8:L11 to J10:L13 (i.e., offsetting our focus by two rows from the start of the template table to make sure the quasi-cumulative probabilities are in the top row of the sub-table considered). We could then use the HLOOKUP function on that OFFSET sub-table and the RAND() function to randomly determine which state to transition to after State 3. If the random value searched for is 0.21 based on the numbers in this case, HLOOKUP will see the first value in the offset sub-table (0.0) as adequate but will view the second value (0.45) as excessive; therefore, looking three rows below the last adequate value will return a 1. Similarly, a random value of 0.48 would return a 2, in this case. In this way, as used in the sample spreadsheet, the transition matrix description of a 45 percent chance of 3 to

1, and 55 percent chance of 3 to 2, is fully captured. This is a nice example of the compound use of multiple functions in Excel; not the most elegant, but effective and fairly straightforward.

As a final note, there's nothing stopping us from adding in more complexity that accounts for unique costs (and variation in costs) for being in each state, or for having a single job stay in progress for some excessive total amount of state visits. These structures are often commonplace in complex system simulations that evolve over time. The same macro-based approaches to iteration and recordkeeping apply with simulations where such stochastic processes are embedded.

Chapter 8 Supplement: Simulation Control Made Friendly

Excel provides two set of mechanisms by which to develop visually appealing and user-friendly interfaces. One set is referred to as ActiveX controls; the other as form controls. Often you can get the same task accomplished with both. Both allow developers to add elements such as check boxes, option buttons, drop-down menus, and so on to their spreadsheet as alternatives to changing values in cells. Form controls often provide a simpler interface for developers, but ultimately I find that ActiveX controls provide more versatility and a greater range of options for development. We'll stick to the ActiveX controls for this discussion (functioning examples found in Chp8_SampleControls), starting with the basic text box.

Text boxes duplicate the contents of any individual cell in a workbook, but because it's an object unto itself, it can be positioned anywhere in a workbook. This can be valuable because whereas cells in complex decision-support environments may be difficult to relocate meaningfully (without messing up other parts of the design), the location of these text boxes has no impact on what's going on behind the scenes. You could even group the text box with other objects, such as graphs, so that when you move a set of objects in your spreadsheet, the text box moves along with that group. To create a new text box (or any other control for that matter), under the Developer tab, select Insert from the Developer tab, as shown in Figure 8.21.

Click the Text Box icon in the toolbox to generate a new text box at any point in the spreadsheet. When created, you will automatically enter Design Mode where you have a wide range of control properties that you can edit. Right-click on the new box and select Properties to open the Properties dialog box, shown in Figure 8.22.

The most important properties of your new control is the Linked Cell property. This indicates the value shared by both the text box (in this case) and a particular reference cell on the spreadsheet (i.e., if the linked cell is A1, whatever value A1 takes on will show up in the text box. Keep in mind

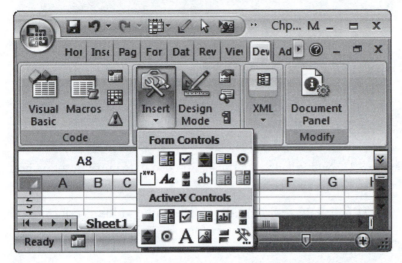

Figure 8.21. Controls available through the Excel menu interface.

this important point: Any formatting in the linked cell will not transfer to the text box; only the value contained).

Consider the example of setting the value in cell E9 to =NOW() {i.e., the current date/time signature} and formatting that cell to show hours:minutes:seconds. Linking a new text box to that cell will copy the value of that date/time signature to the text box – for Excel, that value is a numeric string that, while useful from a system perspective, doesn't mean much to a typical user. In the case of 11:56:42 on January 4, 2006, this string

Figure 8.22. Modifying the properties of a text box ActiveX control.

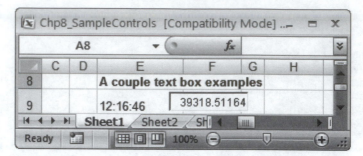

Figure 8.23. Numerical value translation of a date entry by a text box.

is 38721.49771 (see Figure 8.23). Again, the same value is contained in both the cell and the text box, the only difference is in the format by which the value is presented.

On the other hand, if we completely convert the date/time signature to a string of characters (i.e., no longer a numeric value) whose construction is based on a certain formatting rule (e.g., using the TEXT function, = TEXT(NOW(),hh:mm:ss), the text within both the cell and the text box should be consistent. They both contain the same text, as shown in Figure 8.24.

Incidentally, cell linkage with controls works in both directions. If you change the content of that cell in the spreadsheet, that change will appear in the text box. If you type different content into the text box, that cell will take on that value. Keep in mind, however, that this will also erase any formulae that might have been in the cell previously, if that's the nature of how the cell was used.

It is also worth noting the variety of other properties that you could use in configuring your text box, including (refer back to Figure 8.22):

Background and font color/types
If you want the control to take on a 3-D appearance
What aspect the cursor takes on when it runs over the control
Whether the text within the box should wrap
Whether scrolling the text content is available for the box

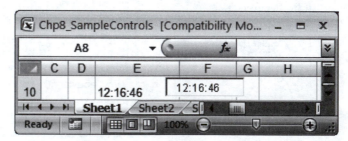

Figure 8.24. Specified text depiction of a date entry by a text box.

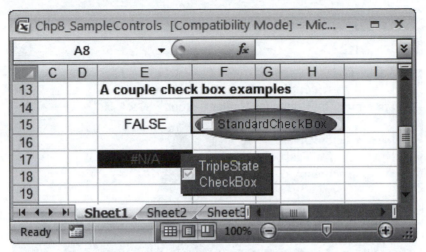

Figure 8.25. Examples of check boxes active in a spreadsheet.

As with cells and other objects, you can also change the name/label of the control for more intuitive reference (i.e., call it CurrentTime rather that TextBox1).

Having a basic familiarity with TextBox creation, we can now discuss other controls that can come in handy for interfacing in Excel. Buttons (under the rubric of controls) are really no more than that – imagine that you can click to start an existing automated set of events. You can get the same functionality from any object (e.g., a drawn circle) to which you assign a macro in Excel. Buttons created through the Controls menu just give you the convenience of something that already looks like a button that should be clicked (something you might have to work a little to create an aesthetic image of using the standard drawing tools).

Check boxes, which you've already seen applied in some past examples, are also a nice convenience control that allows users to toggle between two settings (e.g., 1,0; Yes,No; On,Off; Restart,Stop). As with text boxes, a number of the same standard control properties can be modified (e.g., colors, labels). One unique difference is that check boxes also allow you to add fixed text labels that accompany them on a page (e.g., Restart or StandardCheckBox). Another unique feature of check boxes is the ability to use them in what's called a triple state. In such a case, each click on the box will move the user through the states of True, False, and #N/A (i.e., other). This could be useful, for example, if you had three alternative settings rather than just two that you would like to make available through this kind of object-oriented interface (Figure 8.25).

Option, or radio, buttons add an additional level of complexity that is not present with check boxes. Whereas check boxes typically react independently

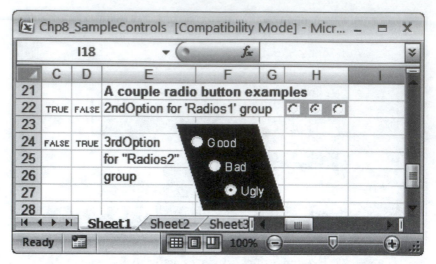

Figure 8.26. Examples of radio button groups in a spreadsheet.

of one another, radio buttons (see Figure 8.26) are designed to be used as one of a set; in other words, each radio button is used to represent specific alternatives, only one of which may be active or relevant at a specific time. An example would be the selection of a single candidate for a specific position during voting, the selection of a specific shipping option for an order, or the selection of a specific accounting classification for filing an item on an expense report.

A critical property is the GroupName. The group name represents the set of alternative radio buttons that each individual button works in conjunction with. By default, new radio buttons created on a worksheet will receive the name of that worksheet as their group name. But similar to all other properties, you can (and usually should) change that (e.g., for one set of buttons that represent interchangeable options, you might use the group name Radios1; for another set of buttons that are not dependent on the choice made in the

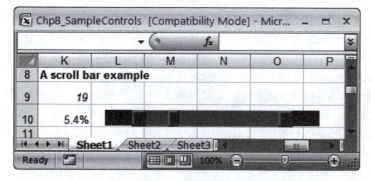

Figure 8.27. Examples of scroll bar in a spreadsheet.

first set, you might use the label Radios2). Specifying different groups for independent sets of radio buttons will ensure that they don't interfere with each others' functionality.

Another item to note here is that the various buttons in a group should typically be assigned to their own individual cells to avoid confusion. So for a set of three radio buttons, three cells in a spreadsheet would be used to capture the state of the buttons (e.g., the second button clicked, and the others not). IF statements are typically used to convert that information into a single result (e.g., =IF(B24,"1stOption",IF(C24,"2ndOption","3rdOption")))

Scroll bars, as shown in Figure 8.27, provide mechanisms by which to select a continuous range of values bounded by an upper and lower limit (rather than just a discrete set of options as described by check boxes and radio buttons). For example you might want to allow a user to specify an interest rate between 5 and 7 percent, a minimum average labor force IQ between 900 and 1,100 (e.g., on the SAT), or a maximal budgetary allowance between $10,000 and $35,000.

A scroll bar might be a nice choice for an interface on such a decision. Excel, however, currently has some annoying limitations. For example, you can specify upper and lower bounds, but those bounds have to be integers. In fact, all values that the scroll bar takes on have to be integers. If you specify a range between 0 and 100 and don't mind the fairly simple task of rescaling to fit the range you are interested in (e.g., 5 to 7 percent), this isn't really an issue. It's just annoying that this limitation is something you need to work around.

Drop-down menus are another nice interface control for situations where a wide range of options might exist (e.g., list boxes or combo boxes). One of the additional properties of these controls requires the specification of a list of alternative options (e.g., presented as a sequence of cells in a column of a worksheet; as shown in Figure 8.28). A combo box with such a reference list specification provides a compact form that can be expanded by the user for item selection purposes.

PRACTICE PROBLEMS

Practice 8.1

Using the approach demonstrated in Section 8.3, build a report that shows not only the average, but also the best (MIN) and worst (MAX) cases for the cost (holding) and stock-out rates (as before, across 200 iterations or trials). Run this 3 times for each of 11 reorder point policies ranging from 60 to 70. The end result should be a table with 11 records, each describing the average, best, and worst cases of cost and stock-out rates. Comment on how average performance might not be completely informative with regard to "best policy" selection.

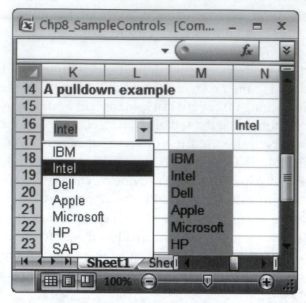

Figure 8.28. Examples of drop-down menu in a spreadsheet.

Practice 8.2

Reconsider the Lobo's Reservations example simulation from the previous practice section. We selected random numbers based on a specific level of variation, and limited ourselves to only a few specifically structured scenarios. But we might want to find out how different the performance of this system might be given alternative overbooking charges and alternative levels of variation (more or less) in customer dollar contributions.

Use three option buttons to depict different possible levels of variation characteristic of the random numbers involved in the simulation (Std Dev = 10, 15 and 20).

Use drop-down menus to allow individuals to choose between the application of three distinct overbooking charges ($220, $250, and $280).

Using a report format similar to that of the previous practice problem, summarize the results of these $3 \times 3 = 9$ possible combinations. To simplify the work, limit yourselves to only the consideration of the case in which 28 reservations are made.

9

Scenario Generation and Optimization

A natural extension of a discussion of simulation, given our existing under-standing of optimization, is how the two methods can be used together. The basic question behind simulation optimization is:

What decision (if any) tends to provide relatively superior results regardless of the uncertainty associated with the real world problems they are designed to resolve?

Simulation provides the means by which to incorporate uncertainty into the evaluation of a specific decision, or a predetermined handful of such decisions; however, this question implies much greater scope. It suggests a formal search for the best decision across a very wide range of possible alter-native decisions. For simulated variants, the term *best* takes into account not just the average/expected value of parameters describing the setting (as would be common in discrete optimization), but also the potentially extreme performance of outliers, be that good or bad. For system simulations, the best would necessarily need to further relate to performance as the result of a sequence of events where the interplay of initial guiding decisions, compli-cated by uncertainty, might be extremely difficult to assess without sufficient simulation runs. The follow-up question then is:

How can we integrate the techniques associated with simulation and optimization in a single solid mechanism for meaningful decision support?

Here again we gain from the robustness of Excel and the availability of addi-tional applications that capitalize on Excel's computational strengths. Specifi-cally, we can return to a more in-depth and nuanced discussion of the various features of RISKOptimizer that, along with Excel, make all of this possi-ble. Although other packages exist that might provide similar simulation optimization capabilities, we'll focus on RISKOptimizer, given our famil-iarity with its usefulness in assisting in difficult optimization problems (see Chapter 7).

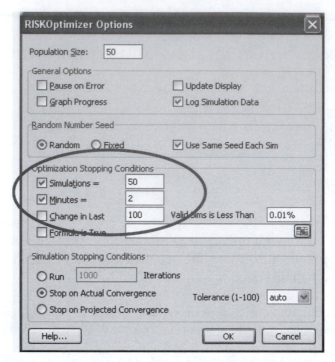

Figure 9.1. Specification of simulation stopping conditions.

9.1 Basic Simulation Optimization Capabilities

There are a number of characteristics of simulation optimization procedures that are available to users of RISKOptimizer. Two in particular are worth mentioning in detail here (some others have already been described in the Chapter 7 supplement).

9.1.1 Optimization Stopping Conditions

As suggested in Chapter 7, RISKOptimizer's search for an ideal solution (decision policy that meets the objective subject to any relevant constraints) can be terminated manually by clicking the Stop button at any point during evaluation. However, users are also given the opportunity to pre-specify under what conditions the application can stop its search; for example, if an individual doesn't have the time to continue to monitor progress and would at the same time like to free up system resources for doing other work on their computer when ideal solutions are discovered. This automatic termination is made possible through a variety of tactics available through RISKOptimizer. These are available under Options when the RISKOptimizer interface is being used to specify the particulars of an optimization procedure. The RISKOptimizer Options dialog box is shown in Figure 9.1.

As shown in Figure 9.1, an optimization search can stop after a given set of decision policies have been examined. In Figure 9.1, if the analyst felt that the assessment of 50 alternate solutions (a fairly small number in actuality) was sufficient to draw conclusions, they might click the box marked Simulations = 50 or change 50 to a more appropriate number. Note here that the term *simulations* in this dialog box is used somewhat misleadingly to represent the number of alternative solutions considered in the simulation optimization. If an analyst wanted the search to stop after two minutes of time, they could specify that under Minutes.

Other stopping conditions include other measures of finality in a search that might otherwise continue for a very long period of time. Change in Last allows the search to terminate when the changes in the performance of subsequent solutions considered becomes less than practically significant (e.g., in the current example, if the average performance of the last 100 decision policies doesn't differ by more than 0.01 percent among those solutions that are valid, or in other words meet all required constraints). The Formula is True option provides a mechanism through which the user can reference any customized calculation within their spreadsheet aimed at assessing the convergence of the search upon a desired solution. This may be used much like a goal seek option in Excel, or may be much more nuanced to the needs of the analyst.

It is also worth noting that users need not rely on any one of these stopping conditions alone, but can have as many simultaneously active as they want. For example, the analyst might want to make sure that the simulation search stops at the 10-minute mark or before, if little practical change has taken place in the last 100 solutions assessed. The check box nature of the interface allows for multiple stopping conditions to be applied simultaneously towards this end.

9.1.2 Simulation Stopping Conditions

Recall from Chapter 7 (where we first introduced RISKOptimizer) that we had specified a single iteration to be run for each solution considered (see Figure 9.2). This, of course, made a great deal of sense because there was no uncertainty built directly into our optimization models at the time.

However, in the case of simulations, the benefit of generating a wide range of simulated variants as part of the complete assessment of potential policies is clear. Any one random number pull can provide a misleading picture of the effectiveness of a policy, particularly in the case of simulated variants where single-period performance can very easily impacted by an unusual random draw. It is therefore useful to be able to require RISKOptimizer to consider a set of possible outcomes in its assessments and overall search for optimal solutions. In the case of simulated variants, increasing

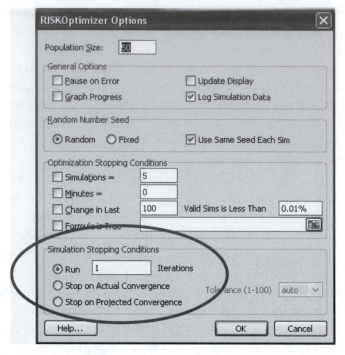

Figure 9.2. Specification of single iteration conditions on search.

the number of iterations specified provides exactly this kind of capability. In the case of system simulations, the use of iterations needs to be thought out much more carefully, as will be discussed later in this chapter. Nevertheless, specification of multiple iterations can be useful for system evaluation as well.

As a side note on the use of multiple iterations for evaluating policy performance that includes uncertainty, one convenient mechanism to ensure policy comparability across even a small set of iterations is that of the Random Number Seed field (also found in the RISKOptimizer dialog box). An analyst can specify that the same set of random numbers is ostensible drawn in evaluating each new policy decision under consideration during the search (see Figure 9.3).

By specifying the Use Same Seed Each Sim check box, the analyst can be better assured that RISKOptimizer will be making apples-to-apples comparisons with regards to the conditions under which each possible policy solution is being judged. This is typically a default setting, but one worth paying attention to again particularly when a relatively small set of random number draws are being specified during solution assessments.

Alternatives to specifying a discrete number of iterations for the evaluation of each policy considered (e.g., generate 100 possible outcomes associated

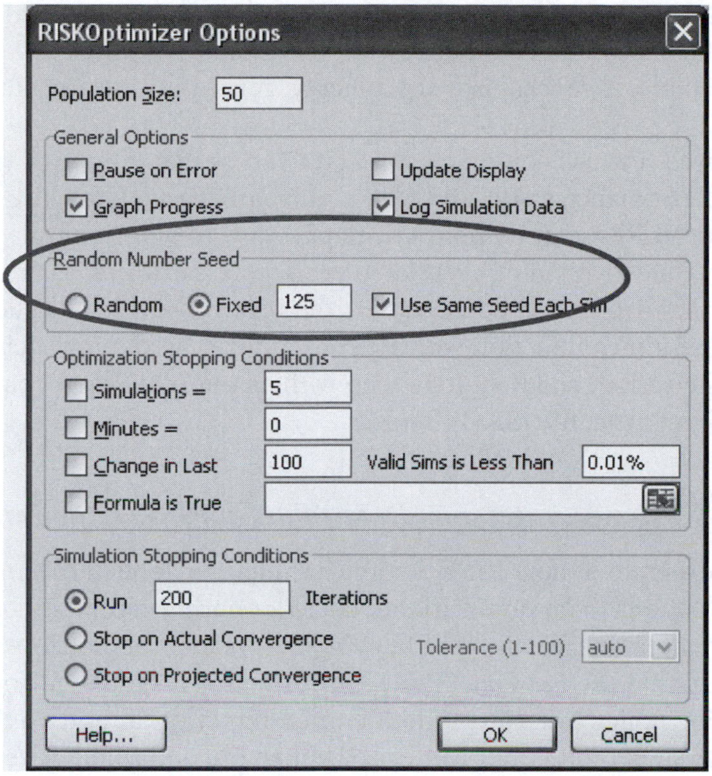

Figure 9.3. Specification of random number generation conditions.

with each decision considered) include the Stop on Actual Convergence and Stop on Projected Convergence options. In cases where you might not know how many iterations to run to get a stable characterization (e.g., average) of performance, you can actually let RISKOptimizer try to figure it out on its own. This takes a little control over the optimization out of the hands of the analyst, but can be helpful if the number of iterations needed to assess certain policies is appreciable greater (and unknown) relative to some more simplistic policies.

9.2 Optimization of Simulated Variants

For simulated variants, iterations relate to new random number draws that in turn provide alternative performance results for a specific decision. This is valuable particularly in cases either where average performance may not be sufficiently informative for decision comparisons (i.e., high average performance may also equate to high variance and hence high risk), or when average performance cannot be assessed based the distribution or interdependence of uncertainty in performance (which is largely why simulation would be useful over discrete assessments to begin with). In Chapter 8, we briefly described the Data Table, a mechanism for quickly generating a large number of iterations.

We showed how we could develop Data Tables that either provided estimates of performance associated with a range of decision policies, as well as (in our second Reservation policy example) how to view multiple potential results associated with multiple related yet distinct performance measures of a single policy. Here we'll describe how the results provided by such a table could be used in conjunction with RISKOptimizer as an approach to simulation optimization, and then follow up with an alternative approach driven more directly through RISKOptimizer.

9.2.1 *Using Averages from Data Tables in RISKOptimization*

As a first example of how RISKOptimizer might be applied toward seeking out best solutions to random variants, consider once again the Lobos Reservations example, specifically the DataTable2 spreadsheet developed for that problem. In that second Data Table, performance is tabulated for a single overbooking policy in terms of both earned direct profit and implied costs of ill-will from overbooking. These are broken out and summarized in Data Table form for 100 random scenarios. If we were interested in only finding a policy to maximize expected profit, subject to a service constraint (on average, only overbooking at most by one table 80 percent of the time; i.e., incurring an average overbooking cost of $400 maximum), we might specify the optimization search in RISKOptimizer as shown in Figure 9.4.

Under Options in RISKOptimizer we'll also request a log of the progress of the solution so we can monitor development over time. Because our iterations are basically being covered by the DataTable, we won't request any more than a single RISKOptimizer-based iteration per decision policy evaluated.

After a few minutes the performance appears to have leveled off. And the best result seems to be a reservation policy of around 20, although the there does seem to be considerable variation between best solution performance and other acceptable solutions (worth noting because there's only one decision variable being modified, in this case).

A closer inspection of the optimization summary log (at least those solutions that met the service constraint) shows that the solution 20 along with other neighboring solutions, e.g., 17 and 18 overbookings, are fairly comparable, and the standard deviation of 20 performance is actually fairly high. In some cases, analysts might look at results such as these and consider implementing options that perform second best simply to avoid high levels of performance risk.

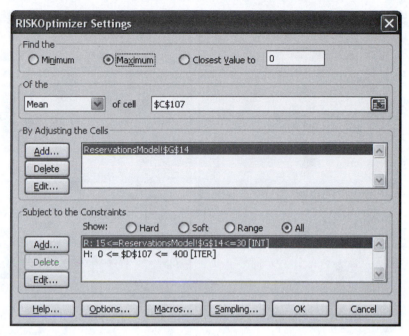

Figure 9.4. Problem specifications for simulation optimization of reservation problem.

9.2.2 *Using RISKOptimizer Iterations for the Same Result (without Data Table)*

An alternative approach to generating the same result is to capitalize not on Data Table functionality for developing simulated variants (i.e., iterations in RISKOptimizer lingo), but instead on RISKOptimizer's built-in iteration mechanism. To accomplish this, we only need to modify the source of the performance and constraint results in RISKOptimizer (the single calculations of profit and cost from the main model sheet) and specify to RISKOptimizer that we would like for it to personally run 100 iterations for each solution considered, just as the Data Table had been providing (see Figure 9.5). Because Data Tables won't be necessary in this approach, those associated sheets could also be deleted from the workbook, and may actually save the processor a lot of trouble and allow the search to proceed more swiftly.

Worth noting is that to get the constraints to apply equally in this case, we will need to specify that we are only interested in meeting the service constraint "on average" (i.e., across all 100 iterations of each policy assessed). We could be more stringent, but our search might yield different results and wouldn't be a fair comparison given that the Data Table approach was basically just looking at satisfying the constraint on average across its 100 trials. We can make this modification to the service constraint by asking that the Mean service level for each policy (across all iterations) be

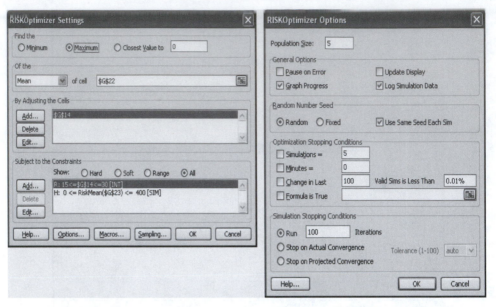

Figure 9.5. Alternative specification leveraging RISKOptimizer iteration capabilities.

considered rather that the final Value (i.e,. of each iteration, or the last one viewed).

Ultimately, the result of an otherwise preferred policy of around 20 bookings is comparable to that derived by the other method and a close inspection of neighboring results similar as well. However, the RISKOptimizer handling of iterations tends to converge upon this conclusion much faster than the Data Table approach.

9.3 Optimization of System Simulations

Before getting into the use of RISKOptimizer with system simulations, it is worth taking a moment to consider the potential for complications associated with relying on iterations for simultaneously both the generation of multiple pulls of random numbers and the development of evolving systems based on circular loop calculations.

Let's reconsider the Lobos Inventory example from Chapter 8 (Chp8_LobosInventory.xls). We've already shown that we can use the F9 key to run through a series of calculations. We've also demonstrated how we can record a macro for repeating a large set of such recalculations to ultimately build a rich and valuable history of the performance of decisions (i.e., reorder point policies) made for the system. For 200 periods, Figure 9.6 shows the kind of result we might generate using the macro we considered in the last chapter (which was designed to effectively recalculate things 200 times).

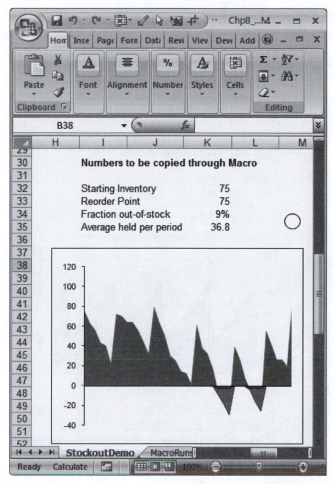

Figure 9.6. Anticipated history generated in single iteration mode.

For richness of description, also I've chosen to track the last 40 periods (following the same method from the Web data acquisition discussion in Chapter 3), and provide a graph showing the inventory positions for those last 40 periods. The presence and impact of variations in demand and delivery lead times is certainly apparent.

Attempting to simply increase the number of iterations conducted in quick succession doesn't give us what we might expect. Adjusting the number of iterations to 200 rather than 1 gives us results similar to Figure 9.7.

Not only are the performance results vastly different than those provided by our macro (64.9 vs. 36.8 inventory held, and 0% vs 9% stock-out rates), so is the overall character of the inventory level depiction recorded and graphed. So what happened? I have to honestly say that the first time I encountered something like this, I was little thrown. In part because I didn't expect it, and in part because I didn't have any immediate intuition as to why it was

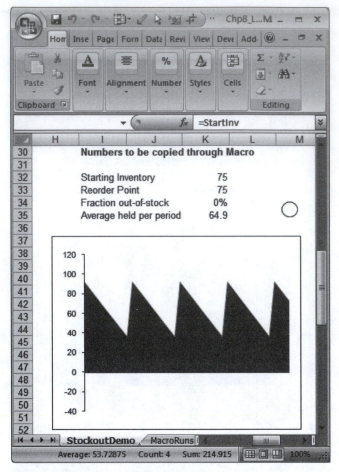

Figure 9.7. Example of unintended results of the application of multi-iteration mode.

happening. Looking carefully at the graph, it would seem as if a uniform set of calculations was taking place in repetition without the impact of newly (periodically) drawn random numbers. It seems as if any random number generation that we may have started with simply did not continue as iterations were being calculated.

But why would that happen? The answer lies with the way Excel views the application of iteration mode. Iteration mode largely exists to update cell calculations that are co-dependent on previous values contained within those same cells (or on other self-referencing cells that they in turn reference). In other words, iteration mode exists to allow for the iterative calculation of cells that are dependent on circular loops. Other cells that are not dependent on the system of circular referencing are simply not going to be updated multiple times when multi-iteration settings are on.

To illustrate, let's consider a much more simplified scenario where we simultaneously want to make use of both random number generation and some sort

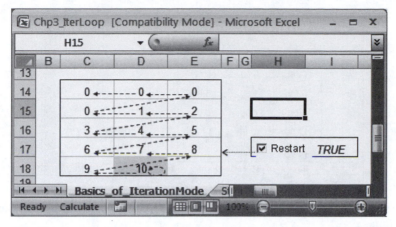

Figure 9.8. Previously depicted results of multiple iterations in a linked system.

of system evolution (and recordkeeping). To keep things simple we'll look at a variant of the first example we used back in Chapter 3 when introducing iteration mode. Recall the following table shown in Figure 9.8 used to illustrate how a simple one-point self-increment could be developed and propagated across a set of cells above or in the same row left of a self-referencing cell (again only when iteration mode is active).

First let's substitute the former contents of D18 (i.e., formerly containing =D18+1) with something that makes use of the random number generator (for example, =D18+RANDBETWEEN(1,5)). By doing so we retain the circularity so critical to the use of iteration mode in developing living records, while at the same time we allow for a random numbers-generating mechanism. At a single iteration setting, new random numbers are pulled and the record updated. A multi-iteration setting (10 iterations in quick succession) will update 10 cells in the rest of an otherwise empty table upon Restart, based on those 10 random pulls. The result is shown in Figure 9.9.

Close investigation of Figure 9.9 shows that the differences between the cells in the order of their tabulation differ in magnitude as would be expected with new random number draws (e.g., 21−18=2, 18−17=1, 17−13=4). So everything seems to be working as planned.

But imagine instead of generating the random number within the self reference call itself, we used =D18+K14 and placed =RANDBETWEEN(1,5) in cell K14. If we weren't considering the use of a multi-iteration setting and simply electing to use something like F9 to generate random numbers and propagate our living record, there would be no real difference observed in our results (10 hits of F9 in a single iteration setting would provide a table with similar variation between cells as that provided in Figure 9.9).

However, under a multi-iteration setting (again, 10 iterations in quick succession), this structure only generates a single random number. It will make

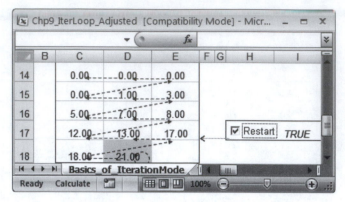

Figure 9.9. Demonstration of integrating random number generation into a circular loop system.

use of that same number throughout all cell updates in the table, but lack the kind of variation we would otherwise anticipate. We'd get the results shown in Figure 9.10.

Close inspection of Figure 9.10, using the external random number generation and reference and a multi-iteration setting, creates a table where the cells tabulated in order differ by exactly 4 (a single random pull between 1 and 5) throughout.

Why? Certainly cell D18 is still referencing itself, and all related cells depending on D18 would also be part of that circular dependency and thus subject to consideration during Excel's iteration-mode based updates. However, as stated earlier, random number generation (in cell K14 in this case) is not taking place in a cell that is dependent on a self-reference. It is being used by a cell that contains a self reference, but that doesn't matter to Excel. As far as the application is concerned, there is no obvious need to update this

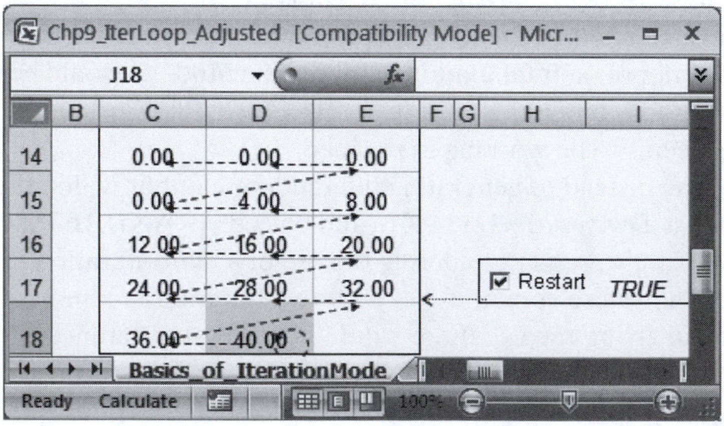

Figure 9.10. Propagation of random number whose generation is not part of a circular loop.

cell in accordance with the settings of iteration mode (i.e., the multi-iteration settings don't apply). Pressing F9 once forces 10 iterations of the cells in the table dependent on D18, but K14 is not dependent on any self-reference whatsoever and is updated only once (only one random number is pulled).

In part this is a nice way to distinguish the nuances of iterations (as specified in iteration mode for example) from that of recalculations in Excel (as activated by F9, for example). At the same time, the issue encountered is something that can easily be adjusted for. Here, if we need to make sure K14 contains a self reference to be included in the activities of iteration mode, why not just add a self reference to that cell? Something as simple as throwing in a +K14*0 (yes, itself times zero) would do the trick without having any impact whatsoever on the output of that cell. It's a simple tricking of the application, and may seem pointless from a purely mathematical perspective, but it is meaningful from an Excel logic perspective and the bottom line is that it gets the job done. Using this minor addition in multi-iteration mode will, in fact, give us exactly the kind of result we saw when the random number generation was embedded in cell D18.

Because this is precisely the kind of problem that the original version of the Lobos Inventory model faced when we attempted to use it in under a multi-iteration setting, the same kind of solution should apply. It is worth noting that because several calculations are dependent on the same randomly generated set of numbers, it does make sense that they be generated external to other calculations (e.g., if in a given period multiple calculations rely on a randomly generated lead time, they should all be referencing the same randomly generated lead time for that period). If an appropriate dummy self-reference term (such as K14*0 in the simpler example) is introduced into each random number generating cell, then the Inventory model will act exactly as would be desired under a multi-iteration setting. Chp9_LobosInventory_Adjusted includes this change (and that's the only change). The results under a 200-iteration setting are now comparable to the results provided by the macro (running in single iteration mode), as shown in Figure 9.11.

The only challenge left in using RISKOptimizer for system simulations is in ensuring that the system is Reset on the evaluation of each decision scenario (in this case, each combination of order-up-to point and another terms that might be viewed as potentially adjustable decisions, such as order quantity and even lead time averages if alternate carrier options exist at cost).

Note: What we have done here to capitalize on the multi-iteration setting has implications beyond a single simulation of this system. As we are about to discuss, such a capability can be useful in a search for optimal policy characteristics, but can also be useful in the comparison of a specific performance measure across a small discrete set of policies. Similar to the first example used on the Lobos Reservations case in

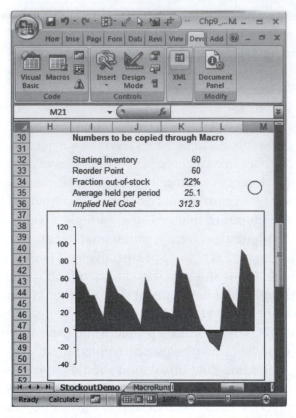

Figure 9.11. Possible spreadsheet setup for inventory system simulation optimization.

Chapter 8, the adjusted Inventory workbook can be modified to allow for proper Data Table tabulation across a discrete set of order-up-to levels. We would have to add an additional somewhat awkward conditional statement to Reset the system whenever iterations reached their limit (200 here), but otherwise we could use a similar procedure to that first discussed when introducing the Data Table tool to provide end-of-simulation values for comparison. Chp9_LIwDT_Adjusted provides an example of how this might be accomplished.

9.3.1 RISKOptimizer with Calls to a Reset Macro

To demonstrate how a Reset macro could be used in conjunction with RISKOptimizer for simulation optimization, let's first consider how we might actually develop such a macro. Basically we'll use the same approach we took when recording a macro in Chapter 8. All we want here is a macro that will set the value of the reset (or Restart) cell in the workbook (cell H18 in the inventory workbook) equal to False, let the spreadsheet recalculate the numbers, and then equal to True. That's all. And all we need to do to make such a macro is to start recording a new one, enter False into cell H18, press Enter, press F9, and then enter True into H18, again followed by pressing Enter and another F9 (just to get things started right). Stopping the recording at that

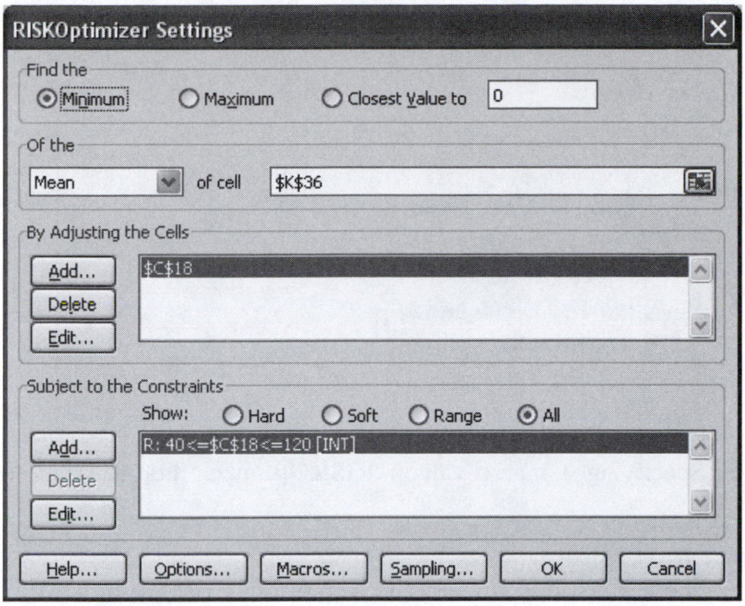

Figure 9.12. Specifying a macro call in RISKOptimizer before each solution is considered.

point will give use what we need to initialize each new investigation (i.e., this is basically the initialize system step denoted in the simulation flow charts in Chapter 8). In the discussion to follow, we'll assume we haven't been creative in naming the macro and have gone with the default label of Macro2 for this simple automation. (Note that this macro is already available in the Chp9_LobosInventory_Adjusted file.)

9.3.1.1 Use under a Multi-iteration Setting

To make the setup in RISKOptimizer as simple as possible, let's define a single objective that integrates the two costs represented in this system – holding costs and shortage costs. Let's just assume for now that every unit of inventory held per period on average costs twice the amount as the goodwill lost from each day that we are out of stock because we assume all customers will ultimately be served, albeit not instantaneously, via backorder. That is, let's create a Net Implied cost in cell K36 equal to 2*C35+C31. We'll use that sum as the objective function we're aiming to minimize. Because these two components of the cost function trade off against one another and are non-linear functions of our policy, it is likely that the combined objective function will be nonlinear as well with considerably high costs appearing at both ends of the reorder-point policy spectrum (another trait well suited to the use of RISKOptimizer).

What we specify to RISKOptimizer as far as the objective, decision variables, and constraints might be something as simple as shown in Figure 9.12,

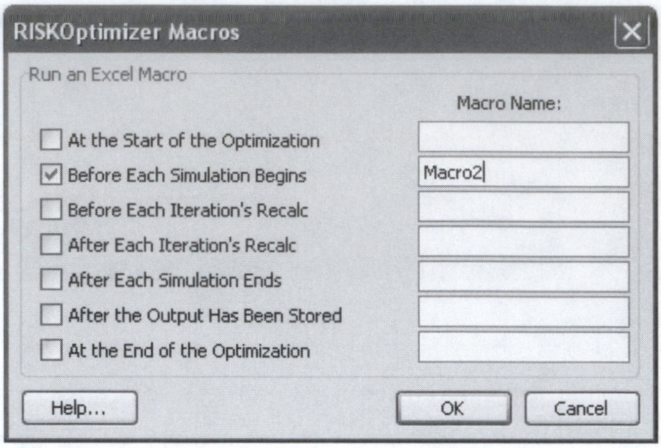

Figure 9.13. Specifying a macro call in RISKOptimizer before each solution is evaluated.

assuming we have reason to suspect the best policy exists somewhere between a reorder-point of 40 and 120, and the existing automatic calculation of reorder quantity in cell (C28) doesn't need reconsidering.

As far as making use of the Reset macro before simulating each alternative policy, we'll want to specify a little extra under the Macrosbutton in the RISKOptimizer Settings dialog box (Figure 9.12). Click this button to open the RISKOptimizer Macros dialog box, shown in Figure 9.13. We want the system to be reset before each new system simulation is run, so we'll specify exactly what is shown in the figure.

After one minute, given the objective and everything else specified in the system model, the best reorder-point solution found was around 60 (i.e., inventory reorders placed whenever the inventory level reaches or goes below 60 units). A graphical inspection of the simulation output log shown in Figure 9.14 provides the same overall observation.

9.3.1.2 Using RISKOptimizer's Built-in Iteration Mechanism

RISKOptimizer also provides an alternative mechanism for iterating us through the 200 periods with which we're interested. To demonstrate, our setup will involve making sure we are running Excel in single iteration mode (as opposed to multi-iteration mode). Instead we'll specify these 200 iterations by clicking the RISKOptimizer Options button to open the RISKOptimizer Options dialog box (Figure 9.15). As shown in the figure we'll specify 200 iterations in the Simulation Stopping Conditions section of the dialog box.

This essentially tells RISKOptimizer to recalculate the spreadsheet (i.e., pull random numbers, refresh totals, re-assess conditional statements,

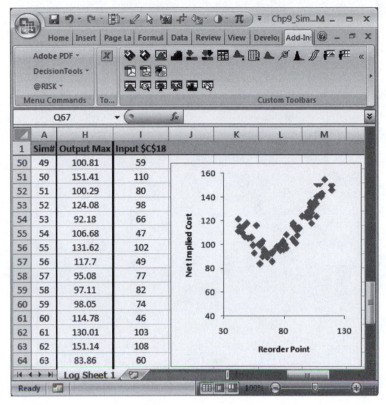

Figure 9.14. Reviewing nonlinearities inherent to the solution space encountered.

generate a new period's worth of data) 200 times before moving on to the consideration of an alternative solution.

At this point, our analysis approach needs to be a little tricky because RISKOptimizer is going to view every single iteration it generates as a possible policy outcome. This isn't exactly what we want because we know that in reality each iteration simply represents a single period, and performance in any one period may be extremely misleading (and highly variable). What we're interested in is average performance across the 200 periods. The average inventory held early on (e.g., periods 1 through 5) will tend to be very high compared to the average account after 200 periods. Furthermore, the number of periods of stock-out can never be more than the number of periods considered, thus early iterations by RISKOptimizer will also have much fewer of these than the final total after 200 iterations. RISKOptimizer's averages of the numbers it sees across all 200 of its iterations will therefore not reflect the ending values we would otherwise be recording for this system. Neither would the minimum or maximum values.

Although there's no easy way to cut out the earlier iterations of RISKOptimizer (as is fairly common practice in simulation analysis where starting

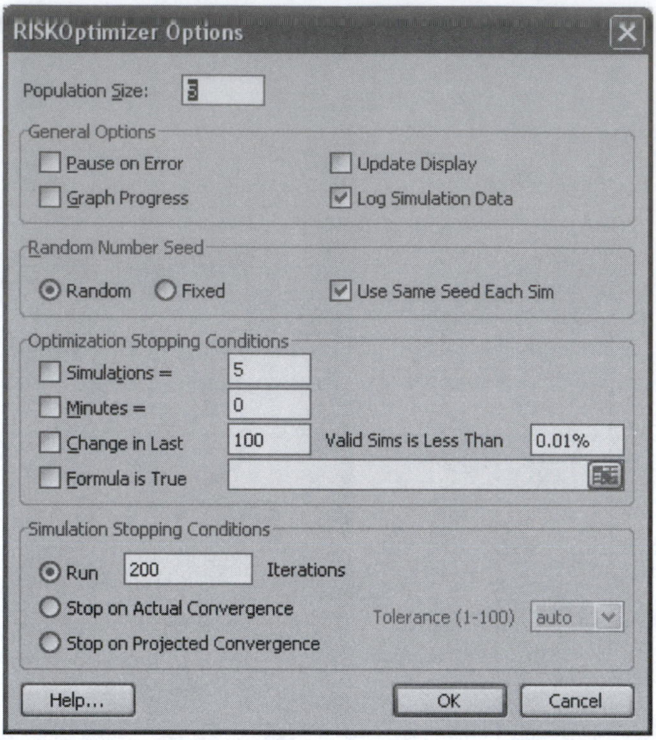

Figure 9.15. Specifying the use of RISKOptimizer iteration for a system simulation.

conditions are misleading), there are ways to cut out early numbers through directly modifying Excel calculations. In this case we could capitalize on our knowledge of how we're calculating our objective function to modify the averaging calculation in cell C35. We know the number of periods out-of-stock must be a nondecreasing function of time (i.e., that number can only increase as subsequent periods are iterated). We could, for example, substitute into cell C5 =IF(C32>=199,C34/C32,0) to make sure that the positive cost contributions of holding inventory are taken into account only in the objective function at the end of the 200 iterations. The Maximum (not the Average) values provided by the RISKOptimizer log will then be most representative of the kind of system summaries we're looking for. This doesn't help RISKOptimizer find best solutions for us per se, but it does help us make sense of the RISKOptimizer log for visual inspection of where best solutions may reside.

Note: Structuring objective functions differently than in this example could bypass such a less-than-ideal approach to capitalizing on RISKOptimizer's built-in iteration capabilities. Because we are mainly interested in simply demonstrating the nuances of RISKOptimizer her,e however, we'll leave such a consideration up to the intrepid reader.

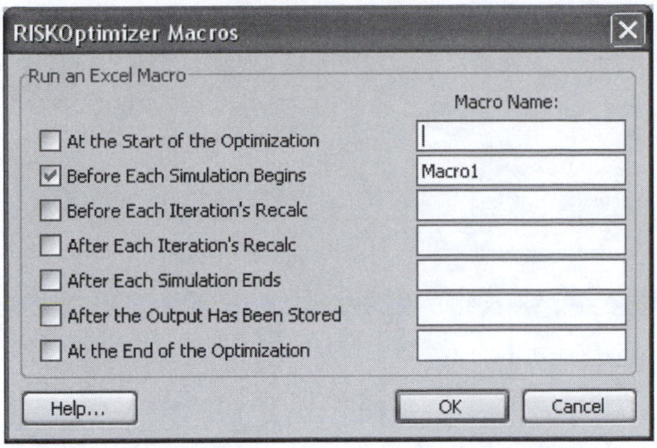

Figure 9.16. Alternate pre-evaluation macro call in RISKOptimizer.

9.3.2 RISKOptimizer with Calls to a Recalculation Macro

RISKOptimizer's macro calls can also be used to prompt the Visual Basic-driven iteration of the system across 200 periods (i.e., as made possible by the macro written in Chapter 8). To illustrate, we should again make sure that we are running in single iteration mode. Our setup in RISKOptimizer will be the same as in the previous example, as far as objective, decision variables, and constraints.

The nature of our macro calls will change. We'll want to initialize at the start, call our Macro1 from Chapter 8 (Figure 9.16) every time a new policy is considered, and then call our new reset function every time a simulation ends.

We might stop the optimization after one minute to see how we're doing. Figure 9.17 shows an example of the log of solutions considered during that one minute period, along with a graph describing the nature and variability of the relationship between the reorder-point policies considered and the objective function (Net Implied Cost). Given the objective and everything else specified in the system model, the best reorder-point solution found was around 61 (i.e., inventory reorders placed whenever the inventory level reaches or goes below 61 units). Note again that this is essentially the same answer we got in the past two approaches, validating in Excel the old adage . . . there's more than one way to skin a cat.

PRACTICE PROBLEM

Recall the project scheduling problem from Chp7_ProjectScheduling. In reality, the time to complete specific tasks can only be truly estimated and is automatically viewed as associated with some level of uncertainty. In each of the cells where

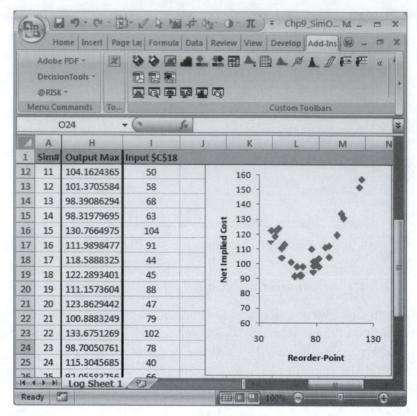

Figure 9.17. Again, reviewing nonlinearities inherent to the solution space encountered.

estimated completion times are being tabulated (E6:E15), introduce an additional term +RANDBETWEEN(1,4) to allow for the simulation of such uncertainty. Use a RISKOptimizer procedure similar to that originally applied in Chapter 7 for this problem, but additionally specify that 10 iterations (i.e., 10 simulated variants) are considered for every solution considered. After five minutes of run time, use the RISKOptimizer log to comment on the nature of the performance variability of the final solution suggested relative to other best solutions encountered along the way.

10

Visualizing Complex Analytical Dynamics

The visualization of analytical dynamics comes naturally to tools developed in Excel. This is largely due to the dynamic nature of graphs constructed in Excel. For example, if we wanted to depict the range of possible outcomes associated with specific decisions for which outcomes had a describable level of uncertainty or variation, it would be simple enough to introduce a random term into tabular forms of such estimates and then graph those tabular forms. As always, pressing the F9 key would simply draw another random number from the built-in generator, and augment associated data tables and plots to represent such the volatility of those outcomes.

For example, based on the Data Table generated in the Lobo's Reservations case, we could depict the variable nature of our results graphically using the high-low-close plot (tricked out a bit) provided in that workbook. Every time F9 is pressed we would see how much the variability in outcomes across policy types was subject to change (based simply on different separate and independent sets of random data draws). The result, as shown in Figure 10.1, would depict an alternative array of outcomes that could be associated with a set of decisions. Similarly with the second Data Table example in that case, shown in Figure 10.2.

This in itself might be entirely adequate in providing insights regarding the sufficiency of the number of variants examined. If the results don't change much, the best policy (or any possible relationship between associated outcomes) is probably well represented.

In this case the system being visualized is assumed to follow dynamics that are essentially devoid of memory; that is, systems where future conditions are independent of past conditions. But most systems in practice do have a memory of some kind. For that reason it is worth going over a few mechanisms through which to build memory into system visualizations. There are many forms of such memory, and the complexity of these forms ultimately impact the complexity and richness of the visualization to be designed. We'll start out with the simplest form and work our way up to more complex forms.

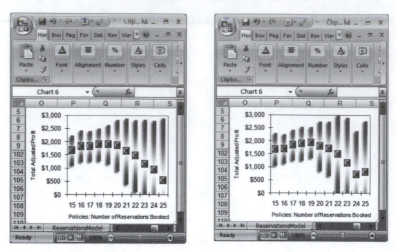

Figure 10.1. Profit variation graphed in two randomized (F9) instances.

10.1 Random Walks

One form of memory concerns position, or what we might call the state of an element within a system. Upon a single iteration, the state (or graphical position) of the element might change slightly. Even if the magnitude of the change is entirely independent of state, the new state represents a new starting point for any other change to follow. When changes are entirely random and independent but subsequent states are clearly linked to prior conditions, a random walk occurs. This is illustrated in Chp10_RandWalk&FrctnlessBox (Figure 10.3).

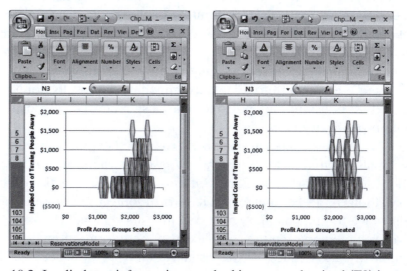

Figure 10.2. Implied cost information graphed in two randomized (F9) instances.

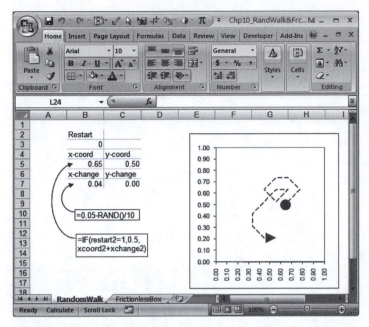

Figure 10.3. Example of random walk dynamics graphed.

Although seemingly uncharacteristic of common experience, there are many cases in which such models provide shockingly sufficient descriptions of the kind of dynamics we might observe in the real world – feeding patterns of pigeons, the physical meanderings of a drunken college student, the socio-ethical meanderings of sober financial professionals, and so on.

10.2 Frictionless Boxes

Some systems involve much more defined mechanisms for changes in the state of an element. This could be called directional or trajectory memory. In such cases, both current state and directional tendencies are critical in determining future states and trajectories. The simplest example of this is a frictionless box where an element set in transitional motion maintains its trajectory until certain boundary conditions are met. It then partially reverses its trajectory (ricochets) based on what boundary condition is met. An illustration of this is provided in Chp10_RandWalk&FrctnlessBox and shown in Figure 10.4.

Once again, although a zero loss of energy or momentum seems unlikely as characteristic of mechanical systems, prior trajectory dependency and deflection responses in general are common characteristics of many physical, social, and economic systems. It wouldn't take much to incorporate features such as loss of momentum or additional more complex boundaries (for deflection) into this kind of a model.

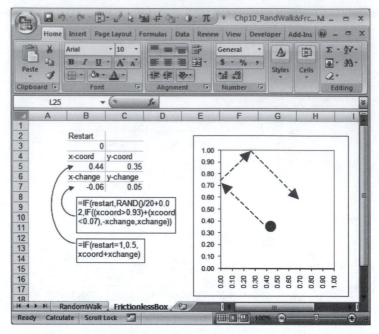

Figure 10.4. Example of frictionless box dynamics graphed.

10.3 Path-Directed Flows

The notion of systems that retain memories of both state and direction opens the door to still more complex and potentially meaningful graphical visualizations, including those that retain memories of progress between states along much more nuanced trajectories. For example, consider the visual simulation provided in the Chp10_Lobos FloorPlan workbook (see Figure 10.5).

As in the previous examples presented in this book, opening this workbook and holding down the F9 key will allow the visual simulation to cycle through. Seeing this in action, an initial reaction might be to view this as far beyond the skill of someone just getting the hang of developing tools in Excel. But the building block and ideas on which this visualization is based are straightforward. We've actually covered them all in one form or another already.

Pasting images in place of scatter plot points (the images of the waiters and mariachis in Figure 10.5 are just points in a scatter plot)

Pasting a background for a plot (that's the restaurant backdrop).

The apparent motion of the points along paths; there's the iteration mode at work, again used in the evolution of a living record, in conjunction with the transition matrix concept introduced in Chapter 8 and a little bit of careful graphical design.

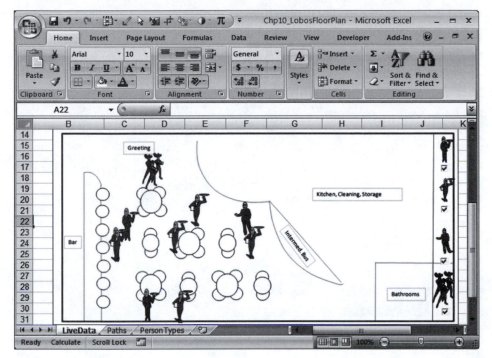

Figure 10.5. Example of multi-element path-movement by graph.

Easier said than done? There is some complexity in this last point, but like all processes, it's not something that can't be broken up into a set of logical steps.

10.3.1 An Introduction to Visualizing Path-directed Flows

Let's take a look at a somewhat more simple illustration of how these tools are used together. (We'll get back to the specifics of this particular example in a bit.) At this point let's not attempt to take into consideration physical proximity in the graphics. To keep it simple, let's just represent the three steps/states of a process as three points plotted to a graph. For structure we'll make use of the same transition matrix example introduced in Chapter 8. In the Chp10_TransMatrixRvstd workbook, the worksheet labeled TransMatrix+StateChangePlot (Figure 10.6) provides the same structure as discussed in Chapter 8 with the addition of only a few new elements.

The additions include three sets of x–y coordinates (in various shades of gray) to spatially distinguish the three states on a scatter plot, as well as a pair of x–y coordinates based on that set of three that specifically captures what state a job resides in at any point in time. Holding down the F9 key updates the tabular data as before, but now also provides a visual representation of job progress between these states.

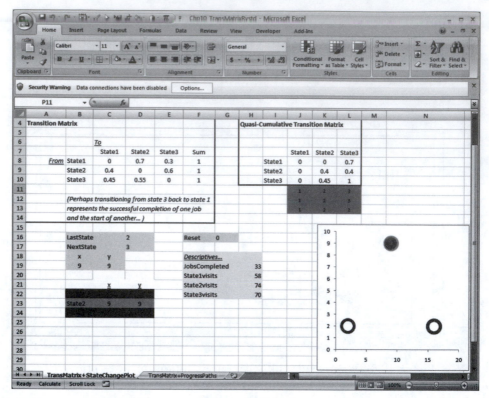

Figure 10.6. A simple state-to-state transition plot.

Although informative, such a visual is still somewhat limiting in its capability to depict flow. Instantaneous movement between states is generally difficult to keep track of visually in this manner, particularly in cases where multiple jobs may be transitioning among the same states at the same time. More gradual progress between transitional states often proves more useful in these kinds of system simulations.

10.3.2 *Visualizing Progress along Paths*

To provide a visualization of transitional progress over much more visually complex paths, we can fall back upon the kinds of capabilities discussed when we introduced scatter plots in Chapter 4. These plots are constructed based on a series of data points. In many cases, the ordering of these points are irrelevant to analysis; in other cases, such as those associated with transitions between states within a process, their ordering is critical to intuitive understanding.

Let's start by considering a single path structure described by a set of x–y coordinates. We'll pick a simple path structure to begin with, for example that of a circular or oval path. For aesthetic purposes we'll illustrate this with a depiction of the Earth moving in orbit around the sun (see workbook

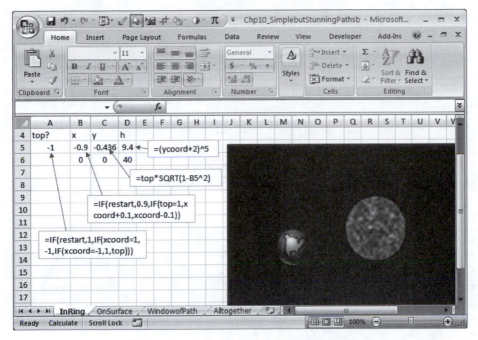

Figure 10.7. Simple nonlinear path dynamics.

Chp10_SimplebutStunningPaths.) In this case the illustration is constructed through the use of a bubble plot and further augmented through the manipulation of size of bubble Earth as it moves along the path.

As shown in Figure 10.7, the path itself is nothing more than an application of the equation of a unit circle ($y = +/- \mathrm{sqrt}(1-x^2)$) in iteration mode, with the value of x changing in small increments either positively or negatively depending on whether the right or left boundaries of the circular path have been reached. The squashed appearance of the circular path is nothing more than an artifact of the squashed nature of the vertical scale.

As can be seen through opening the workbook example and holding down the F9 key, subsequent iterations provide the appearance of the Earth moving in front of the sun and then dipping into the background as it travels to lower and lower y-coordinates in the plot (see Figure 10.8).

Although this may be a decent illustration of technical capabilities, it is still a fairly limited example as far as practical application is concerned. To get more practical, we could capitalize on our knowledge of transition

Figure 10.8. Several phases of a nonlinear path dynamic graph.

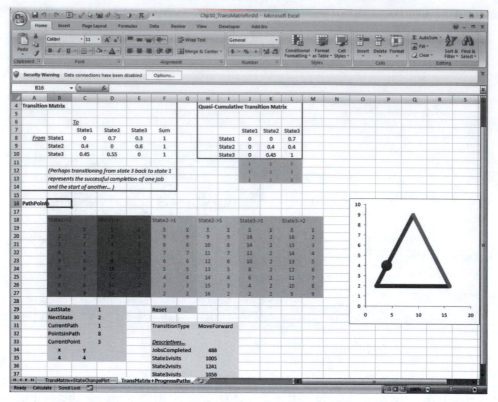

Figure 10.9. The introduction of paths to a simple transition flow graph.

matrices to merge multiple paths into a system depiction over which progress between states can be monitored. Referring once again to the three-state transition matrix example, the TransMatrix+ProgressPaths worksheet (Figure 10.9) provides a further extension where individual points between the spatially represented states are specified. These points outline straight-line paths between these states – i.e., positions of jobs along the paths represent progress in the transition between any two states. Because progress may be either forward (e.g., 1 to 2) or backward (2 to 1) we have six sets of x–y coordinates (three of which are simply reversals of the other three).

Additional features include cells that keep track of which of six paths a job is on, how many total points of progress exist along each path (eight in all cases here), as well as how far the job has progressed along it's path (referenced here as CurrentPoint).

Here the x–y location of the job is dependent directly on path information; specifically a column (path) and row (progress on path) OFFSET reference (see associated worksheet). On each iteration, a job progresses along the current path until it reaches the last point on that path. At that point, the same lookup mechanism initially introduced for determining what next state will

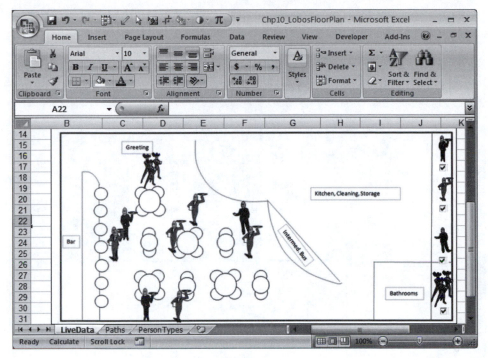

Figure 10.10. Revisiting the multi-element path-movement example.

be transitioned into is used. In iteration mode this is followed immediately by the designation of the next appropriate path and a resetting of the path progress (CurrentPoint record) to 1. As before, F9 demonstrates the iterative progress in this example.

10.3.3 Custom Path Visualizations: Lobo's Floor Plan Revisited

In some cases, the graphical specification of path structures may be pre-established or extremely straightforward in terms of laying out x and y coordinates within a table. For example, perhaps changes in performance follow the arc of a production possibilities frontier or some set of conceptually and practically meaningful mathematical constraints. In many real world simulations, however, the kind of dynamic path movement that is most telling relates to much more complex forms that aren't easily described by a series of formulations. Some of these are based on spatial considerations (e.g., internal or external physical infrastructures of facilities; others may be designed to represent transitions that are conceptually diverse and complex (e.g., representing the processing of new design ideas as opposed to the assembly of prototypes by design, or the retooling of staff in preparation for new work deployment). For example, let's consider an example from earlier in this chapter (Figure 10.10).

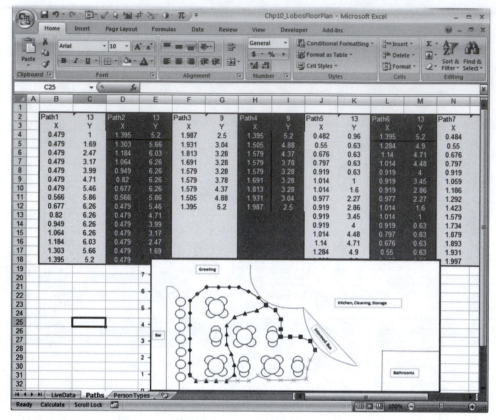

Figure 10.11. Paths specification associated with flow depicted.

Ultimately, this is really nothing more than a more complex variant of the path types we've discussed. In this particular example, to organize what would otherwise be a fairly difficult to manage set of spreadsheet calculations, we are making use of three sheets in a single workbook. One of these sheets simply contains the set of x–y coordinates that specify the pathways that elements can move along in the graph (Figure 10.11).

The visual shown in Figure 10.11 is nothing more than a scatter plot graph containing a line-linked presentation of that tabular data, superimposed on a graphic of a restaurant blueprint. (Approaches to massaging this set of coordinates to fit neatly with the natural paths of a scanned blueprint are discussed in the Chapter 10 supplement.)

On the PersonTypes worksheet shown in Figure 10.12, I specify the transition matrices relevant to this graphical simulation. In this case these matrices specify the probability of an individual shifting onto an alternate path upon completion of the one they are currently on. The same lookup mechanism used to determine where to go next based on a random number pull in the

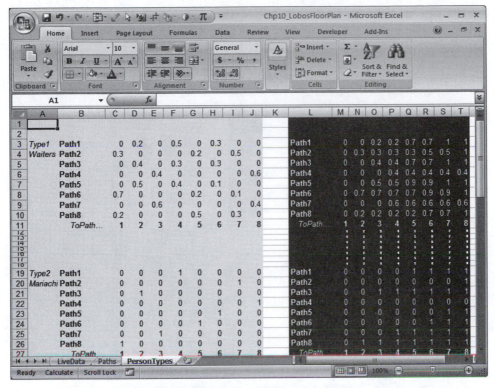

Figure 10.12. Paths specification associated with flow depicted.

earlier three-state example is used here with eight instead of three states. Here we're drawing on the concept of stochastic processes introduced at the end of Chapter 8.

Different people may be described by different types of movement, and so the transition matrices of the busboys are not the same as that of the manager or the mariachi band, for example. Along with these transition matrices are cumulative matrices that are used when Excel actually needs to look up on what next random path the person will embark.

The main page (LiveData, shown in Figure 10.13) is the most complex, and is therefore fully annotated, complete with red triangles on the column headers. Ultimately the logic used there is no more complex than the structures discussed in the examples of the iteration mode. The complexity comes into play only when you consider how all of these elements and techniques come together to form a single integrated system. Of course the caveat here is that even the coolest (or simplest) graphics can get messy at times. When complete graphical depictions limit the capability to get a point across or come to an understanding, partial depictions of representative or critical data are more useful.

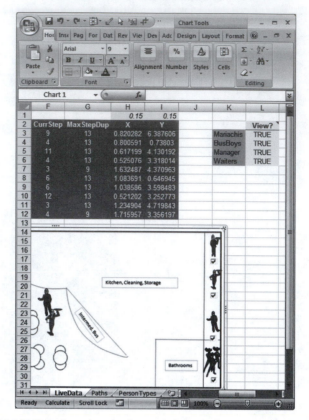

Figure 10.13. Pruning visuals through leveraging the ranges of graphs.

Along these lines, another handy feature of this example is the use of controls to helps provide a graphical pruning mechanism, again with the intent of focusing on only specific elements of the dynamic visualization. Here we see the addition of a toggle associated with each type of entity class (i.e., the waiters, the busboys) that can set to TRUE or FALSE (i.e., 1 or 0). If TRUE, the entities in that class show up somewhere along their associated paths; If FALSE their X–Y coordinates are set to $(-1, -1)$ and therefore out of range for the graph (they don't appear on the portion of the graph that we view). It's a bit of a fake-out, but it gets the job done. Plus it allows for the development of other more sophisticated pruning interfaces (e.g., control-based check boxes as introduced in Chapter 8 supplement).

Chapter 10 Supplement: Visually Derived Paths

Rather than trying to change the visual depiction of these paths through modifying the coordinates in tables, we could rely on alternative visual techniques for path adjustments and design.

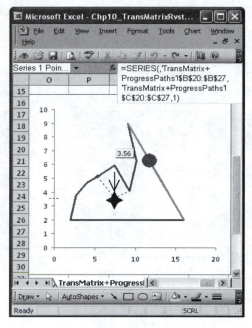

Figure 10.14. Manipulating plotted fixed-value points.

Plot-pulled Extractions

One way involves making use of the graphed-data manipulation discussed in Chapter 4. Depending on your version of Excel, this approach may or may not be available; it is certainly available in the 2003 version. Once again, using the three-state example for illustration, all you need is to select a specific path (set of data) within the graph, select a specific point to adjust, and pull either horizontally or vertically on that point (assuming it related to fixed data rather than a function) until it is in more visually representative location (see Figure 10.14).

System visualizations set up the way we have outlined in this chapter need no more changes for these plot-pulled manipulations to become effective.

In the case of the Lobo's floor plan example, I actually used this very technique. I started with a set of points (0,0), (1,1), (2,2) and then plotted them in a scatter chart. At that point, they're just a single straight line. After choosing the restaurant layout as a background picture for the plot, I started selecting each of those points and pulling them into positions that roughly corresponded to what might be commonly traveled paths within the restaurant layout; for example, note that people don't appear to be passing through walls or over tables in Figure 10.15.

In truth, it takes time to make things seem well spaced. As with the three-state example, some paths on the page are simply the same points of existing paths placed in the opposite sequence (i.e., representing travel in the opposite

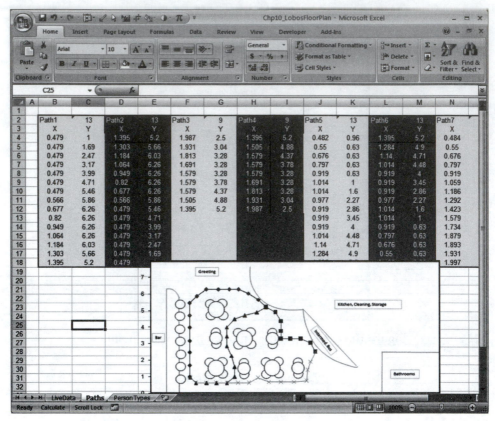

Figure 10.15. Revisiting the point-structure used in the floor plan example.

direction of a given path). To save time when creating these reverse paths, I simply set the first point on the reverse path equal to the cell reference for the last point on the forward path, the second point equal to the cell reference for the second last point on the forward path, and so on. This soft referencing allowed for any later changes to the original path without having to make subsequent changes to the reverse version.

Drawn-path Extractions

A very different alternative approach is to simply draw a path using the drawing objects available through Excel and then extracting coordinate information from the drawn lines. If you have a rough idea of what you want the path to look like, you can use the freeform, curve, or scribble options in the Shapes drop-down menu (Insert>Shapes). If you want the path to approximate a designated blueprint of some sort, there's no need to first insert that blueprint into a graph. When available in Excel, you can simply draw your path over the inserted picture.

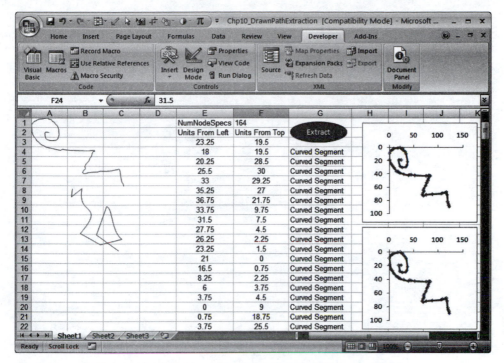

Figure 10.16. Path-point data extracted from a scribble.

Regardless, the real trick is in getting the structure of those drawn paths into a tabular form of which your visual simulation can make use. Unlike plot-pulling approaches, which require a tabular structure, no coordinate data associated with drawn lines is automatically linked to the spreadsheet. Fortunately there are some simple VB codes that can be used to get the data you'll need. The workbook labeled Chp10_VisuallyDerivedPaths also contains a worksheet that demonstrates how coordinate data can be extracted from a variety of drawn paths. Figures 10.16 and 10.17 provide two examples of tabular sets of coordinates extracted from two very difference drawn paths, along with subsequent scatter plots that validate the extraction process.

The following code provides a mostly foolproof approach to extracting path-point data from either of these kinds of drawn paths.

```
Sub ExtractPoints_from_DrawnLine()
    Columns("A:I").ClearContents
    Range("E1") = "NumNodeSpecs"
    Range("F1") = Selection.ShapeRange.Nodes.Count 'Number of node records
            'in in freeform record. Includes curvature data if any.
    Range("E2") = "Units From Left"
    Range("F2") = "Units From Top"
```

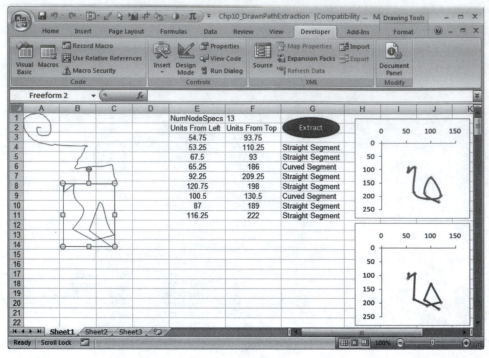

Figure 10.17. Path-point data extracted from a freeform with added curvature.

```
NumTruNodes = 0
For Count = 1 To Selection.ShapeRange.Nodes.Count
    NumTrueNodes = NumTrueNodes + 1
    If NumTrueNodes > 1 Then
        If Selection.ShapeRange.Nodes.Item(Count).SegmentType = 0 Then
                        'Check whether node starts a straight line segment
            Range("G3").Offset(NumTrueNodes - 1) = "Straight Segment"
        Else 'Otherwise, "jump over" curvature data built into freeform record
            Count = Count + 2 'Note: Not typical within a For loop, but an easy
                        'solution in this case
            Range("G3").Offset(NumTrueNodes - 1) = "Curved Segment"
        End If
    End If
    Range("E3:F3").Offset(NumTrueNodes - 1) = _
                Selection.ShapeRange.Nodes.Item(Count).Points
    Next
End Sub
```

For those not interested in learning how to work with Visual Basic code, the program is available for use in Chp10_DrawnPathExtraction, and can be executed on any line drawn in that workbook.

For those who are interested in leveraging the full capabilities of Excel (given that you've gotten this far), as we are about to see in our discussion of the VB Editor environment (Chapter 11), the code can also be copied and pasted into other workbooks, manipulated and expanded upon for more advanced applications.

Section 4

Advanced Automation and Interfacing

11

VB Editing and Code Development

Many effective decision support systems rely not only on the ability of a manager to present information, analysis, and meaningful dynamics (e.g., through graphics), but also on enabling users to realize the intended use of those elements by themselves (without the developer holding their hand).

This is often going to mean providing sufficient documentation that might go beyond just cell labeling and embedded comments.

It may mean coming up with some kind of a customized user-driven help or wizard component as part of the DSS that makes use of not only automated numerical and graphical demos, but also makes dynamic use of other objects such as the images and .wav files that could be incorporated into the workbook.

And often this is going to mean a level of automation that stretches the limits of the kind of work that can happen at the spreadsheet interface alone. In fact, it may be impossible to achieve by using just the top layer of an Excel workbook.

Let's see how macros and the Visual Basic (VB) Editor might provide us with some new options in this regard.

11.1 The Visual Basic Editor

Let's take a deeper look into one of the first macros we introduced. Opening the Chp8_LobosInventory workbook provides us with an opportunity here. To see the code associated with this macro, select the Developer tab on the main menu bar and then select Visual Basic (which will open the general VB Editor screen) or click Macros (see Figure 11.1) and from the associated dialog box select the specific name of the program code you are interested in viewing (in this case, generically called Macro1) and then Edit.

The VB Editor in Excel has its own distinct structure (fairly distinct from that of the Excel spreadsheets). Because any given macro may be specific to

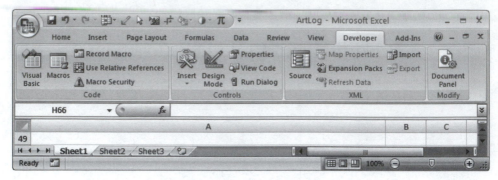

Figure 11.1. The Developer tab and associated elements.

a single workbook, worksheet, or even refer to an included add-in (such as Solver), the VB Editor provides a mechanism to categorize the macros that are associated with any workbook currently open in Excel. That mechanism is the Project window that appears to the left of the VB Editor interface (shown in Figure 11.2).

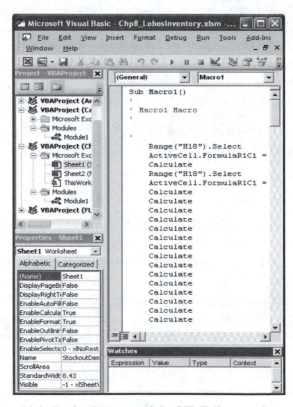

Figure 11.2. Basic elements of the VB Editor environment.

11.1.1 Confronting Code

The critical feature of the VB Editor is the code window (shown to the right of the Project Window in Figure 11.2). In this and all cases discussed in this text, the code we're interested in will be stored in the Modules folder in the VBA project window. If you don't see any code at this point, open that folder and double-click on Module1. The code associated with the Chapter 8 workbook should now appear. When you record a macro, this is precisely the kind of stuff Excel writes for future reference (i.e., for repeating or editing the actions you've recorded). This is also where all ground-up code development takes place (in lieu of macro recording). This is a useful point, in part because not all useful code can simply be generated through macro recording alone.

Admittedly it's probably one of the most intimidating areas for new developers, particularly those without computer programming backgrounds. But don't give up yet. As an experiment, let's try to interpret the language Excel and the VB Editor use to keep track of some of the actions we may have recorded. Table 11.1 shows an abridged and annotated version of the code written and used in the Chapter 8 example.

Again I've fully annotated the code (the text in Table 11.1 is not actually present in the code itself), but even if you didn't have this annotation, do you think you could have guessed what some of these lines did? Some are fairly obvious, or at least suggestive (e.g., Range("H18").Select, Selection.Copy, or Selection.EntireRow.Insert). VB capitalizes on simple elements of the English language, making it easy for even laypersons to navigate. Some code is more cryptic, but in general we could get a sense of what's happening here by attempting to read through the code as if it were steps in a set of cooking instructions.

The bottom line is this – you'll find that recording and editing macros is one of the best ways for non-computer programmers to learn to do some amazing things with code (perhaps more so in Excel 2003, but still very handy in Excel 2007).

11.1.2 Checking for Bugs

There are resources available to help pinpoint where things go wrong in code, and believe me they will, again and again and again. For every minute that beginning (and even advanced) developers spend on coding, they may find themselves spending about that same amount of time (often much more) figuring out where they went wrong and what they can do to resolve it. There are a few features available that can help in this process.

The first feature is the ability to "step-through" a macro line by line, as opposed to just letting a macro run until it ends (or breaks down). In VB Editor, after a specific macro is selected and the blinking line cursor appears

Table 11.1. *Annotation and Code for Chapter 8 Example*

Annotation	Actual Code
Name/Start of macro	Sub Macro1()
	'
Notes	' Macro1 Macro
	'
Selection of active cell	Range("H18").Select
Specifying "reset/reinitialize"	ActiveCell.FormulaR1C1 = "FALSE"
Call to Recalc (e.g., F9) to reset	Calculate
Reselection of active cell	Range("H18").Select
Specifying "start simulation"	ActiveCell.FormulaR1C1 = "TRUE"
Call to Recalc to iterate	Calculate
	Calculate
	Calculate
~200 of the same lines (for 200 periods iterated	:
	Calculate
	Calculate
Select key cells	Range("K32:K35").Select
Copy them as a set	Selection.Copy
Select the "record" sheet	Sheets("MacroRuns").Select
Select a starting cell there	Range("B2").Select
Paste the copied cells there (note that the "_" is used to denote code statement continuation on next line)	Selection.PasteSpecial Paste:=xlPasteValues, Operation:=xlNone, _SkipBlanks:=False, Transpose:=True
	Application.CutCopyMode = False
Insert new row in anticipation of next record paste	Selection.EntireRow.Insert
	Sheets("StockoutDemo").Select
End of macro	End Sub

in the code (e.g., as for editing), pressing the F8 key will step the developer through the code line by line. Each line will be highlighted in yellow, signifying that the particular line of code has just been or is being processed. A yellow arrow also appears at the side bar of the code window to emphasize the current line (see Figure 11.3).

As an alternative to using F8, some developers prefer to allow larger macros to run for a longer segment of code and stop only for checking when specific points of interest are reached. Those specific points are often chosen by developers because there is some intuitive feeling that something around that point is likely to cause some problem (i.e,. something has either just recently had the possibility of going wrong, or is about to). To insert these breakpoints, the developer can select the line of code of interest, right-click, and select Toggle>Breakpoint (see Figure 11.4). The line then gets shaded maroon and

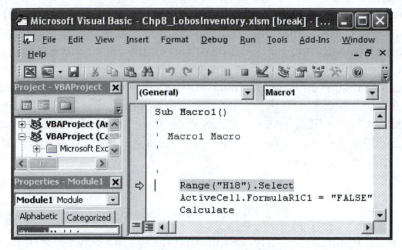

Figure 11.3. Step-through code execution.

a maroon circle appears to the left of the code. Another fast way is to select a line of code and press F9 in the VB Editor, or still more simply by toggling breakpoints on and off by clicking on the bar area immediately to the left of the code.

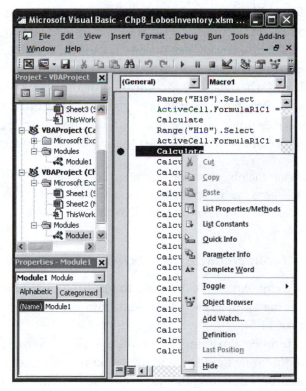

Figure 11.4. Toggling breakpoints in code.

There can be as many breakpoints as there are lines to a code (although there would be little point in adding so many). When added, the developer can start a macro run in the VB Editor (using the Play button). The macro will run up until each breakpoint and then stop until the next breakpoint is reached, the macro ends, or the macro breaks down because of a processing error. At each break, the developer has the opportunity to check what the spreadsheet looks like, and even check on the status of some of the data maintained by the macro (which can provide a wealth of insights that we'll discuss later in this chapter).

11.2 Object Manipulations

At this point it should be fairly obvious that there are many other objects you might encounter, construct, or manipulate aside from just cells in a workbook. Objects such as graphs, buttons, and clips of various types can reside within a workbook, and may ultimately serve as the primary vehicles for users to interface with a DSS. Yet as with cells there's often much more to these objects than you might first expect.

Similar to cells, all objects have a certain set of properties that can be manipulated. Many developers refer to the full set of properties of any object as a record, although the structure and content of those records may be very different depending on the objects. For example, objects such as check boxes are specifically designed to possess properties that a simple circle drawing would not. Check boxes contain a property that describes the cell to which they are linked, and whether they are checked or not checked, for instance. At the same time, simple circle drawings possess other attributes like line-type that check boxes don't (at least not in an identical form). Regardless of these nuances, there are some properties that all of these objects share:

Name/Label: What the object can be referenced as
Location (x,y): Where the object is located in a spreadsheet
Visualization (e.g., size, color, and shading): What it looks like

11.2.1 Incorporating External Objects into Workbooks

Let's see what we can expect if we decide to import a picture into our work-book. Start by going to Insert>Picture and then browsing for an image to import (see Figure 11.5).

For my own reference, I'm going to rename this object SampleImage (using the same labeling/naming field I would use to name cells and cell ranges). In doing so I'm essentially updating the name attribute of that image. The image is shown in Figure 11.6.

Figure 11.5. Importing pictures into Excel.

Note that when the picture is selected in Excel, the Picture toolbar displays at the top of Excel. The items on that toolbar represent other attributes of that object's data record (e.g., color, brightness, orientation, size, line thickness).

You can also insert other kinds of audio-visual objects, such as sound and video clips (generally found under the Object button through the Insert tab in Excel 2007, see Figure 11.7). We can edit elements of a sound clip (e.g., where we want it to start or stop) in the same way that we could edit different attributes of imported images. Figures 11.8 and 11.9 display the subsequent object selection and specification steps associated with inserting a wave sound object, for example.

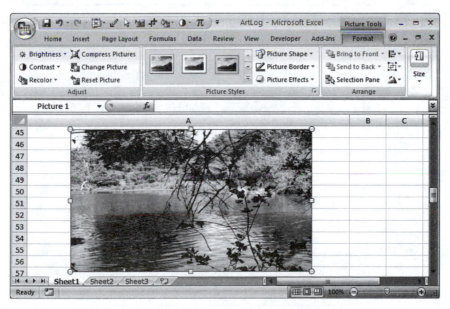

Figure 11.6. Example of picture import and available editing tools.

Figure 11.7. Access to general object importation.

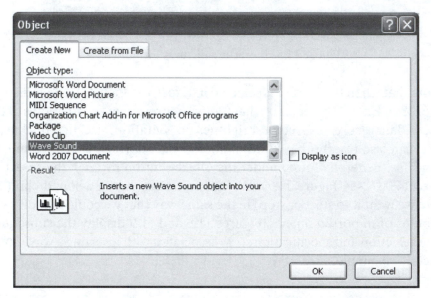

Figure 11.8. Navigating the object import selection interface.

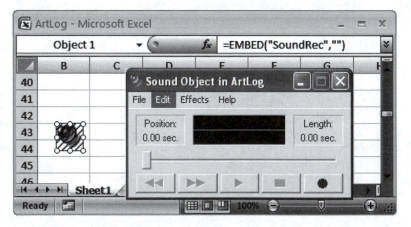

Figure 11.9. Working with imported .wav file objects.

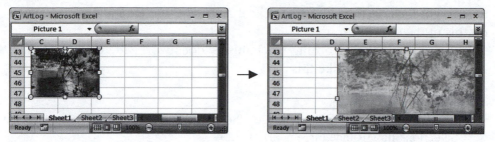

Figure 11.10. Editing a picture object while recording a macro.

For future reference, I'm going to use the labeling/naming field to rename this object as SoundClip. At this point it might also be worth inserting an actual sound file into the newly created template, using the Edit>Insert File option in the dialog box depicted in Figure 11.9 (to re-access the dialog box just right-click on the newly imported object and selecting Open from the shortcut menu).

11.2.2 Object Macros

Given our existing discussions on the development of macros for repeating common actions, let's use one of the new objects we've imported to see what Excel will allow us to record on objects rather than just cells. Pick any random cell on the spreadsheet. To make sure that the object is not yet selected, we want to record the selection as well). Then start recording by selecting Macros>Record Macro to open the Record Macro dialog box. Enter a name for your macro, such as ImageMacro, and then click OK.

While we're recording, let's try some simple manipulations of the imported image. For example, we might select the image and drag it to the right. We might then pull on one of the corners of the image to expand it a little. Then maybe click the Brightness button in the Picture toolbar a few times to lighten things up. The results are shown in Figure 11.10.

Now let's stop the recording. Try to play your macro by going to the Developer tab (in Excel 2007), selecting Macros as before. This time select the macro of choice and hit Run. If the actions are repeated perfectly, you're probably using either Excel 2003 or a patched version of Excel 2007. If nothing happens, it may be a function of the version of Excel 2007 you are using.

Here is some good news for Excel 2007 users. If you create a macro that manipulates objects (such as pictures) in a previous version of Excel (e.g., Excel 2003) and then use that file in Excel 2007, it should work. Alternatively, if you know the code enough to create a macro that manipulates an object from the ground up using the built-in Visual Basic Editor, you should still be able to get those actions to run in Excel 2007. We will take a look at how to do this in the next section.

In any case, if the recording mechanisms does work, the code recorded should look something like this:

```
Sub Macro1()
    ActiveSheet.Shapes("SampleImage").Select
    Selection.ShapeRange.IncrementLeft 120#
    Selection.ShapeRange.ScaleWidth 2.35, msoFalse, msoScaleFromTopLeft
    Selection.ShapeRange.ScaleHeight 2.34, msoFalse, msoScaleFromTopLeft
    Selection.ShapeRange.PictureFormat.IncrementBrightness 0.03
    Selection.ShapeRange.PictureFormat.IncrementBrightness 0.03
    Selection.ShapeRange.PictureFormat.IncrementBrightness 0.03
End Sub
```

No annotation here, and I'm not going to spend much time walking through this code because it's fairly clear what each line is getting at if you just spend a just few seconds reading through them. For example, some lines clearly have to do with the selection of the object in question (in this case, the image); others clearly pertain to manipulations of the location of the object, the size of the object, and the brightness of the object.

Nevertheless it's worth pointing out at least one less intuitive structure. Specifically, VB actually has a range of Location(x,y) change commands for objects, although in this particular case the VB Editor has defaulted to the use of the command IncrementLeft for the horizontal movement recorded (IncrementTop would be the associated command for vertical movement). When the IncrementLeft command is used, it means that the left edge of the object will be moved a certain horizontal distance. When moved to the right, that distance will be positive (+); when moved to the left, it will be negative (−). So in this case, the code would actually move the object to the right, just like I did during the original recording in Excel 2003. This is a case where the designed use of language-rich syntax doesn't hit home as intuitively as one might have hoped. Just something to get used to.

Perhaps surprisingly, in contrast the code representing the activation and playing of the sound clip is much simpler than the graphic manipulation. Table 11.2 shows the annotated the code clip. It's nice to see that only two lines are really relevant here.

It is worth pointing out that in both of the image movement and sound clip cases, there is considerable reference to something called selection. The IncrementLeft 120# action seems to be just a feature of the selection in the first case, while the Verb Verb:=xlPrimary seems to be a feature associated with the selection in the second case. Both are actually functional attributes

Table 11.2. *Annotation and Code for Basic Clip Play Macro*

Annotation	Actual Code
Name/Start of macro	Sub Macro2()
	'
Notes	' Macro1 Macro
	'
Selection of wave object	ActiveSheet.Shapes("SoundClip").Select
Play sound clip	Selection.Verb Verb:=xlPrimary
Call to Recalc (eg. F9) to reset	End Sub

that apply only to certain kinds of objects. We know they are associated with objects selected because of the use of a period (.) to link their use to the key term selection in all cases. The use of this period will become increasingly familiar to you as a developer as you encounter more and more advanced codes (either ones that you've recorded, been given, or write from the ground up). In actuality this serves a little like the period in the Dewey decimal system used at libraries to get into increasingly more specific features of a larger category of attributes (or drawing on our Principal Components Analysis discussion, it's a bit like specifying how each individual item relates to a higher level factor). This notation can be used in both constructing data storage mechanisms in VB (i.e., items called records) as well as in other functionality that comes standard with selections.

11.3 Syntax and Coding

Now that you've got a taste of what you can record using Excel macros and VB code, we're ready to talk about the basic standards in VB. Literally, all macros/subroutines/programs typically start with the following in the VB Editor.

Sub SubroutineName () 'whatever name you want to use

And end with the following:

End Sub 'always the same regardless of the macro

Everything between those two lines represents what will take place (or could take place, as we'll see in a moment) when the macro/subroutine is run. Remember that we can start the run of any macro directly from the Excel workbook interface by going to Macros>View Macros>Run or by assigning a macro to an object such as a control button or image we've created or imported.

11.3.1 Intro to VB Variables and Types

One of the first things you might want to do in developing a new subroutine to run in Excel is define any variables that you want the VB Editor to keep track of outside of the spreadsheets of the workbook. In other words, we're talking about data that isn't actually stored in any of the cells of the workbook. There are a number of reasons why you might want to temporarily store data this way.

Referencing and modifying data that's present in the cells of spreadsheets actually takes a little longer than doing the same with data stored only by the VB Editor during run-time. If you have a lot of data that you plan to access and base simple calculations on, that can really make a difference in the amount of time it takes for the program to run. You may not want to do this for all the data you use in the workbook; it makes sense to have some of it stored in spreadsheet form, for example if you want to make sure it's retained when you save the workbook. But for some data, this kind of virtual storage comes in handy – at this point I don't expect you to be able to make that distinction.

Also, some data takes on a structure that may be difficult or cumbersome to meaningfully store in spreadsheet format. For example, let's say we want to run some kind of a simulation that takes into account all the restaurant franchises in a niche market that exist in each of the 48 contiguous states. Based on historical data, some franchises open whereas others close over time. Imagine that for the ease of certain calculations we want to make sure our data remains sorted by state and restaurant chain. Storing and changing this data in a spreadsheet over the time window of the simulation would mean either inserting and deleting rows of data (and knowing where to do such deletions and insertions based on state and chain), or adding data at the end of a list and then resorting that list every time new data is added.

That can be a lot of work, even if fully automated. A better way might be to store that data in some kind of an array format in the VB Editor, something that automatically indexes data the way you want (e.g., by state, chain, and franchise #), keeping track of which franchises are open and which are closed. In particular, certain forms of these kinds of variables (called dynamically linked lists) are used extensively by DSS developers.

We'll focus on the simpler forms of arrays here. Let's start by just outlining some of the most basic kinds of data structures in VB: single value variables and single variable data types. Common types include:

Integer: For whole numbers ranging from -32768 to 32767
Long: For whole numbers ranging from -2147483648 to 2147483647
Single: For all numbers ranging from as small as $+/- 1.4 \times 10{-45}$ to as large as $+/- 3.4 \times 1038$

Boolean: For variables that take on the value of either True or False

String: For variables that take on text values (e.g., someone's name)

Note that each of these single variable types can be used to construct a variety of more complex data types. For example, they could be used to build a record, or combination of different variables each of a potentially different type (e.g., the name {String}, student ID {Long}, and class grade {Single} for an individual student). Alternately, they could form variable arrays, which are lists of values for multiple instances of the same kind of variable (e.g., a list consisting solely of individual students' names {An array of Strings}). They could also be used to construct *variable record arrays*, or lists whose entries are each a record that includes a student name, ID, and class grade.

To ensure that the VB Editor is handling data the way you want, define the variables you want it to keep track of right at the beginning of your subroutine/macro. All declarations start with the term Dim and are followed by the name you want for your VB variable and a description of the type of variable it is. For example,

```
Sub SubroutineName ()
    Dim NewInteger As Integer
    Dim NewStudentName As String*50
End sub
```

would create a new subroutine called SubroutineName in which two variables are defined – one called NewInteger that is designed to hold integer-type values, and another called NewStudentName that is designed to hold text-type values 50 characters in length (max). The '*50' designation specifies this, although is often not a requirement for String declaration.

After you have declared, you can use these variables within your subroutine without any doubt regarding how the VB Editor will interpret them. You can now develop additional code that assigns and changes values for these variables. Here's the kind of syntax you might use to assign a value to the NewStudentName variable.

```
NewStudentName = "Jimmilford Jonesburgson"
```

It's valuable to note that the name you give a variable in VB Editor has absolutely nothing to do with any labels/names you've applied in the spreadsheets of the workbook. Regardless, you can easily copy and paste values from VB variables to cells in a spreadsheet, or the other way around. For example:

```
Range("Sheet1!A2") = VBvariable1
VBvariable2 = Range("RateofReturn")
```

This would place the value currently in your VB variable called VBvariable1 into the cell A2 in Sheet1 of your workbook, while setting VBvariable2 to whatever value is currently in the workbook cell labeled RateofReturn.

11.3.2 Declaring and Using More Complex Variables

To create a variable array (list) of strings for storing multiple (say, 25 max) student names, we would use a declaration like this:

```
Dim NewStudentNames(25) As String*50
```

After such a declaration, to set the third name in that list to a name in your workbook, for example, a name you know is in cell B30 of Sheet1, you'd use:

```
NewStudentNames(3) = Range("Sheet1!B30")
```

To create a variable record that represents a grouping of numerous different variable types, you use the following syntax.

```
Type StudentInforRecord
   Name As String * 50
   ID As Long
   Grade As Single
End Type

Sub Macro1()
   Dim NewRecord As StudentInfoRecord
End Sub
```

This is obviously a much more complex declaration, but still something we can get our hands around. The first thing that's happening here is the definition of a new type of variable, one that contains three components of Name, ID, and Grade. This must be typed at the top of the VB Editor code before the subroutine starts. The second is a declaration of a variable base on that new type. Here how we might assign values to two fields of that new variable.

```
NewRecord.Name = "Jimmilford Jonesburgson"
New Record.ID = 555442727
```

Note that each field of the record is designated by a period (.) followed by the name of the field to be used.

Finally, to create an array of records, you could use the following declaration (assuming you already have the new type StudentInfoRecord defined as earlier).

```
Dim NewRecords(50) As StudentInfoRecord
```

You could then modify the 15thGrade in that array (for example) to be equal to say the value found in cell G12 in Sheet3.

NewRecords(15).Grade = 3.45

As a quick example to pull all of these ideas together, consider the following macro code.

```
Type StudentInfoRecord 'defined the new type (record)
   Name As String * 50 'define the first attribute as a string
   ID As Long 'define the second as a whole number
   Grade As Single 'define the third as a decimal number
End Type

Sub Macro1()
   Dim NewRecords(50) As StudentInfoRecord 'define the variable array
      'assuming theres some student data in the second row . . .
      'read that data piece by piece into the first variable in the array
   NewRecords(1).Name = Range("a2")
   NewRecords(1).ID = Range("b2")
   NewRecords(1).Grade = Range("c2")
      'Now copy it into the second variable in the array
   NewRecords(2) = NewRecords(1)
      'Now use those two records to generate a third
   NewRecords(3).Name = Range("a2") + "'s Nemesis"
   NewRecords(3).Grade = NewRecords(1).Grade / NewRecords(2).ID
      'And now modify the record in the second slot once again
   NewRecords(2) = NewRecords(3)
End Sub
```

Ultimately the code outline is a bunch of seemingly random manipulations of information storage devices, but hopefully it allows a little more familiarity with the nature of variables and how different kinds of variable structures interact with one another.

11.3.3 Watching for Changes in Stored Information

All of the variables and types just described are helpful because they provide the means of storing information outside of the spreadsheet proper and the means of storing information in forms other than the piecemeal structure typically associated with spreadsheet records. However, the storage of information in VB-based variables does leave one particular issue to be desired: visibility. Generally speaking, it often appears to those starting out that what happens behind the scenes in VB is a bit clouded in mystery, or at least much more difficult to get a handle on than the kinds of calculations that take place in a spreadsheet.

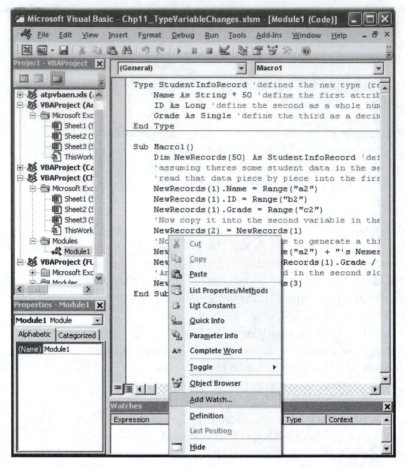

Figure 11.11. Adding a Watch to macro code monitoring.

In reality this may have more to do with the roots of those developers transitioning from spreadsheet environments where data storage units (e.g., cells) are ever present, to VB environments where only specific data storage units (e.g., variables) exist on a need-to-exist basis (i.e., when associated macros are being run). Even when macros are being run and variables are called into existence for the use of storage and calculation, the changes to the contents of these variables may not appear immediately obvious. Fortunately the VB Editor does provide the means of making the values stored and changed within these variables crystal clear to developers who are interested in monitoring their change throughout a macro run. The tool provided to accomplish this is simply called a Watch and is generated by right-clicking anywhere on your code to open a shortcut menu. From there, select Add Watch (shown in Figure 11.11). The process is facilitated if you select the variable of interest and right-click directly on it.

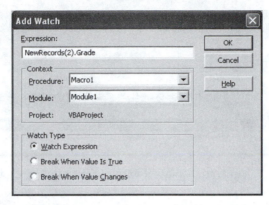

Figure 11.12. Specifying the nature of a Watch.

Selecting Add Watch opens the Add Watch dialog box (Figure 11.12), which enables you to specify exactly what you want to watch as you step through the macro (e.g., using F8, or running the macro with breakpoints active). The Watch then appears at the bottom of the screen (Figure 11.13), as is what you'll want to keep your eyes on for changes in the variables selected. After stepping through to the end of this particular macro run (in Chp11_ TypeVariableUse), the Watch screen should appear as shown in Figure 11.14.

11.3.4 Common Operations with (or without) Variables in VB

With all of these variable declarations, the nagging question remains: How can we complete tasks with data stored in VB variables after we have it? Like the long list of functions already built into Excel, a comprehensive coverage of what we can do in VB is certainly beyond the scope of this text; however, it is useful to at least cover a few examples to illustrate some of the differences, and particularly some of the advantages of doing work in the VB Editor.

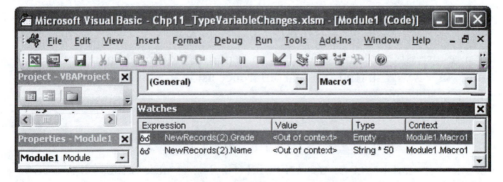

Figure 11.13. The initial display of variable Watches before values are assigned.

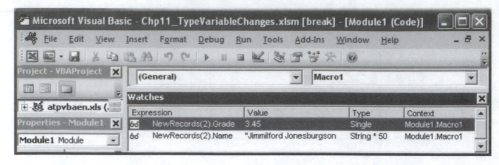

Figure 11.14. Change in display of variable Watches by end of macro.

11.3.5 Syntax for Basic Operators

Many arithmetic functions are the same in VB Editor because they are in the Excel spreadsheets. For example + − / *‸. All of these are the same in the VB Editor.

Others like MOD work a little differently. In a spreadsheet, we use MOD(12,5) to find the remainder of 12 divided by 5 (remainder of 2). In VB code we use 12 MOD 5. Why does the spreadsheet use different syntax than the VB Editor in case like this? There's no good reason, sufficed to say that MS has a huge number of people working for it. Some work on developing spreadsheet functions, others work on VB. Sometimes their approaches differ.

It can be a bit annoying, but here's something to consider: If you really need to know how to calculate something that you can figure out in the spreadsheet but can't figure out with code, you might save yourself some trouble and just do the calculation in the spreadsheet and then simply reference the calculated cell in the VB Editor. This can save you a lot of frustration (Help available on VB functions is much less helpful than the help provided with functions in the spreadsheet).

11.3.5.1 Random Numbers

In spreadsheets we can use Rand() to generate a decimal value between 0 and 1. In VB we use Rnd. No real difference aside from a loss of a vowel and the lack of parentheses.

11.3.5.2 OFFSET

In Excel spreadsheets we use OFFSET(C5,2,4) to access the cell two rows below and four columns to the right of C5. In VB we use Range(C5).Offset(2, 4) to access the same spreadsheet data in the VB Editor.

11.3.5.3 IF Statements

In the spreadsheet we type the following into a cell, for instance, cell D5, to set it's value to 4 when C5=1, and 3 otherwise: = IF(C5=1,4,3). In VB we would use:

```
IF Range("C5")=1 Then
  Range("D5")=4
Else
  Range("D5")=3
End if
```

At first, this may seem more complex than what we're familiar with in the spreadsheet, but it actually represents a fairly robust structure into which a wide variety of actions can conditionally take place. For instance, if C5=1, I might also want to run Solver. I might also want a sound clip to start. I can do that by entering more code into this framework. I couldn't do that just using a spreadsheet's IF statement.

11.3.6 Date/Time Functionality

In the spreadsheet there are a number of ways to get and make use of date/time information maintained by the system clock. For example, the Now() command provides the date/time signature at any given moment. Like the Rand() function, every recalculation in a sheet containing Now() updates the value returned by that function to reflect the passage of time.

What is returned by Now() is a composite of the current data and time. If formatted correctly it should be fairly easy to understand, but ultimately it is just a long decimal number. If formatted like a long decimal number, it will look like one – and one that wouldn't at first glance seem to have a lot of immediate intuitive meaning. Another function, TimeValue serves in a related capacity by translating a recognizable time text string such as 3:30:15 into a long decimal value of the kind that Now() and other time functions actually works with. DateValue serves a similar role with arguments such as Jan 4, 1982.

In VB, multiple tools for accessing and utilizing system clock data are also available. For example the term Now (without the parentheses) can similarly be used to generate a consolidated decimal value that incorporates today's date and time. Also, the TimeValue function works just as it does in the spreadsheet. In VB, however, the combined use of these two functions take on particular relevance because of still more advanced functionality that does not exist directly in the spreadsheet. The Application.Wait function, a mechanism for generating delays during macro runs, is a prime example of how these two can be used together.

Why would someone want to intentionally add a delay to a macro? Sometimes macros run too fast, at least too fast to allow for a meaningful visual demonstration of dynamics. Sometimes it's even desirable to make users wait for calculations, for example because we need to wait for certain online updates. In any event, Application.Wait serves this purpose. As an extremely simple example, if at any point you want to force a one-minute delay in the middle of a macro, just insert the line:

Application.Wait (Now + TimeValue("0:01:00"))

That's it. Easy to customize, easy to interpret – and it works.

11.3.7 Selection Attributes Revisited

We've already taken a couple of looks at the period (.) structure common to what the VB Editor writes when macros are recorded, as well as common to the use of user-defined records for information storage and reference in VB. It's worth taking an additional look at these structures just to reinforce some familiarity. The Chp11_OutliersID workbook provides an example of some fairly simple code in which both functional and descriptive attributes are being used to do some powerful things. We'll focus on the ScatterPlot sheet in this workbook, shown in Figure 11.15 (which also contains examples of the integrated use of a pivot table incidentally).

Opening the VB Editor and the associated Modules folder in this case reveals the following two macros:

```
Sub CreateDatatoPlot()
'Activated by a button assigned to the macro in this case
    Dim Rangetext As String 'need to define a storage place for a line
                            'of text to be created below
    Rangetext = "B8:F" + Range("TotRecords_p_7") 'This term and all it
            'contains must be treated entirel as text to work below
    Range("B9:G2007").Clear 'just clearing out the region of the worksheet
            'where we're gettin the data to be plotted
    Range("B8:F8").Select 'now I'm selecting the range of formulae to copy
    Selection.AutoFill Destination:=Range(Rangetext), Type:=xlFillDefault
            'using the range specified above to only fill in the necessary
            'rows with the copied formulae
End Sub
```

```
Sub GetDataLabel()
'Shortcut Ctrl-k to activate
    Range("HasDataLabel") = Selection.HasDataLabel 'Just for our infor
    If Selection.HasDataLabel Then 'and as a failsafe
        Range("DataLabel") = Selection.DataLabel.Text 'output the point's label
    End If
End Sub
```

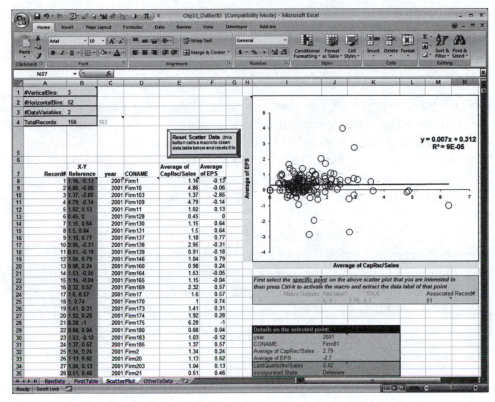

Figure 11.15. Example of graph-point interaction and macro use.

The first of these routines selects a range of cells, which happens to be a set of cells in row 8. It then conducts an autofill using the formula content of that selection to fill in a larger range of cells below it (defined by the string variable Rangetext and based on some specifications described in the associated spreadsheet).

The second routine assumes the user has first selected something and then attempts to access information on that object to return to the spreadsheet. In this case the assumed object is a graphical point on a scatter plot, and the information returned is the label data the point has associated with it. This is particularly useful in this case to identify outliers in a graph and subsequently excluding them from visualization and analysis such as line-fitting.

In both cases we are making use of selections of some sort, and drilling down to capitalize on their attributes. The first is a selection of cells; the second a graphical object. In the first case we are drawing on a functional attribute of a selection (autofill, a verb essentially). In the second case we are drawing on a descriptive attribute (datalabel.text, an adjective essentially). Regardless, VB is able to recognize the appropriateness of our drill down based on the starting point – that is, based on what exactly the selection happens to be, just in the same way that it is able to make sense of the attributes of a record based on how we've defined the nature of the record type definition.

11.3.8 Iteration Structures: Loops

Given a little insight into how these common elements are dealt with differently in the VB Editor, we might assume that there are different, possibly better, ways of dealing with other tasks we've performed in the spreadsheet. And we'd be right. A case in point is the use of Excel's iteration mode as a mechanism for getting us through a series of sequential events. Often this is done better in the VB Editor through what are called loops.

11.3.8.1 For-Loops (fixed-finite iteration structures)

When we know how many times we want some action repeated, or we know how many items we want the same or similar action applied to, no matter what that action is, For-Loops can get the job done pretty quickly. Here's an example of what that Chapter 8 code might look like if all 200 or so of those Calculate lines were condensed using a simple For-Loop:

```
Sub Macro1()
'
' Macro1 Macro

    Range("H18").Select
    ActiveCell.FormulaR1C1 = "FALSE"
    Calculate
    Range("H18").Select
    ActiveCell.FormulaR1C1 = "TRUE"
    For Count = 1 To 200
      Calculate
    Next
    Range("K32:K35").Select
    Selection.Copy
    Sheets("MacroRuns").Select
    Range("B2").Select
    Selection.PasteSpecial Paste:=xlPasteValues, _
      Operation:=xlNone, SkipBlanks:=False, Transpose:=True
    Application.CutCopyMode = False
    Selection.EntireRow.Insert
    Sheets("StockoutDemo").Select
  End Sub
```

A few more than 200 periods seem to get recorded, but that's purely a result of the rest of what's going on in the code and fairly easy to fix. The main point is that the code has been greatly reduced and becomes much easier to both read,

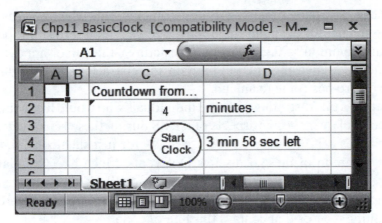

Figure 11.16. Interface for example of use of a While-Loop.

manage, and edit. Furthermore, there are plenty of other actions that could also take place within each iteration of that loop, such as complex calculations or even multiple calls to add-ins like Solver or external applications like MapPoint.

11.3.8.2 While-Loops (Open-ended Iterations)

In contrast, While-Loops are useful when we don't know how many times we want some action repeated, or we don't know how many things we want the same or similar action applied to, no matter what that action is. These loops end when specific conditions are met, similar to the stopping logic used as part of RiskOptimizer's functionality. As an example that combines the use of some of the date/time functions as well as GetEvents, consider a While-Loop used to simulate a simple count-down timer. The Chp11_BasicClock workbook provides such functionality. The main sheet appears in Figure 11.16, allowing individuals to enter in the number of minutes to be counted down from and a button that activates the looped count-down macro.

Before getting into the code for this one, it's probably worth making a general warning statement regarding the use of While-Loops: They are notorious for causing headaches for developers. Although For-Loops have a fixed and certain end, While-Loops may never find the condition needed for stopping. This results in what is referred to as an infiniteloop that might stop only if the user presses Ctrl-Alt-Delete, or when the computer dies – whichever comes first.

Of course there are other ways to build in mechanisms that allow users to force exits from loops of any kind, or at least maintain control during the running of long loop processes. Generally speaking, when macros are running, users are not given much of an opportunity to do other work in the workbook containing these macros. That shouldn't be a problem in many cases where macros get their work done quickly. But when macros take a long time to run, for example when they involve a long series of repetitions of the kind common to the use of loop structures, the cursor appearance in the spreadsheet environment will take on the characteristic hourglass icon until the macro has come to an end.

This can be a bit frustrating for some individuals who would like to maintain greater control over specific aspects of a DSS during these runs. Fortunately, certain clauses can be added to code to allow for just such control. One of the most common of these clauses is DoEvents. Much like Calculate, it is typically used by itself within a program. Functionally, it allows items such as forms and controls on the spreadsheet to respond to actions taken by users while running macros that contain this line of code.

Let's take a look at the code working behind the scenes of the BasicClock example just discussed. The following is a clip of the code, as fully annotated in the file.

```
Sub EfficientClockSub()
    MaxTime = TimeValue("0:01:00") * Range("CountdownFrom")
    TimeSpent = 0 'Initialize this time keeping record
    StartTime = Now 'Note that 'Now' is a predefined term in VB and provides
                'the current system time
    Do While TimeSpent < MaxTime 'Do as long as MaxTime isn't reached
        DoEvents 'Allows forms/controls on the spreadsheet to respond to actions
            'taken by user while clock runs. Allows general access of cells
            'but stops code upon deliberate entry of new data directly into
            'cells
        '**Below this point you might code in things that need to be calced or
        '**refreshed via VB ...
        TimeSpent = Now - StartTime 'Update the time keeping record
        Range("TimeLeft") = MaxTime - TimeSpent 'Here we're just displaying the
                    'amount of time left
    Loop
End Sub
```

Leveraging a DoWhile loop structure, the macro essentially continues to update the amount of time left in the countdown on the main spreadsheet until the system time reaches a point equal or greater than the initial system time plus the length of time originally requested to be counted down from. However, notice that along with all of the date/time elements being used there is a continued reference to DoEvents within the main While-Loop.

As stated, the DoEvents clause allows for certain cursor activity that would otherwise be disabled in its absence. Another interesting feature of DoEvents

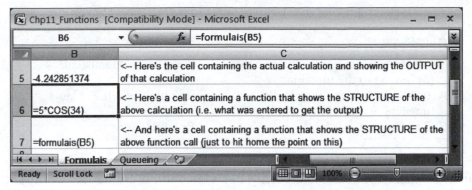

Figure 11.17. Interface for example of user-defined function.

is the fact that direct data entry into a spreadsheet cell while running a macro (which it ostensibly allows) can actually offer/force a direct exit from the running of that .acro (i.e., typing into the spreadsheet with DoEvent can shut down the macro).

This can serve as a convenient exit, but it can also prove inconvenient if the shutdown takes place accidentally. As a word of caution – if you want to allow interfacing with forms/controls (as introduced in Chapter 8) during a macro run, and if you want to use DoEvents to give you that functionality, you might want to make sure that users are not able to accidentally shut down the program halfway through a run. One way to prevent this is to protect the interfacing worksheet against any most types of potentially inadvertent selections and sheet modifications (we'll get into the specifics of sheet protection in Chapter 13). We'll find that we can do this while keeping any cells unlocked for which you want to allow changes through VB or forms/controls changes (hence allowing the specific kind of control desired during macro runs while avoiding errors).

11.4 User-Defined Functions

A natural extension of the discussion we've had so far regarding the value, capabilities, and structures of macros is to spend some time on functions, another development mechanism made available through the VB Editor.

11.4.1 An Introduction to Functions

Figure 11.17 shows an incredibly simply example of a function that writes out the formula content of another cell, something you would typically have to go into a cell directly to see. You will not find this function automatically built into Excel (e.g., not listed under Formulas>Insert Function under a typical install). Instead I created it to provide a simple example of user-defined

Table 11.3. Code and Annotation for Basic Function Structure

Annotation	Actual Code
Name/start of function and arguments (or inputs) to the function	Function formulais(cell as Range)
Actions/calculations taken by the function; output of function	formulais = cell. Formula
End of function	End Function

function that anyone could create. After a function is created or workbook containing its code is opened, it will appear in function listings or at least be recognized in some form by Excel. For the time being however, let's just see what this function is all about. Here's a clip from the Chp11_Functions workbook in which it was coded.

Table 11.3 shows the VB code that makes it possible to use the function formulas in the spreadsheet. Note the structure here, one that is distinct from that of a macro.

This distinction has to do with the purpose/role behind user-defined functions. Their main purpose is to take inputs and kick out individual outputs to the cell that references them. Although what happens within the code of a function may be as complex as what takes place in the code of a macro, the role of a macro in contrast is to execute a set of actions that results in something other than a single value getting returned to a single cell (although that can certainly take place as well, it's usually not the main objective). User-defined functions are just like any other function in Excel, (except they don't come standard – they need to be built by users). In contrast to being activated by a button or a selection from a "macro list", they are called directly from cells within a spreadsheet orother programs in VB Editor, with the assumption that a sufficient specification of inputs is provided for them to do the number crunching they were designed to do.

And as for making sure that the right kinds of inputs are fed into a user-defined function when being used in a spreadsheet, recall that Excel will recognize the function when defined. In other words, you should be able to locate it in the Insert Function dialog box shown in Figure 11.18 (note formulais section of this dialog box) when the workbook that contains the function is open.

Furthermore, Excel will attempt to provide assistance with the inputs required for a user-defined function in the same way that it attempts to provide assistance for all other functions. Note specifically that in Figure 11.18, Excel is suggesting that the key input to formulais is a cell reference. No more help is provided, but perhaps no additional help is needed.

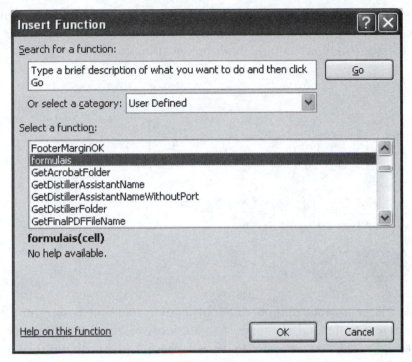

Figure 11.18. Recognition of user-defined functions by Excel.

You could always provide more help in the comments of the function code, but that would require users to open up VB. If you were determined to make sure something other than No help available appeared below your function in the Insert Function dialog box, there are still some options. One way is to start by creating a new macro recording in the spreadsheet, and designating the kind of descriptive help you might want to appear for your existing function. Copy and paste all of the content of that function (aside from the function header and footer) into that macro, delete the original function and then change the header and footer info on the macro to convert it into a function instead. That description should appear whenever the function is selected in the Insert Function dialog box. It seems like a backwards approach, but it's fairly foolproof and gets the job done.

11.4.2 A More Complex Example

For those who remember the queuing equations from any Operations course-work you may have taken, you'll recall that they are pretty hairy. For those not familiar with these equations, consider yourselves lucky – they aren't exactly fun to work with. As an example, the following are some of the formulae needed for estimating associated calculations such as line length probabilities and average wait times for situations where you have multiple servers (c could equal cashiers, clinicians, accountants, and so on) but only limited space (N) to accommodate people waiting.

Finite-Queue M/M/c Model:

$$P_0 = \cfrac{1}{\left(\sum_{i=0}^{c} \cfrac{\rho^i}{i!}\right) + \left(\cfrac{1}{c!}\right)\left(\sum_{i=c+1}^{N} \cfrac{\rho^i}{c^{i-c}}\right)} \qquad P_n = \begin{cases} \cfrac{\rho^n}{n!} P_0 & for\ 0 \le n \le c \\[2ex] \cfrac{\rho^n}{c!c^{n-c}} P_0 & for\ c \le n \le N \end{cases}$$

$$L_s = \frac{P_0 \rho^{c+1}}{(c-1)!(c-\rho)^2}\left[1 - \left(\frac{\rho}{c}\right)^{N-c} - (N-c)\left(\frac{\rho}{c}\right)^{N-c}\left(1 - \frac{\rho}{c}\right)\right] + \rho(1 - P_N)$$

$$W_s = \frac{L_s - \rho(1 - P_N)}{\lambda(1 - P_N)} + \frac{1}{\mu}$$

Here, λ is the average number of people arriving per time (e.g., minute), μ is the average time needed by a server to complete a customer's request, and ρ is the ratio λ/μ. The first function, P_0, then represents the probability of having no one in the system (line plus those being served) at any given moment in time, while P_n represents the probability of having exactly n people in the system. The terms L_s and W_s represent the average anticipated number of individuals in the system, and the average amount of time an individual can expect to spend in the system (again in line and at the counter) before their needs are filled.

Again, the calculations of these estimation terms are not trivial. In particular the summations over a range of values are not particularly fun to do by hand. In a spreadsheet, we could do all the required summations by setting up a table and calculating a sum of all appropriate cells in that table, as shown in Figure 11.19. But that takes up a lot of space even in the spreadsheet, space that we could be using for something else (the Chp11_BigQueueCalc workbook contains the extensive spreadsheet usage in Figure 11.19).

Fortunately, we can easily create a sum of sequential terms in VB through using loop structures such as For . . . Next. Not only does that eliminate the need to take up space in the spreadsheet, it's actually more concisely developed in VB. In contrast to spelling all of this out in the spreadsheet alone, the associated function codes (for all four functions) on the other hand take up space only behind the scenes. The second spreadsheet in the Chp11_Functions workbook, shown in Figure 11.20, gives an example of how functions are being leveraged to provide a much more spreadsheet-frugal approach to this model.

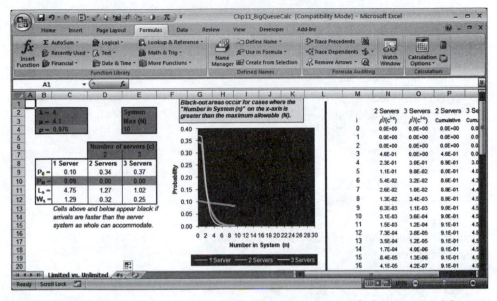

Figure 11.19. Example of extensive calculation space occupied on a spreadsheet.

Additional notes on the newly crafted functions and their arguments are displayed in this sheet in columns M through P, but notice that they really are there only for clarity purposes. The big thing is that absolutely no calculations need to be made in these columns to let the calculations of interest take place. Instead we have the following functions working behind the scenes in VB.

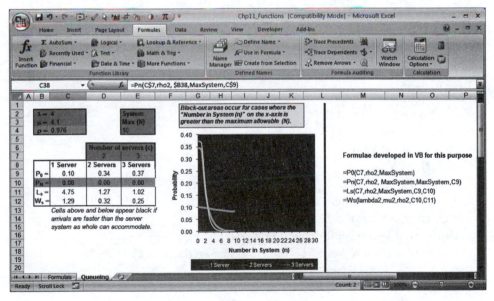

Figure 11.20. Example of function-enabled frugality in the use of spreadsheet.

```vb
Function P0(c_ref, rho_ref, N_ref As Range)
    firstsum = 0
    secondsum = 0
    c = c_ref.Value
    rho = rho_ref.Value
    N = N_ref.Value
    cfact = WorksheetFunction.Fact(c)
    For i = 0 To c
        firstsum = firstsum + (rho ^ i) / WorksheetFunction.Fact(i)
    Next
    For i = (c + 1) To N
        secondsum = secondsum + (rho ^ i) / WorksheetFunction.Power(c, i - c)
    Next
    P0 = 1 / (firstsum + (1 / cfact) * (secondsum))
End Function

Function PN(c_ref, rho_ref, littlen_ref, bigN_ref, P0_ref As Range)
    c = c_ref.Value
    rho = rho_ref.Value
    littlen = littlen_ref.Value
    bigN = bigN_ref.Value
    Pnot = P0_ref.Value
    cfact = WorksheetFunction.Fact(c)
    littlenfact = WorksheetFunction.Fact(littlen)
    If (littlen >= 0) And (littlen <= c) Then
        PN = Pnot * WorksheetFunction.Power(rho, littlen) / littlenfact
    ElseIf (littlen > c) And (littlen <= bigN) Then
        PN = Pnot * WorksheetFunction.Power(rho, littlen) _
                /(cfact * WorksheetFunction.Power(c, littlen - c))
    Else
        PN = " "
    End If
End Function

Function Ls(c_ref, rho_ref, N_ref, P0_ref, PN_ref As Range)
    c = c_ref.Value
    rho = rho_ref.Value
    N = N_ref.Value
    Pnot = P0_ref.Value
    PbigN = PN_ref.Value
    cless1fact = WorksheetFunction.Fact(c - 1)
    rhocpow = WorksheetFunction.Power((rho / c), N - c)
    product1 = Pnot * WorksheetFunction.Power(rho, c + 1) _
                /(cless1fact * ((c - rho) ^ 2))
    product2 = (N - c) * rhocpow * (1 - (rho / c))
    Ls = product1 * (1 - rhocpow - product2) + rho * (1 - PbigN)
End Function
```

```
Function Ws(lambda_ref, mu_ref, rho_ref, PN_ref, Ls_Ref As Range)
    Lambda = lambda_ref.Value
    Mu = mu_ref.Value
    rho = rho_ref.Value
    PbigN = PN_ref.Value
    Lsubs = Ls_Ref.Value
    Ws = (Lsubs - rho * (1 - PbigN)) / (Lambda * (1 - PbigN)) + 1 / Mu
End Function
```

You might think this looks complex and are not sure you want to take this route. It's no more complex than cranking out the calculations within the cells of a spreadsheet. Many of the lines of code here are just referencing cells from which to draw information. Others are absolutely critical calculations that would be present in the spreadsheet otherwise.

And there's still another benefit to developing functions in VB rather than within spreadsheet cells. Building user-defined functions for complex calculations tend to be less prone to errors than a pure spreadsheet approach, particularly when the calculations are bound to be repeatedly used in many ways within a spreadsheet.

PRACTICE PROBLEMS

Practice 11.1

Import both an image and a .wav file of your own choosing into Excel. Create a macro that activates that .wav clip and then use the time functions in Excel to make an image slowly fade away over a 15-second period. Then make the image slowly reappear, again over a 15-second period. Do this either by building the macro from the ground up based on code similar to that showed in the example of this chapter, or through using a version of Excel that allows for object macro recording.

Hint on making an image appear to fade away: You can use several approaches, but one approach is to increase the amount of lighting provided to an image. This is one of the options on the Picture toolbar.

Hint on time functions: For the time functions, use whichever you think are appropriate, but it's actually good practice to do a little snooping around for these because there are multiple approaches to getting this information (see the functions under the category Data & Time). You may find, for example, the NOW() function to be useful, as well as the HOUR, MINUTE, and SECOND calculations. Use Excel's function help to learn how these may help. Table 11.4 shows an example of how you might set up your tabular output in a spreadsheet.

The one point to reiterate here is that the NOW() function will update only if you ask it to, such as by pressing F9 or making some other change in the spreadsheet. In this way, they act a little like the RAND() function. In the VB Editor you can also do this using the one-line command Calculate. Anytime that is used, the workbook is updated.

Table 11.4 *Example Structure for Tabular Output*

	Total	Total	Total
Now	Hours	Minutes	Seconds
2/10/2008 13:26	13	806	48387

Practice 11.2

Create a function for calculating the Y-coordinate associated with the X-coordinate of a circle. Your input should be the value of X, the radius of the circle, and some binary input that designates whether you want the lower or upper half of the circle to be referred to for your value of Y. The standard formula for a circle is:

$$R^2 = X^2 + Y^2 \quad \text{or} \quad Y = +/- \text{sqrt}(R^2 - X^2)$$

12

Automating Application Calls

Many applications such as MS MapPoint and RiskOptimizer can be leveraged through the primary interfaces with which they were designed, but they can also be called from behind the scenes through the same Visual Basic (VB) developer environment discussed in Chapter 11. From a decision support development perspective, there are several advantages to making such calls from behind the scenes. First and foremost, behind the scenes control can eliminate the need for users to become acquainted with alternative interfaces in the course of using a DSS that leverages their capabilities. Another advantage is the potential avoidance of outputs that automatically accompany the use of these applications, but are nevertheless visual and information distractions from the main point of the DSS design. The appearance of seamlessness in a designed DSS is also facilitated by VB-driven automated calls to applications. This has the potential for engendering greater confidence in the developed DSS, as well as in the developers.

This chapter covers several approaches to working with such applications in roughly the order in which they have been introduced in this book.

12.1 Calls to MapPoint

The Chp12_MapPointCall workbook provides a template through which we can demonstrate how Excel, through VB, can leverage some of the functionality of MapPoint. As with all other demonstrations in this chapter, we'll present only a simple smattering of what can actually be done. To start, let's consider a hypothetical need to get information regarding a route starting in Seattle and passing through four additional cities before returning. The workbook outlines these stops, as shown in Figure 12.1.

Clicking on the Click to route button activates a macro that:

1) Activates the MapPoint application
2) Adds the specified cities to a new route

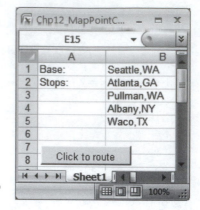

Figure 12.1. Front-end for activating macro call to MapPoint.

3) Asks MapPoint to map and calculate the distance for that route
4) Gives feedback on the covered distance and sequence of the route
5) Takes a snapshot of the MapPoint window for pasting
6) Pastes, crops, and shifts the copied picture

The result is shown in Figure 12.2.

The VB code used to deliver this result is:

```
Private Declare Sub keybd_event Lib "user32"_
   (ByVal bVk As Byte, ByVal bScan As Byte,_
     ByVal dwFlags As Long, ByVal dwExtraInfo As Long)


Sub Route_calc()
```

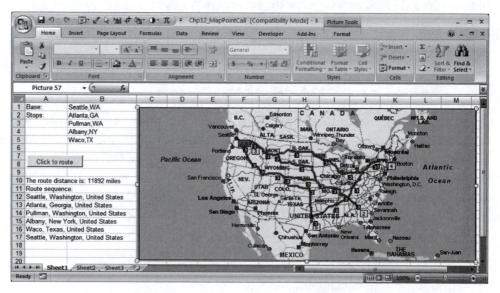

Figure 12.2. Map generation using macro and existing sequence of site visits.

```
Dim objApp As MapPoint.Application
Dim objMap As MapPoint.Map
Dim objRoute As MapPoint.Route

Set objApp = CreateObject("MapPoint.Application")_
 'Set up the Mappoint application
Set objMap = objApp.ActiveMap 'Get the active map
Set objRoute = objMap.ActiveRoute 'Select the active route

'Clear, then add route stops
objRoute.Clear
objRoute.Waypoints.Add objMap.FindResults(CStr(Range("B1"))).Item(1)
For stopnumber = 1 To 4
  objRoute.Waypoints.Add objMap.FindResults(CStr(Range("B1")._
    Offset(stopnumber, 0))).Item(1)
Next
objRoute.Waypoints.Add objMap.FindResults(CStr(Range("B1"))).Item(1)
objRoute.Calculate 'calculate route distance covered
objApp.Visible = True 'Make the mappoint object visible

' ***** Make this code active to optimize the route,_
 if desired and if not already optimized
'objRoute.Waypoints.Optimize
'objMap.ActiveRoute.Calculate 'calculate NEW route distance covered

Range("A11") = "Route sequence:" 'Outputs
For i = 1 To objRoute.Waypoints.Count
  Range("A11").Offset(i, 0) = objRoute.Waypoints.Item(i).Name
Next
Range("A10") = "The route distance is:" +_
  CStr(Round(objRoute.Distance)) + "miles"

    'Here's just a little extra code to implant a screen capture of the
    keybd_event &H12, 0, 0, 0 ' Plant "Alt" key
    keybd_event &H2C, 1, 0, 0
    keybd_event &H12, 0, &H2, 0 ' Release "Alt" key
    CaptureDesktop = True
    objMap.Saved = True_
      'Trick MapPoint into thinking we've saved it (allowing auto-close)
    Sheets("Sheet1").Range("C1").Select
    ActiveSheet.Paste

    'And just to do a little cropping
    Selection.ShapeRange.PictureFormat.CropLeft = 182
    Selection.ShapeRange.PictureFormat.CropTop = 277
```

```
Selection.ShapeRange.PictureFormat.CropRight = 4
Selection.ShapeRange.PictureFormat.CropBottom = 22
Selection.ShapeRange.IncrementLeft -180
Selection.ShapeRange.IncrementTop -270
```

End Sub

This is possibly a bit overwhelming for a novice, but for those who have read through Chapter 11, there's a lot of material here that should seem familiar. For example, references to cell contents using the Range syntax shouldn't be new; nor should the use of an offset with a For-Loop and reference to any of the picture manipulations in the later portion of this code. The two novel areas of code involve the various calls to MapPoint and the calls associated with screen captures of the mapped result (the first three lines of code preceding the subroutine and the four lines of code following the output of the route distance).

Unfortunately, most of these codes are outside of standard macro recording, particularly Excel 2007's approach to macro generation. One could rightly ask, "So how in the world would I learn how to use this code?" For starters, there's nothing stopping someone from editing or copying this code to another workbook towards a similar end. Much of this arcane material, if not available in an advanced programming text, is also available online through various blogs and help sites. For those interested in learning how to get more done in MapPoint (or with screen captures) through VB, one of the best and cheapest ways is to simply pick some of the code from this example as search terms and see what comes up. We'll leave that up to the intrepid reader.

At this point, to advance the discussion of interfacing between Excel and MapPoint a little further given the present code, let's reconsider the result provided. Arguably, the route depicted here seems to be a poor design from a time management (and total distance covered) perspective. Certainly there are better sequences that MapPoint could come up with; however, the macro in its current form isn't asking for MapPoint to perform any optimization. The portion of the code that would make such a request has been commented out by preceding it with apostrophe. It's simple enough to activate it; just remove the apostrophe and click on the Macro button once again.

As the augmented algorithm runs (unfortunately the optimization through an indirect call to MapPoint is not fast as would be desired), the MapPoint interface refreshes and suggests that the optimization protocol has provided a more ideal solution, again based solely on time management and total distance covered. Depending on how much time it takes, Excel may provide the message shown in Figure 12.3.

Figure 12.3. Message relating delay associated with simultaneous application activity.

This designates that Excel recognizes there is still more to be done in the macro, but before any additional actions take place it will need to wait for the work to be completed in MapPoint. Again, given the length of time Map-Point needs to develop optimal routes, this could be a while. But eventually MapPoint should be able to do its work. If all goes well, the final product in this case appears as shown in Figure 12.4.

Note both the updated distance and route sequence as well as the updated mapping of the route. This is certainly something on which a developer could spend more time to make appear more aesthetically pleasing, but not bad in terms of a rough cut at functionality with fairly limited VB code.

12.2 Calls to Solver

In contrast to MapPoint (a potentially stand-alone application), Solver is an add-in and is almost always used only within the context of Excel. Not all add-ins work well with macros, particularly those that are acquired from

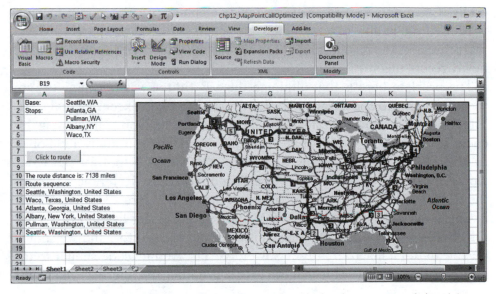

Figure 12.4. Map generation using macro and optimized sequence of site visits.

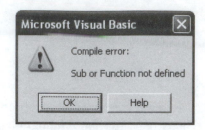

Figure 12.5. Message due to non-referencing.

third parties that did not develop such applications with VB developers in mind. Fortunately for us, Solver is a gleaming exception. In Solver's case we just need to make sure we have our specifications set up the right way (e.g., we need Solver to actually be active in our version of Excel) and know just a little more syntax to get Solver to actually do things by itself.

The following is the kind of code we would get if we simply took a workbook that contained an existing math-programming problem structure and started recording a macro right before we asked Solver to come up with a solution (at least in Excel 2003).

```
Sub Macro1()
    SolverOK SetCell:="$D$4", MaxMinVal:=1, ValueOf:="0",_
    ByChange:="$b$2:$c$2"
    SolverSolve
End Sub
```

Even though the VB Editor created this code, it is not likely to be able to repeat this procedure without us giving it a little more information. In fact, oddly it may not even seem to recognize elements of the code it has just written. If you're able to record the same action into code comparable to that just presented, the results might look like Figure 12.5 when you try to run the newly record macro.

The problem here is that although the VB Editor was told how to turn those actions into code, it wasn't told what to use when executing that code. The Editor needs to know that it should be referencing Solver in running this code. To make the VB Editor aware of this, we need to formally add Solver as a reference, similar to how we added in Solver as a tool for the Excel workbook the first place. In the VB Editor go to Tools>References to open the References – VBA Project dialog box shown in Figure 12.6.

Check the SOLVER box in the Available References list and then click OK. Solver is now formally a reference for the VB Editor, and we should be able to run a macro that uses Solver. NOTE: Adding code similar to the following may provide a mechanism to forego adding the reference manually:

```
ThisWorkbook.VBProject.References.AddFromFile Application.LibraryPath &
"\solver\solver.xla"
```

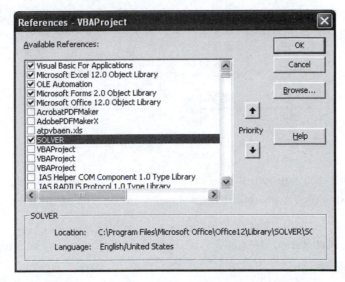

Figure 12.6. Referencing associated applications in VB Editor.

However, depending on how your applications are set up, this may not work for all developers, so don't place all bets on it. The list of Solver-related commands that can be called through VB is as extensive as the number of options made available by Solver. The following is a subset of the more useful commands from a standard DSS standpoint:

SolverSolve UserFinish:=True

This command allows Solver to accept the final solution it comes up with and save the associated values of the solution decisions in the associated cells. This way you don't have to click OK every time a macro running Solver comes up with a solution.

SolverReset

This command clears all Solver contents (e.g., deletes all constraints, objectives, and decision variable references that would typically be retained after each Solver run). Could be useful if you decide to create a program that uses different kinds of constraints in alternative iterations.

SolverDelete CellRef:="$B$2:$C$2", Relation:=4

This command deletes a specific constraint; in this example, one that constrains two cells to be integers (that's what Relation:=4 refers to).

SolverAdd commands

In general, Solver allows for five kinds of relationships to be depicted by constraints as shown in Figure 12.7.

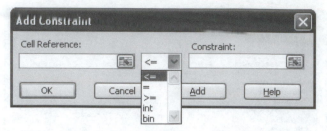

Figure 12.7. Menu interface for editing constraints.

As a result, the following two commands can be used to add individual constraint for the <= (ie. Relation:=1) or integer (Relation:=4) types.

SolverAdd CellRef:="$B$2", Relation:=1, FormulaText:="10"
SolverAdd CellRef:="$B$2:$C$2", Relation:=4, FormulaText:="integer"

12.3 Calls to RiskOptimizer

For problems with more complex structures, or those that involve forms of uncertainty that don't lend themselves to the kind of closed form analysis with which basic Solver's hill-climbing algorithm works well, we've seen that other approaches may be necessary. The use of genetic algorithms, as made available through additional tools such as RiskOptimizer, has already been discussed as an option. It can also be called from behind the scenes using VB code, again perhaps as one of many steps involved in a larger analysis around which a decision support tool is designed. Let's consider a couple of the past examples discussed in the book and how we might more seamlessly automate their interface with Excel.

12.3.1 Work-Group Selection Revisited

Let's again consider the form of the work-group selection problem last formally discussed in Chapter 7. We showed how RISKOptimizer could be used to derive group constituencies subject to criteria that might be outside the bounds of a typical XLStat clustering. (We'll get back to calling XLStat in VB shortly.) To call RISKOptimizer to run its routine behind the scenes, we'll want to have RISKOptimizer formally loaded (much in the same way that we might pre-load Solver, if not already present, before running macros that call it). In addition, as with Solver, a formal reference to RISKOptimizer needs to be made through the VB Editor before the Editor can recognize the code being referenced in any macro calling the application. (Here you're looking for something like RiskOpt.xla to be added in as a reference.)

With that done, we can start to develop some simple code just to get RISKOptimizer to do its thing. Assuming we're using the original Chapter 7 version, perhaps with an additional stipulation that the search stops after one minute (again just to illustrate how this works), the following code would be more than sufficient (taken from Chp12_WorkGroupSelection_VB1).

```
Sub AutoCluster()
   EvOptimize ActiveWorkbook, "myStopRoutine"_
      'Note that EvOptimize is a function
         'that expects a string for its second argument . . . that string entry
         'itself may be another user defined function
End Sub

Public Function myStopRoutine(stopReason As Integer) As Integer
   myStopRoutine = EvBest + EvLogWorkbook +_
      EvLogWorkbookShowOnlyNewBest
   'an addititve specification that basically states we would like to have:
   ' 1) The Best solution found to be saved to the workbook
      'In contrast to EvBest, EvOriginal would keep the original solution
   ' 2) The a log of the search presented in a new workbook
   ' 3) The log should contain ONLY the best solutions discovered during_
      the search
End Function
```

In actuality, the code could be still more simplified, but the structure presented, in which a function is used to specify the nature of the results provided, is a particularly convenient means of suggesting possible extensions of its use. For example, there's nothing stopping a developer from further specifying whether the best solution found should overwrite the original, based on inputs provided by their users in a customized interface. Or whether all solutions encountered should be saved in the logbook (even poor ones or those that might fundamentally violate assumed constraints). Here a few references to designated cells in a workbook interface (or a dialog box along with the use of IF-THEN structures within the function would do the trick.

Aside from manipulating the nature of the output, developers also have the option of manipulating the nature of the problem to be solved by RISKOptimizer as well as the approach taken in doing so. Rather than taking a piecemeal approach to explaining each of the various items useful in developing code that can build optimization problems in RISKOptimizer from the ground up, at this point we'll simply consider a complete set of integrated code. Rich annotation will serve in place of a formalized discussion of the role of each element of code.

Ultimately the kinds of specifications made here are comparable to those that would be made with Solver specifications. To assist in understanding, the following code (from Chp12_WorkGroupSelectionVB2) has been organized in the way we have discussed problem structures already. It starts with a specification of the problem's objective and approach to optimization (e.g., GA stopping rules), the nature of the decision variables, and the potential nature of constraints (if not otherwise built into the objective and/or bounds on decision variables). It concludes with the specification of output interfaces desired and finally the commencement of the optimization protocol (as introduced in the earlier example).

```
Sub RunIt()
    Dim returnCode%

    If SetupModel() Then
    'if setup takes place without error. . .
      EvOptimize ActiveWorkbook, "myStopRoutine"_
        'Note that EvOptimize is a function
          'that expects a string for its second argument . . . that string entry
          'itself may be another user defined function
    End If
End Sub

Function SetupModel()
    Dim mySettings As EvSettingsType
    Dim returnCode%

    returnCode = EvReadSettingsDefaults(ThisWorkbook, mySettings)_
      'creates blank template

    With mySettings_
    'A statement letting VB editor know that much of the following
        'will provide specifications to the existing RISKOptimizer settings
        'everything to follow that is preceded by a "." describes an attribute
        'of "mySettings"

    .CellToOptimize = "sheet1!$P$22" '
    .OutputFunction = EvRiskFuncMean 'What is the nature of the output to
        'be maximized. In optimizations that don't involve simulation, using
        'the parameter EvRiskFuncMean_
          (ie. focusin on the mean performance of
        'a decision policy option) is sufficient. It's usually also the statistic
        'of performance used in simulation optimization. However in simulation
        'optimization, other measures of performance will be different. These
        'include but are not limited to:
        ' EvRiskFuncStdDev:_
          The standard deviation of performance across variants
        ' EvRiskFuncRange: The range of performance across simulated variants
        ' EvRiskFuncPercentile: The value of the approximated P-percentile of
```

'   variants seen. Here the P-percentile would also need to be specified
'   in code such as mySettings.OutputFunction Parameter=0.13
.OptimizationGoal = EvMaximize 'What kind of optimization on above
   'EvMinimize and EvTargetValue are other options. In the latter case the
   ' target would also need specification -.TargetValue=412 for eg.

.PopulationSize = 10 'This relates to how the genetic algorithm works. . . ie.
   'how many past solutions are considered in constructing new solutions_
     moving
   'forward. Relevant for both non-simulation and simulation optimization.
   'See earlier notes from Chapter 7 supplement on GA population size

.StopOnMinutes = True 'Should the search stop after some amount of time?
   'Additive so could simultaneously use mySettings._
     StopOnTrials=True for eg.
   'or.StopOnChange=True
   'or.StopOnFormula=True
.StopMinutes = 1 'For trials - .StopTrials=40 for eg.
   'or.StopChangeTrials=100,.StopChangeMagnitude=5,
   ' .StopChangeIsPercent=True would all need to be specified if you
   ' wanted to stop the search after no changes by >=5% in last 100 trials
   'For "StopOnFormula" - .StopFormula = "sheet1!$P$32>1200"
     for example.
.SimStopMode = EvSimStopIterations 'Combined with below. . .
.SimMaxIters = 5 'For non-simulation optimization, should be as small as
   possible
   ' (ie. 5) since nothing is essentially being simulated. For either the
   ' optimization of simulation variants or system simulations,_
   depending on the
   ' approach taken this number may be much larger.
   ' See the detailed discussion of iterations in Chapter 9 to get a better
   ' feeling for how this might need to be set for different approaches.

.numAdjustableGroups = 1 'Here we outline our decision variables
ReDim.AdjustableGroups(1 To 1) 'Need to define how many variable_
   'groups' exist
With.AdjustableGroups(1)
   .crossoverRate = 0.5 'As noted in Chp7,_
     this and the mutation rate need to be
   .mutationRate = 0.1_
     'specified, otherwise new/better solutions can't be found
   .solvingMethod = "GROUPING" 'or "RECIPE",_
     "ORDER" etc. depending on need
   .numInputRanges = 1 'see below
   ReDim.InputRanges(1 To 1)_
     'Need to define how many variable cell-ranges feed in

```
        .InputRanges(1),Reference = "sheet1!$a7:$a86" ' "WorkerAssignments"
        '   or something like "sheet1!$a7:$a86"
        .InputRanges(1).IsInteger = True
        .InputRanges(1).MinValue = 1
        .InputRanges(1).MaxValue = 4
    End With


    'Hard constraints can also be specified for example:
    '.numConstraints = 3 'if 3 hard constraints applied
    'ReDim.Constraints(1 To 3)
    '.Constraints(1).ConstrainType = EvConstraintHard
    '.Constraints(1).EntryMode = EvEtryModeFormula
    '.Constraints(1).Formula = "ActualSize=20"
    ' . . . contraints 2 and 3 would then also need specification


    .GraphProgress = True_
        'Activate the RISKOptimizer watcher during the search
    .GenerateLog = True 'Make sure a log of the search is being kept


    'Other possible settings for embedded Macro Calls DURING_
        RISKOptimizer search
    '   .RunBeforeSimMacro = True
    '   .BeforeSimMacro = "SomeSuperMacro"
    '   The above lines would call "SomeSuperMacro"_
        before each new decision policy is
    '   evaluated. Particularly useful for simulation optimization (again see Chp9)
    '   Related timing variants include BeforeRecalcMacro, AfterRecalcMacro,_
    '       AfterSimMacro, AfterStorageMacro, StartMacro and FinishMacro. . . _
    '       all associated with the standard RISKOptimizer Macro call interface_
    '       discussed earlier


    End With 'Needed to tell VB editor you are done specifying attributes
        'of mySettings in general


    returnCode = EvWriteSettings(mySettings) 'Need to_
        "write" the specifics to RISKOptimizer
    SetupModel = True_
        'More relevant if we had been checking for errors along the way here


End Function
```

Used in conjunction with code that initiates and stops the actual optimization process, these kinds of specification protocols provide the convenience switching between various optimization problem structures in turn without going through the hassle of restructuring them manually (see example Chp12_WorkGroupSelection_VB2 for the full implementation).

12.3.2 Inventory System Simulation Revisited

Because RISKOptimizer is useful in simulation optimization settings, it is worth reviewing how the code for building and executing an example of such optimization might be structured. For illustration, consider again the Lobos Inventory optimization example from Chapter 9. The same kinds of elements used in the annotated code in section 12.3.1 apply here. With this in mind, and with the interest of providing a contrast in implementation, it is both sufficient and appropriate to present the code that would apply to this case in a similar fashion. A copy of the workbook containing this code is provided in Chp12_LobosInventory_VB. The following is the structure of the setup function (consolidated and free of annotation that has already been provided in the previous examples).

```
Function SetupModel()
    Dim mySettings As EvSettingsType
    Dim returnCode%
    returnCode = EvReadSettingsDefaults(ThisWorkbook, mySettings)
    With mySettings
        .CellToOptimize = "StockoutDemo!$K$36"
        .OutputFunction = EvRiskFuncMean
        .OptimizationGoal = EvMinimize
        .PopulationSize = 10
        .StopOnMinutes = True
        .StopMinutes = 5
        .SimStopMode = EvSimStopIterations
        .SimMaxIters = 5
        .numAdjustableGroups = 1
    ReDim.AdjustableGroups(1 To 1)
    With.AdjustableGroups(1)
        .crossoverRate = 0.5
        .mutationRate = 0.1
        .solvingMethod = "RECIPE"
        .numInputRanges = 1
        ReDim.InputRanges(1 To 1)
        .InputRanges(1).Reference = "StockoutDemo!$c18"
        .InputRanges(1).IsInteger = True
        .InputRanges(1).MinValue = 40
        .InputRanges(1).MaxValue = 120
    End With
    GraphProgress = True
```

```
    GenerateLog = True
    .RunBeforeSimMacro = True 'NOTE that as in Chapter 9 we need to sim
    .BeforeSimMacro = "Macro1" 'several periods to truly assess a "trial"
  End With
  returnCode = EvWriteSettings(mySettings)
  SetupModel = True
End Function


Public Function myStopRoutine(stopReason As Integer) As Integer
  myStopRoutine = EvBest + EvLogWorkbook +
  EvLogWorkbookShowOnlyNewBest
End Function
```

Although the previous examples are designed to illustrate how various VB commands can be used to suite the needs of DSS developers, it is far from comprehensive. Other references, such as Palisade's guide to RISKOptimizer (which accompanies a purchase of their software), provide decent coverage of the various syntax options available for manipulating the optimization protocols through VB. The alternative references are often in dictionary format, but if you plan to be spending a great deal of time automating RISKOptimizer behind the scenes, they may also be helpful down the road.

Note: If you encounter unexpected error messages relating to references to outdated versions of RISKOptimizer or other older settings after you've saved a workbook that references Palisades applications, simply unload all such add-ins and VB Editor references and save the document as reference free. Re-opening and reloading the add-ins and references should restore functionality.

12.4 Calls to XLStat

As we've seen in the previous discussion of XLStat's capabilities, many of the kinds of analysis it provides work naturally very well together. Notably, it is not uncommon for analysis to begin with variable reduction techniques such as PCA, use developed factors as a part of subsequent cluster analysis, and then a follow up with discriminant analysis. Although the re-examination of a specific set of data through these methods may not be needed in many contexts, firms that regularly make it their business to do this kind of sequential analysis with a wide variety of incoming data sets (e.g., information intermediaries, marketing research firms) could find the ability to glean the takeaways from a consistent combined approach all at the click of a single button extremely convenient (and perhaps less prone to errors in data management that can be made between steps).

Fortunately, to accommodate such applications, the developers of XLStat have made it compatible with calls from VB macros, and with fairly straightforward scripting. The following are examples, applicable to the Dodecha case from Chapter 5, for each of the three data consolidation approaches we've discussed.

Principal Components

```
Sub Run_PCA()
    'Must have reference to XLStat-MCA.dll to run
    Call LoadRunPCA(Range("FullData!$B1:$AG116"), 1, True,_
        Range("FullData!$A1:$A116"), NoScreenupdating:=True)
    'The first term above outlines where your data is located
    'The second term, "1", specifies that the data is arranged in attribute
    '   columns and observation rows
    'The third term, "True", specifies that the first row contains attribute labels
    'The fourth specifies where observation labels (eg. ref #s) can be found
    'The last specifies that you want to skip additional prompts and only want
    '   to see the final results
    'Additional optional specifications include PCA Type_
        (eg. other than Peason(n-1), etc.)
End Sub
```

Cluster Analysis

```
Sub Run_Kmeans()
    'Must have reference to XLStat-CLU.dll to run
    Call LoadRunKMN(Range("PCA!$C943:$J1058"), False, 4,_
        WithColLabels:=True, ObsRange:=Range("FullData!$A1:$A116"),_
        NoScreenupdating:=True)
    'The first term above outlines where your data is located_
        (recall it is on PCA sheet)
    'The second term, "False", specifies that the columns of data do not_
    '   represent observations but rather represent factors (hence observations_
        are by row)
    'The third term, "4", specifies the "K" or number of groups to be derived
    'The fourth "True", specifies that the first row contains attribute labels
    'The fifth specifies where observation labels (eg. ref #s) can be found
    'Additional optional specs include Clustering criteria_
        (eg. other than Determinant(W), etc.)
End Sub
```

Discriminant Analysis

```
Sub Run_Discriminant()
    'Must have reference to XLStat-LOG.dll to run
    Call LoadRunDisc(Range("FullData+Clusters!$b1:$b116"),_
        Range("FullData+Clusters!$c1:$ah116"),_
```

Range("FullData | Clusters!$a1:$a116"), NoScreenupdating:=True)
'The first term above outlines where your "group" data is located
'The second term outlines where your predictive data (ie. attribute data here)
is located
'The third term specifies where observation labels (eg. ref #s) can be found
End Sub

As suggested by the comments, the code must be run with XLStat loaded and specifically the associated library files referenced as needed (e.g., XLStat-CLU, XLStat-KMN and XLStat-LOG). Functioning code can be found in the Chp12_Dodecha_VB file under the CodeforRuns module. Additional specifications not outlined here, but of interest to developers, can be made through the menu-driven interface. When specified there, they should be remembered by the application and should exist along with any other specifications made in the code.

As a note on automated calls to Discriminant Analysis, errors in execution may be caused by the presence of the Form19.txt file (typically founding the Addinsoft/XLStat folder). Removing that file prior to run should resolve the issue. Other run-time issues may also occur in workbooks where multiple runs of these tools have taken place. For general assistance with XLStat calls, refer to http://forum.xlstat.com.

12.5 A Final Note on the Value of Linguistics

As a closing personal comment, it is necessary to reinforce that although knowledge of the specific syntax needed to automate via VB is obviously useful, still more critical will always be an understanding of why it should be used. Any well-trained syntax expert doesn't have a ghost of a chance developing something useful in practice unless they also understand what is truly needed in practice, and be able to distinguish that from what is superfluous. Expert programmers can be found. Work can be delegated to them. The most effective professionals analysts aren't those that know all of the code that exists out there, but rather know what can be done (e.g., by hired programmers, if need be), what needs to get done (to benefit real-world practice), and how to integrate and delegate abilities towards that end. It's this general awareness of "the possible," and a specific understanding of how integration can deliver novel, meaningful, and practical results that is the real message here.

PRACTICE PROBLEMS

Practice 12.1

Recall the Atlanta Professional Training example we first brought up in Chapter 6. We used Solver to find an optimal solution to this problem given a single

Table 12.1. *Scenarios for Automated Analysis and Summary*

Revenue Maximizing Enrollments		Total # of hours of communication training for "Geeks"		
		7	11	13
Total # of Analytic hours for "Geeks"	2	{#Geeks} {#Beatniks} {$Revenue}		
	6			
	10			

set of parameters (e.g., revenue numbers, hours required per student per curriculum for both the Geek and Beatnik types).

Now imagine that APT was reconsidering the number hours the Geek students should be required to take in the two categories of Etiquette and Analytics. The director would like to see how much his revenue-maximizing enrollment would vary under nine different scenarios. Each scenario is represented in Table 12.1.

Set up a table similar to this in Excel. It doesn't need to be exact; I've used the Merge cell option under Home>Alignment to combine some cells and make the table look neat.

Now create a macro that does the following:

1) Copy a new set of Geek curriculum parameters (i.e., hours needed) outlined by one of the row and column combinations of Tabled 12.2 (e.g., 6 hours of analytics and 11 hours of tact/diplomacy) into the template we originally used when solving this problem.
2) Run Solver to generate the revenue maximizing enrollment (assuming integer constraints on the number of students).
3) Record the revenue maximizing enrollment (i.e., number of Geek and Beatnik students) and the associated revenue level generated by Solver for that set of parameters in the associated cells of your table.
4) Design your macro so that it does this for all nine scenarios, one after another, so that you generate a completely filled table with only one activation (e.g., one click) of the macro.

Practice 12.2

Use VB calls to MapPoint to get every point-to-point distance between five locations (of your chosing) in the United States. Use that data similarly to the straight line data used in the Chapter 7 routing example, and use VB calls to RISKOptimizer to find the minimum total roundtrip sequence. Assume a single excursion that hits each point in turn. Chose a fixed starting/ending point if you desire to facilitate the search. Limit RISKOptimizer search time to five minutes.

13

Guided and User-friendly Interfaces

As you've probably guessed by now, as we build up the number of variables on which we feel we need to make decisions and continue to add in more constraints to maintain reality and practicality in our decision-making process, decisions themselves can become increasingly complex. Similarly the ability to concisely provide visualizations of what is possible and what is ideal (and, conversely, what isn't) becomes increasingly challenging. Given this complexity and the perceived need in industry to nevertheless pursue means of visually assisting people in decision making, the concept of the dashboard has come into being and continues to gain popularity.

A dashboard, from a general decision-making perspective, is basically a computer interface that allows individual users to simultaneously view various depictions (i.e., presented structure) of data and information as well as various subsets of data (i.e., content) relevant to a particular task and user context. For illustration, Figure 13.1 shows four dashboards that I've personally put into use for research and/or consulting purposes in the recent past.

Two of these are highly oriented toward geographic (specifically logistics) tasks; the other two are designed with project management tasks in mind. You'll notice that each of these consists of multiple frames and multiple control/form-based interfaces. Some make use of parameterization forms more so than others. Some make use of graphs and charts predominantly, whereas others make rich use of tables with key indices summarized. All of them were designed as applications that could function through the use of Excel alone, and are highly mobile from a distributional perspective.

Of course, there are obvious advantages to integrating the wide range of capabilities made available through associated packages such as MapPoint, XLStat, and RISKOptimizer into DSS designs. In reality, high mobility is often not a key requirement of decision support systems and can easily be overshadowed by the need for advanced application integration. The most critical issue, of course, is practical usability paired with honest and ethical

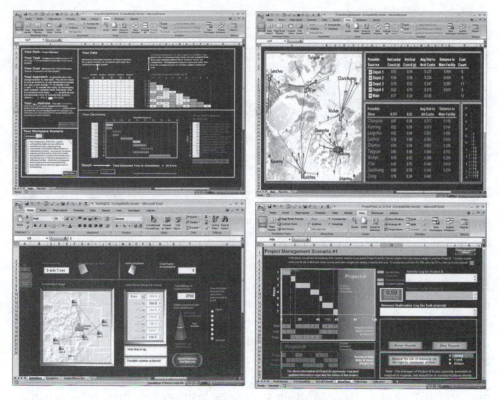

Figure 13.1. Several examples of dashboard developed in Excel.

rigor on the part of developers. Most critical to ensuring these attributes is a detailed understanding of user needs from both a strategic-value perspective (driven by real business goals and decision requirements) as well as from a tactical-use perspective (appropriate context-specific metric depiction and user-oriented visualization/control).

Unfortunately in many cases, it may be impractical to assume that one dashboard design applies to the myriad of users that a DSS is designed to assist. For this reason, still more advanced dashboard designs are increasingly the mark of excellence, allowing individual users to independently choose and alter these depictions and subsets. PivotTables and the use of check-box-triggered pruning mechanisms can be instrumental in providing such flexibility to users. Recall the examples in Chp10_LobosFloorPlan (making use of check boxes) and Chp11_OutlierID (making use of PivotTable capabilities), each of which were designed with such pruning capabilities in mind (see Figure 13.2).

Excel's Change Chart Type and QuickLayout options are a rough approximation of the kind of user customization possible in the structuring of graphical depictions, but nevertheless may be extremely helpful in at least thinking about dashboard flexibility opportunities. Similarly the ability to

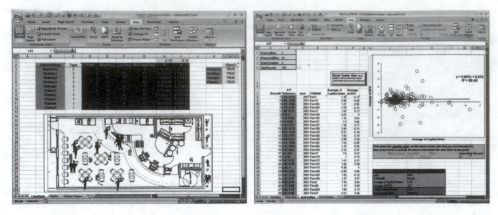

Figure 13.2. Two examples of visualization customization via pruning.

simply adjust the scale of axes in graphs, built and easily accessed through Excel, are also valid avenues of consideration in designing customizable depictions.

Ultimately still greater flexibility comes into play through the full leveraging of macros to reveal customized visualizations on an as-needed basis. The avenues made available through the leveraging of behind-the-scene Visual Basic (VB) coding provide the ability to avoid superfluous data, graphics, and controls that presented in an untimely fashion can lend to confusion, misuse, and fatal professional decision making. Granted, the art of managing access is often one of the last issues considered in DSS design, particularly for those just starting to hone their skills in development; however, it remains a critical element of DSS excellence overall. With this in mind, the following final sections outline approaches to augmenting DSS interfacing along these very lines.

13.1 Interface Locking and Protecting

Under the Home tab of the main Excel menu you'll find the general Format drop-down menu (Figure 13.3) that includes various options meaningful to security measures you might want to capitalize on in your DSS design.

One of the elements subject to consideration when adding protection to workbooks is which cells, if any, should be locked. Locking cells can have multiple implications when spreadsheets and workbooks within which they reside are protected. One is the inability to make modifications to cells that are locked, either manually or through VB without first unlocking or unprotecting in some way through the code. At the same time, calculations and functions present within locked cells can still be updated automatically when sheets are protected, as can graphs based on these calculations. Cells can be

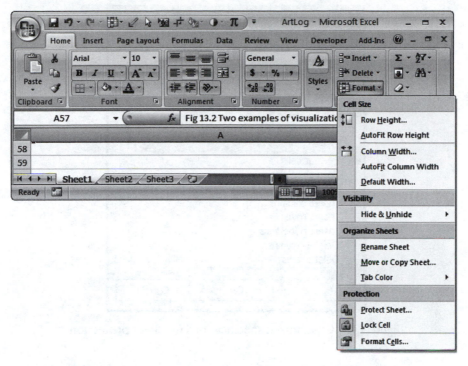

Figure 13.3. Access to interface locking and protecting mechanisms.

toggled between locked and unlocked states through either right-clicking and modifying their properties, or through the Format drop-down menu shown in Figure 13.3.

The same drop-down menu allows for the protection of a spreadsheet in Excel 2007. The Protect Sheet dialog box generated for detailing sheet protection is shown in Figure 13.4.

Note the variety of options that are contained in this dialog box. In general the option to protect (i.e., prevent changes) to locked cells should seem a natural one; however, developers are also given the option to assign a password to the protection mechanism (i.e., so that the sheet cannot be unprotected by those who don't know the password). Developers are also given a slate of check boxes to customize the nature of the protection. These are basically aimed at lessening the severity of the protection (i.e., allowing unlocked cells to be selected, or allowing objects to be edited but blocking most other activities). Chp13_BasicClockProtected provides a follow-up to our previous discussion of the benefits and caveats to the DoEvents syntax in VB. Another mechanism by which to indirectly protect sheets of your DSS from tampering with is simply by hiding them, as shown in Figure 13.5.

The hide and unhide options for rows, columns, and entire sheets are found in the Format drop-down menu. After a sheet is protected, all rows

Figure 13.4. Customized specifications for sheet protection.

or columns that had been hidden prior (but nevertheless might hold vital data and calculations) cannot be unhidden or expanded. It's a way to quickly hide spreadsheet structure without going overboard on interface refinement activities.

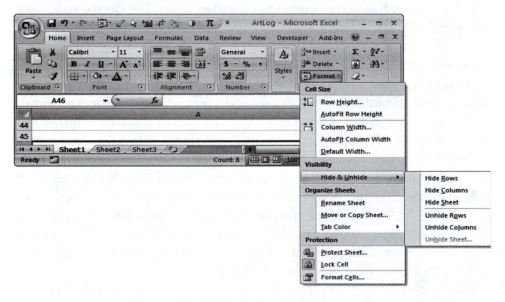

Figure 13.5. Hiding and unhiding interface.

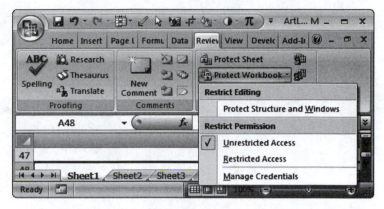

Figure 13.6. Workbook protection options.

If developers are seriously interested in ensuring that hidden sheets remain hidden, an additional level of protection needs to be applied. This can be found under Review>Protect Workbook, as seen in Figure 13.6. Protecting the structure of the workbook with or without a password prevents hidden sheets from being manually unhidden.

13.2 Dynamic Interfacing: Pop-ups/Dialogs

The ability to call up forms and controls on an as-needed basis can be highly effective in the structuring of a DSS interface. It ensures that these controls don't get in the way of other more critical elements of your interface when they are not needed. Also, the ability to withdraw access to these controls can be critical in fool-proofing your DSS against inadvertent changes that these controls could generate.

To start the development of a user-defined pop-up or dialog, enter the VB Editor and select Insert>UserForm. This will generate a new user form. The form toolbox may also appear; if it doesn't, select View>Toolbox from the main header (see Figure 13.7). You'll use this toolbox for a variety of tasks.

In Chp13_FunctionPopup, I provide an example where I've designed a dialog box using a number of basic forms you've already seen (i.e., from Chapter 8). Figure 13.8 outlines/summarizes how most of the various controls were dragged and dropped onto the a newly generated user form, as well as how incidental changes such as name-property changes were made to fit the existing terminology of the QueueEstimator function developed in Chapter 11.

With the dialog box form showing in the VB Editor, double-click on any form component of choice to get access to specifying code for that particular item. Specifically, double-clicking on the Calc button would create a new

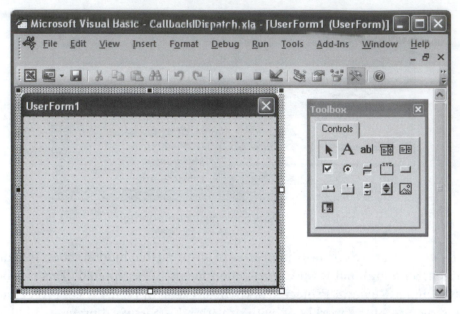

Figure 13.7. User-defined forms and control options toolbox.

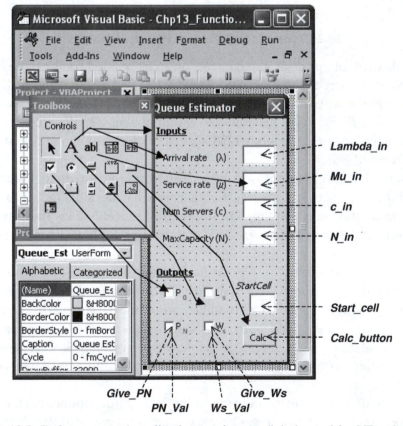

Figure 13.8. In-form control applications and names/labels used for VB reference.

private subroutine for you to edit to your needs (its privacy refers to its designed use specifically in reference to the dialog box interface).

```
Private Sub Calc_button_Click()
End Sub
```

Thankfully these subroutines are coded the same as anything else in VB. The following is what I've developed as a subroutine for the Calc button (functioning code available in Chp13_FunctionPopup)

```
Private Sub Calc_button_Click()
    Dim Lambda, mu As Double
    Dim rho, c, N As Double
    Dim Pnot As Double
    Dim Pn As Double
    Dim Ls As Double
    Dim Ws As Double
    Lambda = Lambda_in.Value
    mu = Mu_in.Value

    If Lambda <> 0 And mu <> 0 Then
        rho = Lambda_in.Value / Mu_in.Value
        N = N_in.Value
        c = c_in.Value
        Pnot = Calc_P0(c, rho, N)
        Pn = Calc_Pn(c, rho, N, N, Pnot)
        Ls = Calc_Ls(c, rho, N, Pnot, Pn)
        Ws = Calc_Ws(Lambda, mu, rho, Pn, Ls)
        P0_val.Caption = WorksheetFunction.Round(Pnot, 3)
        PN_val.Caption = WorksheetFunction.Round(Pn, 3)
        Ls_val.Caption = WorksheetFunction.Round(Ls, 3)
        Ws_val.Caption = WorksheetFunction.Round(Ws, 3)
        Cellposition = Start_cell.Value

        If Cellposition <> "" Then
            If Give_P0.Value Then
                Range(Cellposition) = Pnot
                Cellposition = Range(Cellposition).Offset(1, 0).Address
            End If
            If Give_PN.Value Then
                Range(Cellposition) = Pn
                Cellposition = Range(Cellposition).Offset(1, 0).Address
            End If
            If Give_Ls.Value Then
                Range(Cellposition) = Ls
                Cellposition = Range(Cellposition).Offset(1, 0).Address
            End If
```

```
    If Give Ws,Value Then
        Range(Cellposition) = Ws
    End If
   End If
  End If
 End If
 'Unload Queue_Estimator
 'If active, the above line would hide the dialogue after a one time use

End Sub
```

Close inspection reveals that I've intended to use this single button to activate the full array of calculations specified in the original QueueEstimator (from Chapter 11) but in this case only output those calculations requested by the user, and output the results only specifically where the user has indicated by the StartCell entry form.

To activate this form (i.e., to actually get it to display on request from someone working through the Excel interface), I'll need something to call it into existence. Specifically I'll need another macro defined under Modules, structured such as the following.

```
Sub Call_Estimator()
    Queue_Estimator.Show vbModeless
End Sub
```

If I assign that macro to a simple image I've created or imported (to serve as an activation button), the clean version of the interactive dialog box will appear. Entering the appropriate parameters into the text fields and clicking Calc should give me exactly the kind of output I designed for. And it does. I'll get some summaries of results built into this version of the dialog box, and, depending on what outputs I asked to be copied, I'll get their values written to the spreadsheet.

One note on syntax: The vbModeless term used in the dialog box call is an addition that allows a little more mobility by the user while the dialog box is showing (e.g., allows the user to view other sheets and interact to some extent through the main Excel toolbars). Another interesting feature of vbModeless is that I can move the entire Excel interface out of site while still interacting with the interface. Figure 13.9 shows a clip of the dialog box on my computer desktop. To this extent, dialog boxes can serve as handy and compact specialty calculators when you may want to deal with numerous applications at the same time (aside from Excel).

13.3 Customizing Primary Excel Interfaces

Along with being able to generate pop-up control panels on an as-needed basis, there is also the potential for actually customizing the primary interfaces

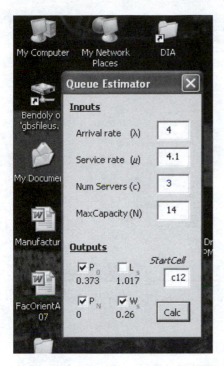

Figure 13.9. User-defined dialog box called and hovering off workbook.

with which Excel users otherwise normally interact. In other words, instead of having a button (which activates a macro or dialog box) residing somewhere among the cells of a spreadsheet, you could place that button where all other buttons already built into Excel reside, such as within the command bar, Quick Access bar, or among the drop-down menus (see Figure 13.10).

It's yet another tactic for keeping work and other items out of the way of the premium space available in the spreadsheet environment. And frankly we can create these kinds of customized additions to the Excel command button and menu environment fairly quickly, both through manual and automated approaches.

13.3.1 Manual Additions in Excel 2007

If the primary development environment is Excel 2007, there is a fairly straightforward approach to adding customized buttons. You can use the

Figure 13.10. Embedded macro button vs. macro buttons integrated with control/menu interface.

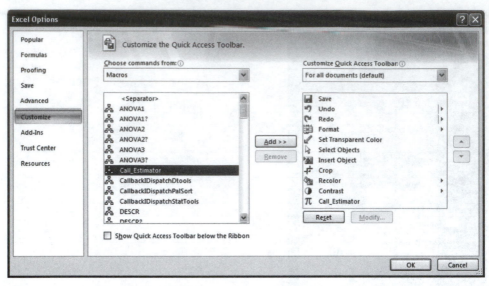

Figure 13.11. Adding macro buttons to the Quick Access Toolbar (Excel 2007).

Office button to access to the Customize screen where any existing tool (including user-developed macros) can be added to the Quick Access Toolbar. The Modify Button dialog box, accessed upon selecting the Modify . . . option shown in Figure 13.11, enables you select a button picture that suits your needs (see Figure 13.12).

Figure 13.12. Selecting button icons for user-defined buttons in Excel 2007.

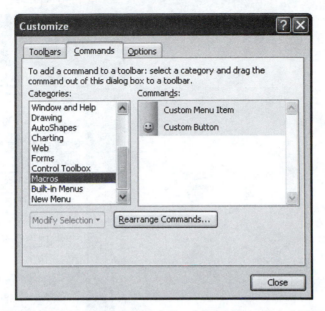

Figure 13.13. Adding user-defined buttons in Excel 2003.

13.3.2 Manual Additions in Excel 2003

Menu bar customization in Excel 2003 is different than in Excel 2007, in part because users seem to have more flexibility in how added elements will appear. The approach involves right-clicking anywhere on the existing command bar and then selecting Customize from the shortcut menu to open the Customize dialog box (Figure 13.13).

Choose the Commands tab, and then select Macros from the Catagories section. Custom Menu Item and Custom Button display in the Commands section of the dialog box, both of which can be utilized to generate changes to the existing toolbar interface; for example, the Custom Button option allows you to place a new button within that interface.

The button doesn't do anything when first added, unlike the manual Quick Access approach in Excel 2007; similar to any button we create in the spreadsheet, we'll need to assign it to a macro or subroutine that we've developed in VB. Not only can we change the icon for this new button, but we can change its name as well. To make these kinds of changes, you'll need to be in the Command Bar Edit mode. Start in the Customize dialog box. In this Command Bar Edit mode, right-click on the newly placed button (in this mode) to access to a range of options, including Assign Macro, Change Button Image, and Name.

It's critical to note that all newly minted buttons must have a name starting with the an ampersand (&). The & won't appear to users, but is critical in ensuring that Excel recognizes the new object. Forgetting or erasing the & can eliminate any work you've done in editing the button, and can be frustrating.

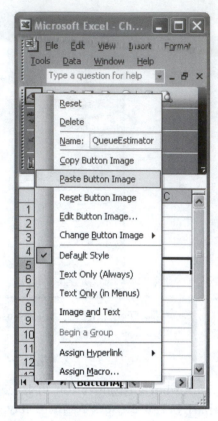

Figure 13.14. Pasting in button icons in Excel 2003.

Another feature present in Excel 2003 but not in Excel 2007 is the ability to edit the appearance of the button icon at the pixel level in the Button Editor dialog box (Figure 13.15).

If you don't have time to be a pixel artist, the Paste Button Image option (shown in Figure 13.14) allows you to take any image or graphic item available

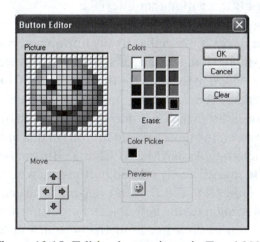

Figure 13.15. Editing button icons in Excel 2003.

and then copy and paste it into that 16×16 square area. You loose some resolution, but the work is quick.

13.3.3 Fully Automating Button/Menu Setups

Aside from their presence in the menu bar, user-designed buttons have a particular nuance to them that distinguish them from buttons that would otherwise be embedded in a spreadsheet. When created, these command bar buttons become registered in a file called Excel.xlb (or something similar, depending on your system configuration), usually in your C:\Windows directory. This allows them to appear in your command bar no matter what workbook you open in the future as long as that workbook is on the same computer. For example, if I reboot my computer and then open a fresh workbook in Excel, that command button should be there. It should have all the properties I assigned it when I last edited it. It'll even know enough to find the macro to which it was assigned, unless the workbook containing the code for the macro has been moved.

The downside is that because the button is defined in that Excel.xlb file and not in a workbook, simply transferring the workbook file (e.g., via e-mail) won't bring that button along for the ride. There are at least two ways around this. You could insist that clients use the specific Excel.xlb file that you use (which seems an unlikely option in most situations), or you could write a macro that creates a set of menu command buttons for your specific DSS (and maybe handles updates in cases where code files are moved around).

For illustration, I'll use a variant of the dialog box generator file discussed earlier in this chapter. The following is how you might structure that kind of installation code in that particular case (functional in Chp13_CustomSetup).

```
Sub AddNewMenuItem()
  Dim CmdBar As CommandBar
  Dim CmdBarMenu As CommandBarControl
  Dim CmdBarMenuItem As CommandBarControl
  Set CmdBar = Application.CommandBars("Worksheet Menu Bar")
              ' Point to the Worksheet Menu Bar
  Set CmdBarMenu = CmdBar.Controls("Tools")
              ' Point to the Tools menu on the menu bar
  Set CmdBarMenuItem = CmdBarMenu.Controls.Add
              ' Add a new menu item to the Tools menu
  CmdBarMenuItem.Caption = "QueueEstimator"
              ' Set the properties for the new control
  CmdBarMenuItem.OnAction = "'" & ThisWorkbook.Name & "'!Call_Estimator"
End Sub

Sub AddNewButton()
  Application.CommandBars("Standard").Controls.Add  Type:=msoControlButton, _
    ID:=2950, Before:=25
```

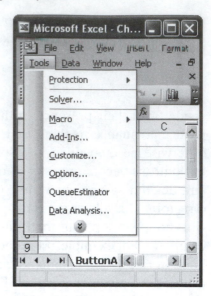

Figure 13.16. Appearance of menu implanted macro call in Excel 2003.

```
     Application.CommandBars("Standard").Controls(25).Caption = "QueueEstimator"
     Application.CommandBars("Standard").Controls(25).OnAction = """ & _
        ThisWorkbook.Name & ""!Call_Estimator"
   End Sub

   Sub SetupBoth()
     AddNewMenuItem
     AddNewButton
   End Sub
```

Running the SetupBoth macro calls the AddNewMenuItem and AddNew-Button macros in turn. The AddNewMenuItem routine adds a new item called QueueEstimator to the Tools drop-down menu, and assigns the Call_Estimator macro (also included in this workbook, regardless of whether we've renamed the workbook) to that menu item. Similarly, the AddNew-Button routine adds a button called QueueEstimator to the command bar. Figure 13.16 shows the final result when this code is run in Excel 2003. Along with the item's presence on the pull-down menu, we also get the smiley face button on our tool bar (not shown in the above clip but present if the code is run in 2003), and we know we can fairly easily modify it.

Interestingly, this code also work if you run it in Excel 2007. The buttons and drop-down menus will appear under the Add-ins tab, under Menu Commands (for the menu item loads) and under Toolbar Commands (for button loads), as shown in Figure 13.17.

Unfortunately, changing the appearance of buttons forced this way into the toolbar in Excel 2007 is not straightforward (at least at this point). You might be stuck with living with that smiley face if you need it to be under Toolbar

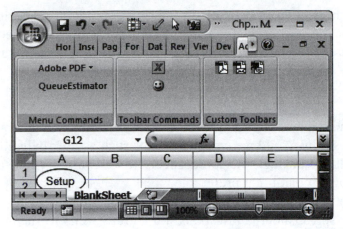

Figure 13.17. Appearance of forced menu and command button implants in Excel 2007.

Commands, but given that you could opt either for the menu item form (text) or the Quick Access form (where you have at least some graphical choices), there's little reason to feel penned in here.

13.3.4 Fully Automating Button/Menu Cleanup

Customized buttons and menu items can also easily be removed manually from use in Excel 2003 by dragging them "out" of toolbars and menus after right-clicking and getting into "Customize . . .". Similarly, buttons can be removed from Excel 2007 by right-clicking and selecting Delete Custom Command from the shortcut menu. Alternatively, if you are interested in providing an automatic cleanup of added customized items and buttons, something similar to the following code could be used in either version.

```
Sub RemoveMenuItem()
    Dim CmdBar As CommandBar
    Dim CmdBarMenu As CommandBarControl
    Set CmdBar = Application.CommandBars("Worksheet Menu Bar")
    Set CmdBarMenu = CmdBar.Controls("Tools")
    CmdBarMenu.Controls("QueueEstimator").Delete
End Sub

Sub RemoveButton()
    Application.CommandBars("Standard").Controls(25).Delete
End Sub

Sub RemoveBoth()
    RemoveMenuItem
    RemoveButton
End Sub
```

Here both menu item deletion and button deletion are described, along with a single macro that might be used to remove both customized elements if present in the workbook (also functional in Chp13_CustomSetup).

13.4 Don't Give Up on the Spreadsheet

If we can build interfaces that reduce user interactions to menu buttons and dialog boxes, why would we create elements such as user-defined functions that are callable through the spreadsheet? If we could get the same result with a dialog box, isn't that preferable?

There's a significant drawback to limiting user interfaces to dialog box menus. The spreadsheet landscape is still a great arena for laying out multiple calculations that are can be updated in real time as other parameters and calculations change, and whose updates can be visualized (i.e., changes depicted graphically) in real time. Replicating that kind of an environment strictly through the use of dialog box is both cumbersome and unnecessary for developers. Similarly, given the fantastic integration between live spreadsheet updates and live graphical updates in Excel, the ability to make abundant use of functions (as opposed to dialog box and button-activated macro-based calculations) should not be underappreciated.

As developers it's increasingly beneficial to be able to offer the best of both worlds in interface designs – allowing routine calculations to be menu driven and providing a function infrastructure that permits a wide range of user creativity and experimentation in the spreadsheet environment.

PRACTICE PROBLEM

Population distributions are often assumed to be normal or bell curved in their shape, with the most common membership of those populations taking place at the center. In statistical terms, this location of greatest frequency is referred to as the MODE.

Often in management we are faced with multiple populations that have some overlap (e.g., clusters of demographically related customers that geographically overlap to some degree). Managers interested in dealing with multiple populations simultaneously may be interest in the associated points of greatest frequency (i.e., where the greatest number of people in the combined population live). However, several forms can arise when combining two normally distributed populations. Figure 13.18 show a couple of simple examples generated in the Ch13_2dists.xls workbook. The first shows a bi-modal structure (one peak representing the global mode); the second with a single composite mode structure. (Numerically the two pictures only differ in the location of the mean of the second distribution: 1 vs. –0.5).

Build your own function for determining the MODE of a distribution resulting from the merger of two normal distributions. Your inputs should be the means and standard deviations for the two distributions, as well as a cell location to dump any

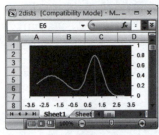 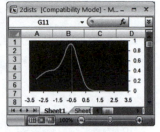

Here the "global" mode is 1   Here it's -0.6 (not quite -0 5)

Figure 13.18. Examples of two compound distributions and associated modes.

resulting output. The output should be the global mode of the composite distribution, and whether a second local peak exists (just give a yes or no response).

Create a dialog box that prompts users to enter the input information into dialog text boxes, and a button that makes VB go through some kind of loop to determine the outputs required. Use a fresh workbook (i.e., not a version of 2dist.xls) for your work. Do not use any portion of the workbook's spreadsheet to store numbers or do the calculations. This exercise should all be done in VB.

To help you, the following is the code needed to calculate the frequency of a single distribution given a mean and standard deviation.

$$f1 = WorksheetFunction.NormDist\,(x, mean1, stddev1, 0)$$

Remember, you'll want to calculated a frequency for each and then add the frequencies together. You can conduct your search by constructing each composite frequency in turn (on 0.01 intervals of X; –3.0, –2.99, –2.98, and so on) and checking whether each new composite has a greater composite frequency than the maximum previously encountered.

Glossary of Key Terms

Cluster analysis *[5.4.4]*: A computational technique used to identify a set of fairly distinct groups of observations (entities, records) in a data set. It operates by attempting to place individual observations in groups whose attribute values are most similar, while simultaneously attempting to ensure that general character of all groups formed are significantly different from one another.

Conditional formatting *[2.2.2]*: A mechanism enabled by Excel by which cells in a spreadsheet take on various visual formats based solely on the nature of their content, and ostensibly the content of the range of cells with which that they were co-formatted.

Conditional logic *[See Decision Trees]*

Constraints *[4]*: Those issues that restrain decision making and the pursuit of objectives; technically they prevent decision variables from taking on certain values either in isolation or in tandem with other decision variables (e.g., relational constraints). Binding constraints in particular work to prevent certain kinds of changes to the best of decision sets (i.e., objective-optimizing decisions) that might otherwise lead to still greater levels of achievement in the objective.

Controls *[8.Supplement]*: A range of mechanisms in Excel through which to develop visually appealing and user-friendly object interfaces for modifying and/or displaying content within a workbook. Controls (and forms) can reside entirely as embedded objects in a workbook, or can appear as needed through the use of dialog boxes/pop-up forms callable through Visual Basic code. In many cases also capable and ideally used in referenced calls to user-developed macros.

Dashboard *[13]*: From a general decision-making perspective, a computer interface that allows individual users to simultaneously view various depictions of data and information as well as various subsets of data relevant to a particular task and user context.

Decision Support System (DSS) *[1]*: An application designed to support, not replace, decision making. Often characterized as providing eased access, facilitated analysis and rich communication, all of which is greatly augmented through intelligent and effective use of visualization.

Decision trees *[2.Supplement]*: Structures that outline sequential systems of compound logic. Useful in mapping the course of decision-making processes, the course of questions to be asked to determine identity or state, or the course of likely events to assess the value/cost of early decisions.

Decision variables *[4]*: The elements of a decision-making process over which a decision maker has either direct or indirect control (e.g., change as a consequence of other decisions made). These variables in turn impact the value taken on by the objective function and thus the relationship between these variables and that function mitigates the pursuit of the overall objective of the decision-making process subject also to the presence of additional constraints on these variables.

Dialog boxes *[13.2]*: Compound user forms that present numerous input and output options on an as-needed basis, appearing only when called for as by the user or as a portion of a macro run sequence. These new form windows are not embedded in the spreadsheets in the same way that many fixed and standard controls may be, and can be designed to float out of the way of the spreadsheet or exist visually apart from the spreadsheet entirely, while simultaneously allowing for continuous interaction with the Excel workbook that generates them.

Discriminant Analysis *[5.5]*: A statistical method aimed at making use of a select set of predictive attributes to attempt to create some simple formulation that places specific observations/records/entities (characterized by those attributes) into groups (e.g., clusters) to which they are though to belong.

DoEvents *[See Loops]*

Drawn-path extraction *[10.Supplement]*: A technique through which developers can leverage standard object drawing capabilities to derive graphical paths and path coordinates that can subsequently be used to develop path-direct flow graphics as a feature of a system simulation visualization.

Filtering *[See PivotTable and section 4.2 in general]*

Forms *[See Controls]*

Formulae *[See Functions]*

Functions *[2.6]*: Built-in formulae that can be executed within cells of spreadsheets. Under most scenarios functions (similar to most graphs built in Excel) are automatically updated when changes take place in the content of workbooks or when forced updates occur, e.g., through the use of F9 in the spreadsheet or Calculate in VB code. These functions can also be automatically updated in conjunction with Web query and iteration mode functionality (also see User-Defined Functions).

Genetic algorithm *[See RISKOptimizer and Chapter 7 Supplement in general]*

Heuristic *[5]*: Codified approaches to developing ideas, decisions, and/or solutions to problems. Fast and frugal heuristics employ a minimum of time, knowledge, and computation to make adaptive choices in real environments. Heuristics in general typically do not guarantee optimal solutions, but can be extremely capable in developing high-performing solutions (relative to random decision making).

Hill climbing *[See Solver]*

Iteration mode *[3.5]*: A calculation mode in Excel that allows for the stepwise calculation of functions within a spreadsheet that are based on previous calculations, even if the calculation referenced is stored in the same cell in which the called function resides (i.e., circular loop calculations). In Excel, the sequence of cell calculations under iteration mode is very specific, and needs to be understood before accurately used.

Labels *[2.3]*: Text that can be associated with cells, cell ranges, worksheets, or objects embedded within an Excel workbook, for use in referencing these items in an intuitively meaningful fashion. Labels are also useful in both locating items in workbooks with considerable added content, as well as referencing these items from behind the scenes through Visual Basic code.

Link Data Wizard *[See MapPoint]*

Living data records *[3.5]*: Data records that typically consist of a range of cells containing data that are updated on an iterative basis. These records typically represent sequences of calculations or observations, and typically have some temporal meaning associated with them.

Locking *[See Protecting]*

Loops *[11.3.5]*: VB code structures designed to allow for iteration as a part of a subroutine's (i.e., macro) run. Two commonly used loop structures include fixed-finite repetition loops (For-Loops) and condition dependent repetition loops (While-Loops). Given that loop structures are often associated with lengthy run times, the availability of flexibility and auto-exit mechanisms such as DoEvents script can become highly useful to DSS developers.

Macros *[8.3]*: Subroutines coded in Visual Basic, often generated through the recording of changes within the spreadsheet environment, that enable specific changes to the workbook content, structure, and associated elements (e.g., dialog boxes) to take place. Only a limited set of activities can actually be directly recorded and translated into VB code; however, a wide range of actions can be coded for directly through use of the VB Editor. External calls to applications and add-ins are also possible through the use of macros. Activation of macros typically take place through the use of either embedded buttons, customized menu items, or control-key shortcuts (or indirectly through calls by other macros).

MapPoint *[3.2]*: A Microsoft application that provides geographic visualization as well as mapping and routing capabilities. Although typically associated with a purchased database of geographic data, the use of tools such as the Link Data Wizard allows for regular imports of data from Excel spreadsheets. MapPoint graphs can also be imported to function as Embedded Maps in an Excel workbook.

Names *[See Labels]*

Objective *[4]*: The main pursuit of a decision-making process. Entirely context and orientation specific, and often unique in form depending on the nature of the problem faced by the decision maker. Also entirely dependent upon the range of decisions available for consideration, as well as the constraints placed upon the decision-making process. Typically viewed as compound calculation (e.g., expected total satisfaction, average total risk) to be maximized, minimized, or set as close to a particular value as possible.

Objects *[2, 11.2]*: In general, non-cell elements imported or created in the Excel spreadsheet environment. Objects can include elements from imported images and sound clips to MapPoint embedded map graphics. All objects have a unique set of attributes that may differ largely from those available to other kinds of objects; however, all can be characterized by position, reference label/name, and specific visualization. Such attributes and many more can be manipulated either through menu-driven interfaces or VB code.

Optimization *[6]*: The process by which values of decision variables are altered computationally (or derived mathematically) to obtain the best possible results in an objective function, subject to constraints on both decisions variables and the objective (as well as on any computational method used to drive the process).

Path-directed flow *[10.3]*: The flow of elements through a system based on a structured network of paths and interpath flow dynamics (logic and stochastic mechanisms). Graphically, the mechanism through which entities travel along meaningful attribute space in their transitions between interpretable states (points on a graph).

PivotTable *[4.2]*: A compound filtering mechanism available in Excel that enables the summarizations of multiple related records based on similarities across specific attributes. These attributes can be organized along rows and columns, and specific values of attributes associated with specific blocks of data can be filtered to allow focus and comparison on key subsets of data. As with other tools in Excel, PivotTables do not automatically update themselves when input data changes (manual or coded refreshing is needed).

Plot-pulled extraction *[10.Supplement]*: A technique through which developers can leverage graphical plotting capabilities (e.g., those of Excel 2003) to derive graphical paths and path coordinates that can subsequently be used to develop path-direct flow graphics as a feature of a system simulation visualization.

Principle Components Analysis (PCA) *[5.3.2]*: A statistical technique that attempts to create a reduced subset of attributes based on a larger set of potentially highly related (and perhaps redundant) attributes. The result is typically a condensed set of higher-level concepts that can ideally be used to more efficiently distinguish the nature of observations in a data set.

Protecting *[13.1]*: In general, a means of preventing certain kinds of changes from taking placed in a developed spreadsheet or workbook as a whole. A critical part of the protection mechanism involves specifying the extent to which actions are limited under protection, and whether or not certain cells are locked from modification. Password protection is an option in both spreadsheet and workbook protection cases.

RISKOptimizer *[7]*: An application developed to search out solutions to highly complex problems, often characterized by features such as nonlinearity and discontinuity in the objective function (as well as within relational constraints that involve decision variables under consideration). Moreover, the tool is designed to enable searches across simulated scenarios of complex problems where various attributes of these problems are subject to uncertainty. To tackle these problems, the application makes abundant use of genetic algorithms as a robust globalized search method (see Chapter 7 Supplement), thus avoiding some of the difficulties that hill-climbing procedures might encounter. Callable both through menu interaction and/or through VB code.

Simulated variants *[8.1.1]*: Generally a set of structured problems or decision making scenarios that are equivalent in structure but differ in the actual values of the parameters used to describe them. Extremely useful in what-if analysis, where the conditions of a problem-solving context (thus the value of decisions constructed) are highly dependent on certain elements of uncertainty.

Simulation optimization *[9.1]*: The task of seeking out optimal solutions to complex problems involving either critical elements that are known to be characterized by uncertainty and/or sequentially dependent across time (e.g., as in system simulations). Generally speaking, simulation optimization is an iterative process that involves multiple randomized assessments of a range of decision policies. RISKOptimizer provides an example of an application designed to conduct such searches.

Solver *[6]*: The standard mechanism provided through Excel to conduct a search for optimal solutions (values of decision variables) to an objective function, subject to constraints. Solver is technically an add-in tool, subject to the same strengths and limitations of many other tools in Excel. In its most typical use it pursues optimization by means of a hill-climbing mechanism (local sensitivity search). It provides rich details regarding the nature of its final solution with respect to its view of the search through elements such as Answer Reports.

Stochastic processes *[8.4]*: Processes in which key elements (e.g., workers, jobs, patients) have the potential for passing through multiple states prior to completion/exit. Each state is associated with a particular probability of being visited in turn depending specifically on what the state the element has most recently been in (among other factors). System simulations often make abundant use of stochastic processes in an attempt to capture real-world dynamics. The visualization of changes within simulated systems can also leverage stochastic structures to provide rich depictions of these dynamics.

System simulation *[8.1.2]*: Generally the computational representation of a complex set of sequential interactions, designed in an attempt to more realistically capture the inter-temporal (across time) dependencies of the processes and resources involved in real-world settings. The performance impact of decisions applied to these systems typically are assessed across multiple periods; therefore, such multiperiod computations must be built into any search for ideal or at least improved decision making for the modeled settings.

Tools *[2.6]*: Additional mechanisms that are often built into Excel to facilitate the organization and analysis of information in workbooks. These include mechanisms by which to sort information and conduct complex statistical computations, among others. Unlike other features of Excel, however (such as most functions and graphs), the functionality of these tools are typically not characterized by live updating (i.e., changes in the content of workbooks, including the data that they are intended to operate on, do not typically alter their results automatically). Although other means by which to automate updates of their results exist, this is a necessary caveat to consider when relying on their use.

Types *[See VB Editor]*

User-defined functions *[11.4]*: VB code that allows inputs to be specified, complex calculations made, or information derived, and individual results to be posted to cells or other macros that make calls to the code. In spreadsheet usage these can operate more or less like any other function built into Excel, including providing automatic updated to results as data relevant to it's calculations are modified (also see Functions).

Visual Basic (VB) Editor *[11]*: The fundamental interface that allows developers to view, edit, and generate code (e.g., macros and user-defined functions) for use in Excel-based DSS. A critical key to leveraging the various capabilities of Excel and linked applications in a seamless and integrated manner. The VB Editor includes multiple mechanisms through which to facilitate development include debugging tools, help mechanisms, and step-through execution (as needed). Key to the leveraging of complex code structures is an understanding of the role of user-defined variables and variable types that can make the best use of data resources and calculations toward a particular programming goal.

Appendix – Shortcut (Hot Key) Reference

Popular Function Keys (*F#*)

F1 Key	Help	**F7 Key**	Spell Check
F2 Key	Edit cell content	**F9 Key**	Recalculate
F4 Key	Toggles hard references ($)	**F12 Key**	Open Save As dialog box
F5 Key	Find and Replace dialog box/Go To tab		

F6 Key Press twice – Activates key-driven menu (provides guide to F6-# shortcut commands; e.g., F6-f opens the Office Button menu)

Some Popular CTRL-# shortcuts
(assuming not overwritten by user-defined macro shortcuts)

CTRL-A Select entire worksheet

CTRL-B Toggle bold text (CTRL-2 does same)

CTRL-C Copies the item or items selected to the Office Clipboard (can be pasted elsewhere using CTRL-V)

CTRL-D Copies down the top cell in a range of selected cells to rest of range

CTRL-F Displays the Find dialog box

CTRL-G	Find and Replace dialog box/Go To tab (as does F5)	**CTRL-1**	Displays Format Cells dialog box
CTRL-H	Displays the Replace dialog box	**CTRL-2**	Toggles bold text (CTRL-B does same)
CTRL-I	Toggles italic text	**CTRL-3**	Toggles italics (CTRL-I does same)
CTRL-K	Insert/dit Hyperlink dialog box	**CTRL-4**	Toggles underline (CTRL-U does same)
CTRL-L	Displays the Create List dialog box	**CTRL-5**	Toggles strikethrough text
CTRL-N	New File	**CTRL-6**	Toggles display of objects

CTRL-O	Open File	**CTRL-7**	Toggles display of Standard toolbar (2003)
CTRL-P	Print	**CTRL-8**	Toggles symbol outline display (2003)
CTRL-R	Copies right the left-most cell in a range of cells to the rest of range	**CTRL-9**	Hides the selected rows
		CTRL-0	Hides the selected columns
CTRL-S	Save file		
CTRL-U	Toggles underlined text	**CTRL-LeftArrow**	Go to end of column
CTRL-V	Paste the contents of the Office Clipboard	**CTRL-Home**	Go to top of worksheet (A1)
CTRL-W	Closes selected workbook window	**CTRL-End**	Go to end of worksheet
CTRL-X	Cut the selected item	**CTRL-PageDown**	Go to next worksheet
CTRL-Y	Redo the last undone action	**CTRL-Spacebar**	Select the entire column
CTRL-Z	Undoes the last action		
CTRL-;	Insert current date	**CTRL-&**	Applies the outline border
CTRL-:	Insert current time	**CTRL-_**	Removes the outline border
CTRL-~	Applies the general number format	**CTRL-^**	Exponential format (two decimals)
CTRL-$	Currency format (two decimals)	**CTRL-#**	Date format
CTRL-%	Percentage format (no decimals)	**CTRL-@**	Time format
CTRL-!	Number format (two decimals)	**CTRL-'**	Copies formula from cell above into active cell
CTRL-`	Toggles display of cell values vs. display of formulas in the worksheet	**CTRL-"**	Copies the value from cell above into active cell

Some Popular ALT-# shortcuts

ALT-=	Autosum	**ALT-F11**	Opens Visual Basic Editor
ALT-F8	Opens Macros dialog box		

Index

Date Due →

Books returned after due date are subject to a fine.

1/4/10		
2/4/10		
2/11/10		